Praise for *The B*

From the beloved author of Dandelion Mama, this long-awaited memoir is the story of how trust merges with betrayal, how love merges with loss, and how pain reveals itself as the catalyst for our most essential growth.
—Kathryn Lynard, author of *The Year My Son and I Were Born*

Tracy McKay's powerful memoir, *The Burning Point* is the kind of discourse that I want to replace the heroic pioneer stories I grew up with. I want to understand the lived reality of modern Saints who have walked through the darkness this world often offers. I want to be inspired by those who have fought to find meaning as they've struggled to wend their way in tears of anguish, watching loved ones wrestle with the most destructive demons of our age.
—Steven Peck, author of *The Scholar of Moab*

For every woman who makes the heartbreaking but utterly necessary choice to leave, to start over, to make a new home, for her kids, for herself; for every woman who will wake up alone this morning and do by herself the hard work of holding a family together; for every woman who puts one foot in front of the other, this book offers a safe space of wisdom, warmth, and understanding. Tracy McKay writes like the best friend you always dreamed of, the one who sits at your kitchen table and plainly, lovingly tells it like it is.. ...
I can't wait to give this book to the heroic women in my life who go it alone.
—Joanna Brooks, author of Book of Mormon Girl

A new standard-bearer of the modern Mormon memoir, this book weaves together disparate social threads such as single motherhood, disability, drug addiction, education, and religion into a vulnerable and deeply reflective tapestry of struggle, despair, and redemption that is not only emotionally compelling but highly readable. Highly recommended.

—Jacob Baker, Instructor in Philosophy at Utah Valley University, PhD Candidate in Philosophy of Religion and Theology at Claremont Graduate University

Also by Tracy McKay

Seasons and Reasons to Celebrate
A Book of Mormons: Latter-day Saints on a Modern-Day Zion
(Edited with Emily W. Jensen)

the burning point

a memoir of
addiction, destruction, love,
parenting, survival, and hope

Tracy McKay

BCC
PRESS

The Burning Point: A memoir of addiction, destruction, love, parenting, survival, and hope Copyright © 2017 by Tracy McKay

For information contact
By Common Consent Press
4062 S. Evelyn Dr.
Salt Lake City, UT 84124-2250

ISBN-13:978-0-9986052-1-0
ISBN-10: 0-9986052-1-2

By Common Consent Press is a non-profit publisher dedicated to producing affordable, high-quality books that help define and shape the Latter-day Saint experience. BCC Press publishes books that address all aspects of Mormon life. Our mission includes finding manuscripts that will contribute to the lives of thoughtful Latter-day Saints, mentoring authors and nurturing projects to completion, and distributing important books to the Mormon audience at the lowest possible cost.

This book is dedicated
to the women of the Relief Societies of the
Belle Terre and Evergreen Wards of
The Church of Jesus Christ of Latter-day Saints.

and to the women of

Feminist Mormon Housewives
By Common Consent
Mormon Mommy Wars
I can never repay you for all you have done.

And to Mo,
who never let the other shoe drop.

The More Loving One
W. H. Auden

Looking up at the stars, I know quite well
That, for all they care, I can go to hell,
But on earth indifference is the least
We have to dread from man or beast.

How should we like it were stars to burn
With a passion for us we could not return?
If equal affection cannot be,
Let the more loving one be me.

Admirer as I think I am
Of stars that do not give a damn,
I cannot, now I see them, say
I missed one terribly all day.

Were all stars to disappear or die,
I should learn to look at an empty sky
And feel its total dark sublime,
Though this might take me a little time.

"Love is the burning point of life, and since all life is sorrow-
ful, so is love. The stronger the love, the more the pain."
—Joseph Campbell

1

The Edge

OCTOBER 4, 2009

There is a scene in one of the Indiana Jones movies where the scary guy reaches out and plunges his hand into the chest of the human sacrifice, and then pulls his clenched fist out holding the still-beating heart. Left behind is a gasping, vacant void where his heart had been.

How can something hurt so much? How can you remember to breathe when pain obliterates even your vision and you find yourself a shadow—a yawning chasm of aching sorrow and grief?

How do you love someone so much, so entirely, and yet find yourself standing at the rocky, sharp edge of having to let them go?

I don't know.

But here I am.

IN MY MIND, THEIR NAMES were Harold and Maude. They were yellow swallowtail butterflies living in the poplar trees lining my back fence. Perhaps there were more than the two of them, but I seemed to only see the pair, fluttering and floating through the eddies and currents while the leaves started to yellow and fall. I would smile when I saw them from my kitchen window. Even now, when I see a yellow butterfly I think of them.

Leaning against the wall outside the same window, I clutched the phone to my chest. In desperation, I had called my friend to see if she could help me with my three children. The copper-haired boys were eight and six, and my precocious daughter was three. My husband had been unemployed for almost two years, and for weeks I had been planning to fly to Houston for a quilt and textile show. It was one of the biggest shows in the country and, through a series of small miracles, I had been accepted as a new vendor. Every hope I had for the future meant that I had to get to Houston.

But that morning, after three years of struggle, half a dozen stints in rehab, and two hospitalizations, my husband had relapsed. Again. There was no way I could leave our kids with him. The last time he'd relapsed, it had taken him barely three days to go from first use to overdose. To anyone looking at me this warm fall afternoon, I was leaning against a sun-dappled wall, watching butterflies in my back-yard. Inside of me, the 641 days of carefully propped-up walls and cultivated stories about my life were crashing into brittle, irreparable shards.

What am I going to do?

My family and friends knew things were rough. Some of them even knew more than just the surface tension about the drug problem, but I had tried to shield my loved ones from the gritty, in-the-trenches reality of what opiate addiction looks and feels like when you're bleeding out on its sharp thorns. I would gloss over my reality, I avoided friends and phone calls, talked vaguely about *bad days*, and circled back around carefully to the acceptable *brave face*. There wasn't much left of my fragile and diminishing hope that he could pull out of this years-long trajectory toward the ground.

I was watching the butterflies, lost in my own painful thoughts, when from somewhere I heard, *"You can leave now."* It was clear, bright as a bell, but nonexistent. It was a roaring wave of emptiness, like cotton-stuffed ears ringing with sound. I looked around, almost afraid, my skin prickling anxiously, wondering who was in my yard. There was nothing but empty grass, the yellowing trees, and a yawning stillness. Suspended.

There are moments in life that transcend time, when everything stops, the birds hold their song, and the enormity of the silence is deafening in its vastness. There are moments where a person can, ever so briefly, see the curving arc of the horizon and feel the curling crest of the wave of time under their feet. Thank God those moments are fleeting, because our earthly hearts can't breathe in that paralyzing intensity for long.

Harold and Maude swooped down again, the birds chirped, the breeze ruffled the golden poplar leaves, and the sky was a beautiful early October blue. The ground was solid under my feet and the wall warm at my back. I exhaled.

I no longer wondered what I was going to do.

For the first time in years, my brother was visiting from California. He had brought his family in their new SUV on the two-day drive up to Washington. Walking back into the house, still holding the phone to my chest, I found him sitting at the kitchen table. "Can we talk?" I asked quietly. He nodded. It had been a rough couple of days, and he was no fool.

I sat down across from my brother and spoke the hidden horrors of the last couple of years. I allowed my pain and sorrow to spill over the kitchen table, and once I tapped the seal, I could not stop until I got to the present: "David relapsed again this morning. When I picked him up from the clinic, he was high already. He's upstairs unconscious now."

My brother didn't say anything. We could hear his wife in the playroom with the kids—his and mine—and he just nodded again while I continued.

"I have to get to Houston. I have to get the kids somewhere safe so I can go to the quilt show and get work—but I can't leave them with him...."

My brother finally interrupted, "Sis. I knew it was bad, but this... it's worse than we imagined. We can get the kids to Mom's—I can take them with us back to California. But you can't go on like this. You just can't."

"I know. Oh God, how did we get here?" I cradled my head in my hands.

He sat looking across the table at me. "It doesn't matter now." His voice was sad.

"I need a lawyer," I said quietly, peering at him through swimming eyes.

"You need a lawyer."

🕊

David lay in an unconscious narcotic-induced haze in our upstairs bedroom while I quietly gathered the children's footed pajamas and favorite blankets and shoved them into their monogrammed duffel bags my mother had given them for Christmas. My brother was in the basement with all of the kids telling his wife about the hurried change in plans, and she took charge with action and efficiency. Within the hour, the three of us had their car packed for the long drive back to California, and were loading the kids into their transplanted car seats for what my brother and I were opting to call a *special visit to Grandma*.

I leaned deep into my brother's car, gently pushing a favorite stuffed cow aside so that I could take my oldest son Jeffrey's face in my trembling hands. "I love you. I will be at Grandma's in a few days to get you. This will be a great adventure. Please help Uncle Eric and Auntie Jackie with Bean and Abby—with Bean especially." I felt guilty at not only the sin of omission, but at the heavy burden I was placing on his young shoulders, and for what I knew was coming but could not yet let him see.

I kissed my fingers and lightly touched Bean's cheek. He didn't like kisses. Autism means different boundaries for my second son, and as badly as I sometimes want to hug him, I love him best by simply smiling. "Be a good boy on your adventure! I love you."

Abby was so little she didn't really know what was happening. From her car seat she kicked her legs happily and clutched the purple and white blanket my mother had crocheted her when she was born. Every grandchild had one. I smiled at her rosy cheeks. "Grandma can fix the holes in your blanket when you get to her house. I love you." I kissed the top of her head and looked away. I didn't want to scare them with tears.

My brother hugged me tightly in the driveway.

"I'll call you along the way. It's going to be okay. Call a lawyer now." He kissed my cheek and got in the car, waving his arm high out the window. "Love you, Sis—wave at Mama!"

I could see the outlines of my children through the dark tints on his SUV windows, but not the details of their faces. I imagined my smile was brave, and I waved animatedly as they honked and pulled slowly away.

I stood in the driveway for a long time—maybe part of me is still there—staring at the place the car vanished on the horizon, the pale pavement warm on my bare feet. Time was stretched and compressed, silent and roaring that day. The sky was blue. The leaves were starting to change. My children were safe.

There are gaps in my memories, but little things billow up. Lost images, things I thought were gone. The scent of elderflowers. A yellow butterfly. A birdcage with a blue singing parakeet. Poplar leaves against azure sky.

I walked back into the too-empty, too-silent house. I could hear David snoring through the ceiling, but there was no movement.

At my desk, I sat down and wrote a letter to my parents—my dad, my mom, and my stepdad. I had phoned my mother when Eric and Jackie were packing the car, so she knew that things were bad and that the kids were on their way. But the letter peeled back the layers of pain and sorrow I had spent three years trying to hide. I spelled out the horror of narcotics, the relapses, the hospitalization, the things I had skimmed up against in our conversations but never directly addressed. I laid it all out, open and raw. I never meant to hide from anyone, but for a long time I had hoped to repair my marriage, and I didn't want my family to think badly of David. Opening that vein and letting the blood flow was a concrete move from which I knew there was no return. When I wrote that letter, I surrendered my last remnant of hope.

I will never know what happened in that backyard. The only thing that I know for certain is that, in the space of a bare moment, I moved from years of instability and unrelenting fear into a space of irrevocable action. There were no more questions. There was no more waiting. There were no more excuses. There were simply facts and the action required to deal with them.

The next day I filed for divorce.

I knew he was an addict when I married him. He was open about his problems, honest to a fault. He felt that frankness was the only way to deal with his demons. The only time that his honesty ever failed was when the pain was too much.

He talked frequently about the mental illness in his family and his troubled childhood and early home life. He openly used drugs to help him feel more normal and to interact with the world. He used them intentionally, with spiritual and psychological aims, and he was frank about it. He told me that once when he was a teenager he purposely sparked a joint in his mother's kitchen, hoping desperately that she would stop him. She didn't. And his heart broke. He had a complicated relationship with her for the rest of his life.

He talked freely about his drug use and occasionally took a kind of wry delight in making other people uncomfortable if they were obfuscating or pretending that they were somehow better than he was. He had a powerful gift of insight, but not everyone wants to be seen or to have a light shined on them when they are hiding.

While he might have had a handle on his spiritual and psychological bases, the physiological reality of drug use eventually tripped him up. Drugs sank their claws deep into him physically, and he wasn't able to control that drive, that need for dopamine and the chemical cocktail that his brain craved just to feel normal, not even high. To nobody's surprise he couldn't will himself not to need them anymore, even when he didn't want them anymore.

His struggle to overcome the physical addiction was a shock to him. He'd always been able to outsmart things, but the physiological effect of drugs wasn't something that responded to reason. His body was crippled by a chemical dependency that his mind couldn't overcome. He found a path out of that hell by submitting his body to rigorous physical training. He started exercising and then weight-lifting. As a big man, he slid into that role naturally and with ease; heavy training allowed him to overcome and conquer what his mind could not manage. His strength was unearthly.

David had been clean and sober for nine years when he relapsed, but I always knew the risk. There is no point at which an addict isn't an addict anymore, and anyone who's had an unfortunate front-row seat to addiction has this truth written on their heart.

I missed it. I had grown complacent, and maybe he had too.

I honestly didn't think anything of it the first time. I should have caught it. I knew better. But I was standing in the kitchen holding Abby. My milk had let down with her squirming, the boys were arguing about trains. Bean was undergoing testing for autism, Abby wasn't sleeping well—because no four-month-old sleeps well—and Jeffrey was having trouble using the potty reliably. I didn't just have my hands full; every part of me was full.

David leaned against the kitchen counter holding a bottle of pills that the dentist had given me after a root canal. Hydrocodone. They nauseated me, and I had shoved them to the back of the kitchen cabinet where we kept medicine away from little hands.

He had tweaked his back a few days earlier lifting weights and had been chewing through the ibuprofen. He shook the bottle of pills from across the kitchen and asked, "Do you mind if I take these?"

I remember frowning while bouncing Abby on my shoulder and squeezing my elbows into my sides to keep milk from soaking my shirt. I was annoyed at the boys fighting behind me, and I needed to feed the baby.

I struggled to focus, looking down at my fussing infant. "Whatever. I'm not taking them." I stepped over the mess of trains and little boy arms and legs, reaching under my shirt, the baby already nosing and grunting for her meal.

I'm not sure there is anywhere else I can pinpoint such a precise moment of loss. I heard the bottle open. He did it right in front of me in our kitchen, just like he did with his mom so many years earlier. All those years, all that experience, all those meetings, all that love. He never hid anything. Right in front of me.

And I missed it.

The morning I sent our children off into the horizon with my brother, David had scheduled minor outpatient surgery for an ongoing knee problem. The procedure was at a surgical clinic, not with his regular doctor where his drug history was well-documented. I called the clinic ahead of time to remind them of his history, I called his primary care physician and asked him to please follow up, and I called the nurse at the clinic after he was in surgery, who assured me he was a *Tylenol Only* patient.

A nurse wheeled him out to the portico where outpatients were loaded into their waiting vehicles. She was cheerful and kind as she handed me his paperwork. "What did you give him?" I asked, shuffling through the papers, until my fingers landed on the scrip. "Oh, God…Oh God, no….Did you give him narcotics? Please tell me you didn't give him any narcotics. He's an addict. Oh God no, you didn't, please…"

The nurse was defensive and looked perplexed. "We asked him if he was in pain. He said he needed something stronger than Tylenol. It will be fine; these are really well tolerated." She pushed his wheelchair toward the open car door.

My vision swam, and I thought I was going to faint. I grabbed the open door with icy hands. David was already in a familiar haze, his eyes dilated and unfocused as the nurse was helping him into the passenger seat. I stood shaking, discharge papers clutched in my hands. Outside, I was pale and trembling; inside, the ground was breaking apart in a heaving landslide.

Three years earlier, after he had blown through the pills from my dentist, he went to his dentist, and then to our primary doctor to get his own prescriptions. And then he called around for a refill. He admitted to me he was doctor shopping and that he knew it was a slippery slope. We weathered that together at home, the two of us battling to get him back on track. While it was scary, we caught it early, and I knew with all my heart that he could stay sober. So did he.

David had everything to fight for. He was a loving and engaged father; he doted on his kids. He was the type of dad who would tirelessly give piggyback rides, play flashlight tag, and add his warm laugh to bedtime stories. He was big and generous with his love, with his encouragement, and with his time. He came home to a wife he loved and to children who adored him. The family life I offered to him was something he treasured, something he had always wanted. Just as he afforded me space to heal and grow, I did my best to protect the fields around his heart.

We were in escrow on our second home when the next relapse came. One quiet afternoon, I got a call from the bank questioning a new $5,000 charge on our credit card. I told them it must be a mistake. It wasn't. David had found a way to buy pills on the internet. We managed to pay down the debt, close escrow on our new home, and get him into a twelve-step program. He lasted longer that time.

The next blow came when he tried to hide his relapse by having pills delivered to his work. He wasn't meeting goals or managing his team, and he was fired. Looking back, there are so many things I should have seen, so many markers indicating the pitch and desperation of the slide, but I wanted to believe he was going to be okay. And he knew I wanted to believe in him. We were like a twisted O. Henry story.

I foolishly kept thinking things couldn't get worse. When you love an addict, you wonder where the bottom will be, where they cannot fall any further. After you fall long enough, hitting the rocks of the bottom starts to sound beautiful. At least at the bottom you will know the fall is over, and you can finally trust your footing and find your bearings.

We were nowhere close yet.

One spring Sunday, I got up before the kids to put a pan of cinnamon rolls in the oven. I wanted to surprise them, and things were so lean by that point that a pan of cinnamon rolls would be a treat. David was fighting another relapse, and I had spent several nights with him on the bathroom floor. Those horrible scenes you see in the movies, with the vomiting and the shaking and the sweating and chills? It's accurate.

I had left him in a fitful sleep, and after I pulled the warm rolls from the oven, I went back upstairs to check on him. He was sitting up in bed, but his head was rolled back, his eyes half-lidded, and there was an open bottle of pills spilling across the nightstand and onto the floor. I had no idea where they had come from. In his right hand he held a large pistol. *I didn't even know he owned a gun.*

Petrified, I backed out of the room as quietly as I could, not thinking but reverting to instinct. I silently woke the kids, wrapped them in blankets, told them they must be very quiet because Daddy was sleeping, and we tiptoed down the stairs. My heart was hammering in my chest and my ears were rushing with racing blood. "Please God just let us get out of here safely please let us get out please let us get out...."

I passed Abby, wrapped in her blanket and rubbing her eyes, to seven-year-old Jeffrey and asked him to strap her into her seat while I buckled Bean. I kept glancing over my shoulder, every muscle taut and strained, holding my breath against my thumping heart, waiting for him to appear in the doorway. I pushed the button to open the garage door and cringed at the horrifically amplified noise as it rolled slowly up its metal track.

As I backed out of the driveway and turned the corner of our street, I started to shake. Relief flooded my body and my vision swam. I had no idea where I was going, but we were out. I kept looking in the rearview mirror expecting to see him. The kids were peering at me with wide eyes from the back seat of our Suburban. I lied to all of us and said, "Hey guys, everything is going to be okay. We're going to visit some friends from church and get some breakfast."

I couldn't think what else to do. I couldn't think at all. I drove toward our friends' house, knowing they would forgive me the early hour and be able to help.

That afternoon, while the kids and I were safe, three men from our church went to my home. David was awake and welcomed them in. They told him why his family was gone and offered him an intervention requiring in-patient care. David agreed that he needed help, and they took him to the hospital. Once he was gone, another pair of men—one of them an off-duty law-enforcement officer—went back to my home and combed the entire house. They found a duffel bag hidden in the back of David's closet filled with bags of narcotics from pharmacies in Russia, China, Taiwan, and India. And they found several guns hidden in various places around the house. It was so much worse than I ever imagined, *and I knew what to look for.*

They collected everything. The bags of pharmaceuticals were taken to the hospital where the doctors cataloged everything but admitted they didn't even know what some of it was. To this day, I don't know what they did with the guns. I decided that if David were ever to ask me, it would be better if I honestly didn't know what happened. He never asked.

David willingly spent twenty-one days under hospital care.

I looked blankly at the naïve little nurse telling me *it would all be okay* after she just gave my addict husband narcotics and pushed him into the passenger seat of our family Suburban with three car seats in the back. *What version of okay do you mean? In what world does an addict on a death-spiral taking one from the strong pile lead to happily ever after?* Waves of nausea and anger alternated, as I struggled to fit the key into the ignition and see through my furious, panicked tears.

That was relapse number eight.

I drove home pleading the entire time to an unseen God to help me do the right thing next, while David nodded in and out of consciousness.

The house was silent. The kids were somewhere on the road to California, and David was upstairs. But as far as I could tell, he hadn't moved. I had half-heartedly attempted to wake him while my brother was packing to tell him the kids were leaving, but the narcotics had stolen him. He was breathing, but I couldn't wake him. I suspected he had stashed a two- or three-day supply from the clinic nurse and took them before I arrived. I wished I didn't know about such things.

The wind rustled through the trees in the backyard, but instead of giving me familiar comfort, it exacerbated my aching heart. The small blue and green parakeets were chirping happily from their cage in the sunroom, but it felt all wrong. Golden autumn light pooled on the floor under the window, amplifying the unnatural silence echoing through the empty house. *My empty heart.* There were whispers of memory on the edges of my vision everywhere I turned, but they were fleeting, transparent, veiled and yellow, like old photographs curling in the sun. Nothing seemed real.

As I sat at my desk staring out the window with the letter to my parents on my screen, the cursor blinked patiently at the end of my name. I hit send and pushed myself wearily back from the old wooden desk. I had picked it up at an estate sale back during a happier time, and it was where I had discovered and tested out my fledgling writing and design wings. Learning to write had been an unexpected joy and had allowed me to build and be a part of a community of other writers, thinkers, and friends. I ran my hands over the smooth wood and wondered if there was any part of this scary new reality I could share with the world. For the time being, the answer was "No. Not a thing."

I stood in perfect isolation.

It was time to talk to David. I had erected razor wire around my heart, higher with each subsequent relapse, but I still loved him. I still saw in him the vibrant, joyous man standing on the edge of the Pacific Ocean, singing the sun into the darkening sea while he waited for me. I would have traded nearly anything in the world to be able to choose a different path. I would have given almost anything to make him better, to release him from the opiate nightmare that had destroyed our family—had destroyed Us.

But I would not trade our children.

Part of the reason I told my brother everything, why I wrote my parents the letter laying it out, was that I needed to burn all escape routes. I didn't entirely trust myself to let him go. With the letters, there was no taking refuge in the fact that no one knew what was happening, no hiding in the increasingly desperate and vain hope that he could recover. To protect our children, I had to get us out.

I could not afford to see him haloed in my mind by the beach sun, smiling at me sitting next to him on the train trestle in my floating skirt and ankle bells. Those days were gone, and if there was the slimmest hope for him to recover, it might lie in my letting go. I do not attribute nobility to my actions in retrospect—my marriage was over.

I hoped that maybe, just maybe, in losing everything we worked so hard to build, he might find that beautiful core that existed somewhere inside and grab onto it. But I couldn't afford to leave anything hanging on that hope. It was an empty hook, nothing more.

I steeled myself, knowing this conversation was going to suck more than anything I had ever done, and I walked upstairs.

2

Rust Never Sleeps

SEPTEMBER 11, 2009

Tears are salty like the sea, and like the tireless sea, they rust even the finest iron over time. Only tears aren't tireless. Oh no, they are not. Tears weep and sop and wring out, and leave one like a sodden rag, taking with them the energy to even make more.

If a soul is dry, wrung, dusty, will the rusting stop? I wonder, when the old iron belt was in full roar, and the smelters lit the night like stars all along the Great Lakes, what happened to the slag as it was raked from the molten metal? Did the iron care as the refiner's fire burnt off parts of itself? Did it ever cry "enough!" only to be lost forever in the warped curls of heat rising from the unending fires?

DIVORCE WASN'T SUPPOSED TO HAPPEN to us. We were different—everyone tells themselves this lie. We all believe we are different. Everyone who finds themselves on the precipice where I was standing must wonder the same thing. What the hell happened? We imagine ourselves different, but we all have the same heart.

ϗ

1990

I shoved the stack of flat cardboard pizza boxes against the counter with my hip, and added another folded box to the pile on the shelf. I worked quickly and efficiently, wondering idly how many boxes I had made over the last couple years. I knew the teenage boys in the kitchen were watching me as I fluidly folded and stacked box after box. I was young and hadn't yet realized vanity wasn't a basis for an identity, and that the power I derived from it was made of ashes and dust.

I liked to proclaim loudly—*why was I always so loud in my stupidity?*—that I preferred the drama-free friendships of men. I was simply repeating things I'd heard my grandma say, but it naïvely escaped me that my grandma was alone and not terribly happy. I was the proto-manic pixie dream girl, before such a traitorous creature had been given a name.

"Hey Trace, come out here." My boyfriend Max, who also was my boss—*because of course he was*—poked his head into the kitchen. His blond dreadlocked hair was pulled back into a ponytail under a black baseball cap, and he had a red canvas apron tied over his sweatpants. He was everything my mother hated, and that made him perfect.

Shoving the last of the empty boxes onto the shelf, I glanced at the small gold Mickey Mouse watch on my wrist. Nearly eleven. Freshly eighteen, I didn't need to be cut loose at ten o'clock anymore. I liked being there later—it was extra money, but it was also quieter, and easier to talk with friends sitting at the long wooden bar waiting on their late-night pizzas.

From the TV over the bar, Norm and Cliff were perfectly mimicking my real life as I pushed through the swinging doors to the front. A motley collection of friendly faces turned as I walked in. The regulars were nice and small talk made the evenings pass quickly. A little harmless flirtation meant better tips, and since I was eighteen, I could legally pour their beers. I had discovered dudes tipped better when a young woman could hold several pitchers at once—a fact I was happy to exploit.

Max was holding up the bar, talking animatedly. It was his thing to be unimpressed by people and keep up a façade of detached coolness at all times. *Totally annoying.* But right then, he was talking with someone he wasn't even attempting to be cool with, which piqued my interest.

I leaned on the open ice machine and idly reached down for a piece to chew. "What's up, Max?"

"Hey Trace, I wanted to introduce you to an old friend. This is Big Dave. A lot of people are afraid of him on account of how big he is, but he's alright." He moved aside and gestured extravagantly. "Dave, this is Tracy. Tracy, Big Dave."

I smiled around Max's oddly grand posture, and looked toward Dave. "Hi, I'm Tracy." I held out my hand.

Big Dave reached forward and smiled. He was a large man, Max wasn't kidding. His hand engulfed mine, but he had kind eyes—wide open, gold-flecked hazel, with long lashes. His brown hair was thick and shoulder-length, streaked with the remnants of summer sun, and he wore a full beard. He was dressed conservatively—a button-up collared shirt under a coat, which was surprising. Most of Max's friends looked like Max—a bunch of prismatic hippies and punks. This guy absolutely wasn't that.

"Why are people scared of you?" I said without thinking, and looked from Dave to Max, perplexed. "I don't understand. There is nothing to be afraid of in this guy."

Dave laughed—a rich genuine laugh that rose from deep in his chest. "Don't listen to Max. Most of what he says is complete crap."

I liked him immediately. "It's nice to meet you, Dave. I'm not afraid of you." Max *was* full of pretentious crap a lot of the time, and there was something about Dave that was immediately familiar and genuine. *Safety.*

He seemed so much more of a grownup than anyone else I had met through Max. "How old are you?" I blurted out. *Dammit.* It wasn't just the clothes, it was the way he held himself. He had good posture—he didn't lean on the bar like everyone else. His large hands were strong and clean, and he had laid an American Express card on the counter for his tab—I didn't know anyone with a credit card, let alone an American Express.

"Please, call me David. I'm twenty-four. I work for Apple. I have two much older brothers and an older sister. And I'm a Pisces." His eyes glinted mischievously.

"I'm sorry. I didn't mean to be rude…." I stammered.

He raised his glass toward me and chuckled as he took another sip. "Not at all. I like your forthrightness. You're different, too. I can see you."

"What?" I wrinkled my nose. "You see me? What's that mean?" He didn't look at me the way the beer-filled men at the bar did. He didn't look at me the way the teenage boys in the kitchen did. He didn't look at me the way anyone else did. He didn't make me feel invisible and consumed at the same time. He looked at my face, and he asked my mind to respond. I had absolutely no idea what to do with that level of engagement.

He continued to look amused but utterly unflustered. He reached into a satchel on the stool next to him, pulled out two dog-eared books, and set them on the bar. I read constantly, and I loved meeting another reader. *Of course he reads.* He could see me trying to peek at the titles, so he twisted them around for my ease without ever breaking form.

"It means, I think I know you." He slid the book with Jung on the spine toward me. "Max is right about very little, but he is right that not many people react to me the way you did. I'm used to defenses, to wariness. I don't fully know why, but it happens. You immediately proclaimed yourself unafraid. You have no idea how rare that is in my life."

I picked up one of the worn books and turned it over, shrugging as nonchalantly as I could manage, though my heart was suddenly thumping. "There's nothing to be afraid of, right?"

He let loose a roar of a laugh. "Sister, if only more people understood that!"

What did he mean about fears? I knew he wasn't talking about himself. We barely knew each other, but the conversation had already taken a turn for the deeper waters I craved with friends. Idle chit-chat drove me mad, and I was terrible at small talk. Books were almost always more interesting. In order to mine some philosophy and psychology, I had started taking classes at the local community college during the day.

He spoke softly, "Let me guess: you're eighteen. I know that because Max is not a fool—well, he can be, but that's another conversation. You know Max isn't right for you, but he serves what you need right now, which is a way to separate yourself from your parents, maybe your mom specifically. You're smarter than many of your friends—which doesn't mean you're making smart decisions, but you know who Jung is already—and you feel isolated because of it. We are the same this way."

I stood, eyes wide, mouth slightly parted, clutching the book, and staring at him.

"It's okay," he smiled gently. "We all do what we need to do to get by. There's no need for fear or guilt. It just is what it is. You're okay."

I felt naked, vulnerable, and it took a moment to realize I was still standing behind the bar in Jake's, while the *Cheers* bumper music played from the overhead TV and dishes clattered noisily on the other side of the wall.

Who was this guy? And why could I suddenly not imagine life without him?

❧

Things with my family were hard at that point. I thought my mom didn't understand me at all—*hello, every teenage girl ever*—she didn't read books, wasn't interested in art, and rolled her eyes at her melancholic daughter. Years later, I would better understand my mother's helplessness in the face of a mismatched and complicated daughter, and how sometimes difficult emotions manifest in equally mismatched ways, but that was still lifetimes down the road.

My parents had divorced that year, right as I graduated from high school. My graduation party was a chaotic tempest of family tension, divorce papers, surprise relatives, pressure to look happy, and enough stress that I ended up in the hospital with abdominal pain instead of at Grad Night with my friends.

At first, I had tried to be supportive of both my parents. But my mother had had me very young, and she found herself in her mid-thirties suddenly single, quite pretty, and getting a lot of attention. The space for me disintegrated in the rush of her new friends, new life, and new boyfriend. I wasn't mentioned in the divorce papers, since I graduated before they were filed. There were agreements about my younger brothers, their time, holidays, money…but I was nowhere. The sting of being invisible compounded my sense of loss. The vacuum filled quickly with a scathing, self-righteous fury—a defensive skin over a foundational fear and abandonment issues that would plague me for years.

And all of that made Max appealing. I had always been a good girl. Even when my friends were sneaking out of their bedroom windows at night to meet boys, I had stayed inside the lines. My high school boyfriend and first love was one of the genuine good guys. He was kind and thoughtful and loyal and honorable. He was cute and drove a muscle car, and he had loved me. He was my first everything. Then my parents' divorce tore the stability of my world violently apart, and it became clear that all the good things break, and so I had broken him, too.

Jung had lots to say about that. When I thought of my high school boyfriend, I couldn't carve out a place where someone so good belonged. It was much safer to push the good boy away. *Go, find some nice girl who deserves you, it's not me. Here, I will prove it to you....*

And so I started dating Max. He was five years older and not in school. He didn't own a car—he was a hipster before there was such a thing—and he rode his bike everywhere. He listened to punk and thrash metal, and shook his appropriated blond dreadlocks in mosh pits. He worked late and didn't get up before noon. He lived in a bachelor apartment with two other guys who appeared to have similar life goals, and where there was usually a bong on the coffee table and leftover pizza in the otherwise empty refrigerator.

Max was the perfect backdrop for me to work out my tragedy. Then I met David.

The conversation that began over the wooden bar continued late into the night on the sidewalk behind Jake's. Max's mountain bike leaned against the alarmed back door while my old red Volkswagen Bug was parked nearby, its small windows slowly fogging in the cool California night.

David had produced a pink candle while we talked. He dripped wax onto the curb and planted the taper in the soft puddle, holding it carefully until it cooled into place. The three of us talked as the wind tossed the flame around, and the wax slowly trickled down into a pretty, pink stalagmite.

David pulled a silk-wrapped deck of tarot cards from his coat pocket. "When is your birthday?" He shuffled the cards with ease, looking intently at me.

"October. Why?" I considered tarot cards and palm reading to be harmless party tricks, but it was always fun to hear things about yourself.

He laughed and cut the deck, "Because I already told you I'm a Pisces, and I want to know what you are. Shuffle the cards." He held the deck out.

I took them gingerly, and instead flipped them over and fanned them out to see the artwork. They were beautiful and not structurally very different than any playing cards—four suits, and an expanded royal court. I said as much.

He burst out laughing—he had such an easy, ready laugh. "Most people don't catch that quite so quickly. Yes, they are—earth, air, fire, and water. Here, lay them out like this…" He smoothed the silk handkerchief, arranged the cards from my hands in a cross formation, and looked down to study them.

I don't remember what the cards were. I don't remember how late we sat there, how long David looked at the cards, or what Max was doing. What I do remember is David looking at me over the dwindling candle flame and saying very quietly, "You are…you are much more than you know."

"I know I don't believe in tarot cards." I smiled at him.

He grinned up at the sky. "Of course you don't! It doesn't matter if you believe or not." His eyes were mirthful, softening his words. "The truth doesn't care about your belief. Cards. The stars. The Bible. Open up a book and point to a word. It doesn't matter—they're all telling our stories. What matters is our willingness to see. Unless we are willing to see, we remain blind."

1991

David rented the third floor in an old Victorian in a tiny beach town on the north rim of Monterey Bay. The house badly needed painting, but was still grand in her redwood construction, impervious to the constant fog and intermittent heat of the coast. Morning glory and jasmine vines covered the front porch, mixing with the scent of warm redwood and salt air in a heady perfume.

The front door was heavy, the original hardware still intact and stubborn to move in its antiquity. Inside, it would take a few moments for your eyes to adjust to the dim parlor. The wood carried the patina under its dust of decades of polish and beeswax, and breathed the memories of a million seaside days. I would fantasize about restoring that house for years after David had moved out.

On the third floor, under the angles and squares of dormer windows and walls built as afterthoughts, there was a bathroom with a pedestal sink and a claw-foot bathtub large enough for a grown man. And there was David's room.

From the dim upstairs hallway, you were blinded when you opened his door. His space was austere in its simplicity, starkly more so juxtaposed against the heavy darkness of the Victorian architecture. He had painted the entire space white—the floors, walls, ceilings, and sashes. White. While the paint was drying, he had burnt dozens of sticks of incense, and the aromatic smoke had dried with the paint and mingled with the crisp salty air caught by the open windows. There was no adornment on the walls, simply his bed under a low west-facing dormer, and his prayer mat and altar facing east. Everything else was perfectly clean and spare.

It was a January morning when I found myself sitting in a pool of sunlight on the white floor. I was waiting for David to finish his morning prayers. He tapped the brass bowl on his altar three times and snapped his mala beads.

"Did you see the 'For Rent' sign across the street? On the upstairs window, next to the piano shop?" He placed his beads on the table next to his prayer scroll and looked quizzically over his shoulder at me.

The week before, I had moved out of my mom's house in one drama-filled night. It had been a rash decision, made in anger and frustration and colored by the deeply growing schism between the mother I remembered—and still missed—and the woman who had taken her place after the divorce. *Happens to everyone, Sweetie.*

I had been bouncing between friends' couches, my stuff thrown hastily into cardboard boxes at Max's apartment.

"No, let's go look!"

Passing from the brightness of David's upstairs attic rooms down through the heavy dark Victorian, and out again into the brilliance of the seaside daylight had become something of a joke with us about passing between worlds. We pulled the heavy old door closed behind us and squinted our eyes against the white daylight. It was winter, but it was California winter.

I had found a choice parking spot a few doors down, and my red Bug glittered in the sunshine. I had recently painted the cover of *Aoxomoxoa,* a palindromic Grateful Dead album, on the front of the hood.

"You did this?" David stopped to admire my work.

I was suddenly self-conscious. David was a grown-up with an engineering background and a real job. He listened to jazz and public radio. I felt so childish, painting my car for a band. "Yeah, I did… I like the Dead. I know it's silly…" I trailed off.

He grinned widely and looked intently at me. "You like what you like, own it. There's too much pretension and snobbery in the faces people try to cultivate. Just be who you are. Besides, the Dead are awesome songwriters and some of the best storytellers we have."

He started to hum a melody I knew well, and when he caught my eye, he beamed at me and perfectly sang the lyrics from *Terrapin Station:*

Counting stars by candlelight, all are dim but one is bright;
The spiral light of Venus, rising first and shining best,
From the northwest corner of a brand new crescent moon,
While crickets and cicadas sing, a rare and different tune

His eyes twinkled with joy at my clearly visible surprise. "The Dead are poets. Never be ashamed of what you love. It speaks to you. Come on, let's go see the apartment."

We walked down the narrow street toward the piano store, and I scrawled the number down on the "For Rent" sign. It was a second story walk-up, so we couldn't peer in the windows, but the building was newer and looked vacant.

We walked the three blocks toward the beach, David humming softly, but allowing me my silent thoughts. I didn't know how to find a roommate, and I had never rented an apartment before. The year before I had stayed in the dorms at CalArts as part of a program for gifted kids in the arts. It was a great experience, but it was the closest I had come to living on my own until the week before. I missed my brothers, and I didn't really know where to start in taking care of myself as an adult.

The sun hit the sparkling water from the east, making the whole bay glitter. During the summer, the town was thick with tourists and summer rentals, the boutique shops overflowing, and the beaches packed with sunburnt visitors. But during the winter, it was quiet. The beaches were deserted and the shops and restaurants kept shorter hours. If you walked down to the water first thing in the morning, you might encounter perfectly smooth sand left by the high tide of the night before, marred only by a jogger and his dog. I loved winter in California.

David turned just before we got to the sand and headed for his favorite café to order two Indian teas with milk.

"Come on, I want to show you something." He handed me one of the teas.

We headed up the street and walked along the slow, wide river making its way to the sea before we veered back into the neighborhood. He made a sharp left and turned into what looked like someone's garden. I paused, not wanting to trespass.

"Come on, it's okay. I promise." He turned and made his way through the garden and headed up a steep hilly path behind the flowers.

The camellias gave way to ghostly, giant eucalyptus trees as I followed him up the rocky path. At the top of the hill was a single set of train tracks. The heavy creosote coated ties lay on a bed of sharp gravel, their oily scent mingled with the pungent eucalyptus leaves. To the east, the tracks curved and disappeared around a eucalyptus lined bend. To the west, the tracks continued across a giant old redwood railroad trestle.

David was ahead of me, carefully stepping on the ties as he made his way over the trestle. "Do the trains still come?!" I yelled to his back.

"Yeah, but the morning train already came through, and the next one isn't until late afternoon. We're safe."

The trestle carried the train tracks over the wide, lazy river we'd been walking beside earlier and continued on to the north. To the south and west, Monterey Bay glittered deep blue. David sat down on the ocean-side edge of the trestle on a little bump-out with a railing, high over the river below, and slipped off his Birkenstocks—the only outward appearance of hippie he allowed himself. He dangled his feet and patted the spot next to him.

"Come. Sit."

I folded my skirt between my knees and held onto the old wooden railing. The view was beautiful—you could see all the way to Monterrey. In the summer the fog would obscure the horizon, but that morning, it was clear. I sat down next to him gingerly and sipped my lukewarm tea.

He squinted at me over the top of his cup. "So Jung says the scariest thing we can do is to accept ourselves. That we do almost anything to avoid facing our souls."

"I think that's a mighty big thought for a Saturday morning." I smiled.

He nodded. "Ha! It is. But there's a weight behind your eyes. When I was saying my prayers this morning, I could feel your heaviness. Tell me what you're mad about."

I was mad about everything. I was mad about my parents' divorce. I was mad about my mom. I was mad at my dad for not making her stay. I was mad at everyone for lying to me about my parents. I was mad at my mom for living a second adolescence when I was supposed to be having my first. I was mad that I was on my own and didn't know what to do. I was so mad at my mom and dad for abandoning me.

He listened. "Yeah. That's a lot of mad."

I stared at the ocean, anger still coating my thoughts.

He rested his hands on the railing and looked toward the sea. "One of the things I have discovered is that 'mad' is often a disguise for more complicated emotions. We're hurt, so we default to 'mad'. We're afraid, but it's easier to be 'mad.' That sound familiar?"

I scowled at him, and he laughed. "I told you I could see you."

"So what do I do?" I pleaded.

"Ah, no. I can't give you your answers. You have to figure that out, but a good starting place is learning to accept yourself. Anger is your default. Instead of punishing yourself, be kind. Acknowledge that, accept it, and don't get stuck. So many people get stuck." He tipped his cup, swallowed the rest of his tea, and shook his head.

"I hate my mom." I stated flatly. "I hate her for what she's done to me."

"Yes. I believe you feel that way, but here's the thing. . .her path is hers. Your choice doesn't lie in what she's done or not done, but in what *you* choose to do. If you are going to allow yourself to be who you are, you must also allow others—*including your mom*—to be who they are. Acceptance isn't about you. It's universal."

I was perplexed. "But she did some wrong things. She did things she taught me not to do. I don't want to accept that." I felt childish again for the second time that morning.

He smiled again. "And? So what? She's human. You hate the fact that you have to be a grownup now, and you don't want to. That may not be fair, but it's real. Your mom is also a person, trying to sort out her own life and identity—remember how young she had you—and ironically, that has nothing to do with you. I know that's hard to hear."

I frowned and fiddled with my cup. I wanted an ally. I wanted someone to say "She's bad! You're being treated unfairly!" and that's not what David was giving me. He was insisting, gently, that I look at the big picture. *That's what he did. No easy way out.*

He was watching me closely. My face was like a picture show, always transparent to what was going on beneath. Dammit.

He picked up a stick from the stones around the railroad ties and smoothed out some dirt. He drew a series of circles connected by lines. "In the Kabbalah, a form of Jewish mysticism, there are eternal and unchanging paths to God. There are paths of mercy. There are paths of severity. At every juncture, we have a choice in which path we will take. The choices we make determine the life we lead, and our relationship with God. We can make it hard. Or we can be willing to learn. God is patient. He's got all the time in the world."

He laughed at himself, tossed the stick over the railing, and we both leaned forward to watch it fall downward, drop into the moving river, and head slowly toward the sea.

When I talk about the complicated unraveling of my marriage, the questions inevitably arise: *Why did you stay so long? Why did you give him so many chances? Why didn't you leave the first time he relapsed?*

I asked myself those same questions. There is no one simple answer. I didn't leave because I loved him and we had three children and a life we had built together. I didn't leave because of who he was to me. I didn't leave because I could see him and I wasn't afraid of him, even twenty years later. I didn't leave because I had seen him conquer his demons in the past. I didn't leave because I knew he could do it. I didn't leave because I believed in him. I continued believing...until that day when I didn't anymore.

The complicated answer to those questions is that I left when I was told I could—by whatever means one wants to ascribe to that moment. Maybe it was inspiration. Maybe it was common sense. Maybe it was just that I finally hit my own breaking point.

What I do know is that because of how it happened, because I knew I had given everything I had, I was freed from the doubts that plague many people during a divorce. I never wondered if I could have done more.

Even when it got worse, I knew I was okay.

There is peace to be found in that kind of center. David taught me that.

David loved a young woman enough to show her the path of mercy. He allowed his love for me to warm my footsteps as I matured, and to leave the path of severity behind. I owed him as much, and I gave it freely.

I still have no regrets.

3

Piece - Work

OCTOBER 7, 2009

Exhaaaaaaaling. NOW.

Holy crap. Wednesday had to be one of the hardest days of my life. I made it, but it was sketchy. Thanks to a super-kind friend with the ability and means to jump in and roll up her sleeves. I have a new helper for Houston. Many, many, many of you reached out to me yesterday—and I am more grateful than I can express right now. My original friend who was going with me has a child in the hospital with the flu, and I'm sending my prayers her way tonight.

There is much more going on, of which I am yet unable to share. But trust me when I say it matters, and that I feel it when so many people offer their prayers on my behalf. It's humbling and powerful.

I leave for the airport in six hours, and I'm not even done packing. Ready or not, here I come....

WHAT HAPPENED NEXT WAS THE perfect storm of chaos and deadlines holding me together while my heart was utterly smashed. I didn't have time to think about how badly everything hurt. I had too much to do to consider the desperate nature of my situation.

I had three days between telling David that I was divorcing him and my flight for Houston. Three days to pack my bags for a national show in which I was a new vendor, to bring everything to decorate my booth, to pick up my patterns and trade-show materials from the printer, and to get it all into two suitcases. This was a bare-bones operation; there was nothing shipped ahead in containers, no fancy booth construction, no custom signs or lights. There was me offering my work and creativity and maybe a bowl of candy with which to woo potential customers.

In that same three days, I had to find and hire a lawyer and get all the paperwork started. I also had to make sure that I hadn't violated any laws by sending my children to California prior to filing. There was barely time to breathe. I cried the whole time, but I never stopped moving.

With each relapse it became clearer that I was going to have to support our family. When we had gotten married we both worked, and I had the better career in purchasing management; he was working in construction, having given up on engineering for his sobriety. When I was pregnant with Jeffrey, I realized that I wanted to be the at-home parent. I made this decision willingly, and David supported it happily. But it was also a decision that haunted me as I looked for ways to return to the workforce.

When Jeffrey was eight months old we moved from California to Washington State. Living in the Bay Area on one income was simply not possible, and we knew moving was a natural consequence of our decision to live on one income. We were able to buy our first house in Washington while still living in California, so when we arrived, ragged and haggard from a two-day drive with a baby and towing everything we owned, it was to an actual home of our own.

Being a stay-at-home mom with a baby can be isolating in the best of circumstances, but being a displaced stay-at-home mom in a new state left me without family, friends, or the support structure I had built over a lifetime in California. In an effort to create something of a social life and make friends, I joined a quilting group.

I didn't know how to quilt, but I had a sewing machine, and I was desperate to talk with grownups about something besides babies. The group met once a month at different friends' homes where we exchanged tips, ideas, and patterns and socialized for a couple of hours, usually over dessert. Over time I picked up skills from the women in my group, and I realized I had a knack for it; I made my first original quilt for a woman at church.

When I took the finished quilt to the meeting, my friends asked me to write down the pattern. They were so complimentary, and they encouraged me to go to the local independent fabric shop and talk to the owner, Jackie, about possibilities and marketing. They were more optimistic than I was, and they were my first cheering section.

I was nervous as I entered The Quilting Bee the first time. The shop was busy, bigger than I imagined, with classrooms full of sewing machines and gorgeous fabric lining the walls. My quilt was rolled up in a bag as I wandered among the brightly stacked bolts of beautiful cloth. There is a discernable difference between high-end cotton and the thinner, mass-market fabric available at chains. The Quilting Bee was my first experience with finer wovens, and I marveled at the colors, patterns, and variety. It was clear that the staff had taken great care in selecting the immense inventory of fabric. The notions and displays were beautiful, and stunning quilts lined the softly lit walls over warm wooden shelves. I was completely intimidated.

I took a deep breath and asked to speak with Jackie.

Jackie was a cheerful sprite of woman with more energy than ten people. She saw something in my work, and much to my surprise, she immediately placed an order for forty-eight patterns. She offered to test my pattern writing skills and have one of her staff make my quilt first—proofing it, double checking my instructions and measurements, and making sure everything was precise. She also sent me home with a pile of cuts from her beautiful bolts of fabric and told me to go and make more quilts. She became my mentor.

That established our relationship. I would take her my new sketches, and she would give me feedback and allow me to take cuts of new bolts of fabric to make my best sketches into quilts. Her staff would test my new pattern, and her store would then have the exclusive local rights to my new designs. I'd bring my completed sample to the store where she would hang it with the new pattern for sale. I was able to create new designs with the most beautiful, current materials—fabric and trim I could not otherwise have afforded—and I was able to generate income for my family. I created more than twenty original patterns in cooperation with The Quilting Bee.

It was Jackie who told me about Quilt Market in Houston and suggested that I apply. It was also Jackie who wrote my letter of recommendation.

It's a tough market to get into. I had never shown my designs anywhere except *The Quilting Bee* and my little sewing circle. But I had a cache of patterns I believed were good, I knew the directions were precise and easy to follow, and I had a group of people I respected and admired cheering me on. I submitted my portfolio and was accepted.

No one knew what was happening in my personal life, but they all believed in me professionally. It was enough.

Monday had been the Rubicon—the day of David's surgery, the day I finally moved from uncertainty to divorce, the day I sent my brother off with my children, and the day I wearily set my feet upon the stairs. My flight to Houston was scheduled for early Thursday morning. Time crushed in.

The one indulgence I allowed myself was to hammer out a quick blog post. I had started a blog four years earlier on a whim—before I was pregnant with Abby and before Bean had been diagnosed with autism—and it had quickly grown to be a lifeline of support and community. It began as a journal project, writing about mundane family life, imagining it as nothing more than something my children might someday enjoy reading. I would have treasured knowing what my grandmother thought when she was home with three small girls, and I hoped that some of my offspring might feel the same.

My blog, which I had named *Dandelion Mama* on a whim, morphed into something more as I documented the emotional journey of learning about autism advocacy with Bean's diagnosis and of how that affected our family. My writing was mostly a collection of short personal essays, but I had tried not to shy away from the hard parts. I opted for honesty instead of putting forth cultivated, pretty images of family life. I had written obliquely about the struggles in my marriage, but I had also chosen to leave some things private. David's struggles were his, and while I wrote about things being really hard and living on unemployment, I didn't address the causes of the pain. People could see it—readers and friends knew that things were hard—but I held just a few too-personal, too-painful cards close to my chest. I still believe this was the right choice at the time. I wanted to protect David's dignity if and when he managed to pull out of the nosedive. His heart and fall were not fodder for a blog.

But I did write about my own pain and sorrow. I was fair game.

Inside I was breaking apart. I was a raw nerve ending, arcing and shorting out in little electric bursts, leaving ash and soot trailing behind me. My eyes were red and swollen, but it was a shock to glance in the mirror and otherwise still look like the same person. Nothing about me felt the same.

Monday night was maybe the longest night of my life, and I got very little sleep. David had left for his mother's house at my request, and I spent the small hours wandering the empty rooms, curling up in my daughter's small pink and yellow bed because I couldn't bear the cavernous emptiness in my own bedroom.

Tuesday morning dawned with no room for emotional indulgences or inactivity. If I was going to manage a national trade show in two days, I had to lock the emotional mess inside of me behind a steel door and start getting crap done. My first job was to find a lawyer.

I called Legal Aid to see about low-cost options. There was a three month wait to have a consultation, and I didn't have that kind of time. What woman does in a crisis? I needed to have something in place to protect us before I brought the kids back from California the following week. My children were out of state, and I had a husband who was in a drug-induced downward spiral. I called the women's shelter to see if they had any resources; they did, but again, there was a months-long wait. There are very real obstacles to getting legal help when you are poor. In the middle of my own hell I found myself aching for women trying to extricate themselves from dangerous situations. My situation sucked, but my kids were safe with my family, and I wasn't in immediate danger.

I knew Mr. Stenzel from church. He was a friendly, kind man who had visited with me more than one Sunday when I had been tending a wiggly toddler or fussy baby out in the foyer during services. He was also something of a family law legend in our community. I called him next.

David's years of drug abuse, combined with his unemployment, had left us with almost nothing—it was actually worse than nothing, but I didn't know that yet—and Mr. Stenzel knew that I was without resources. He took my case anyway, for a flat fee, on which he said I could make payments. I'm still grateful to him for that kindness. He explained that he could not legally represent me without a nominal retainer, and as soon as I got that to him he could file papers and get the process started. Mercifully, Washington was a no-fault divorce state, and it would only take ninety days if there were no contestations or problems. I would also be immediately protected from David's financial decisions upon filing.

That afternoon, David's uncle volunteered $250 to use as a retainer for Mr. Stenzel's legal services, and the process of dissolution began.

I met Emily through my sewing group. She was a divorced grandmother, her children were grown, and she owned a small publishing company that printed a national travel directory of quilting and sewing stores. It was a niche market, but a good one, and she loved her work. She kept a small office staffed with capable women and a permanent graphic designer.

Emily had watched as I grew my fledgling business, designing and assembling all my patterns at home. She was part of the cheering section that encouraged me to first approach Jackie at The Quilting Bee, and she was kind and generous with her support. When I was accepted into Quilt Market Houston as a vendor, she offered the services of her shop to help redesign the covers and packaging of all my patterns. Previously, I had been gluing Costco-printed photographs of each quilt to a one-color printed cover, which I folded, stuffed with the pattern, and inserted into a clear hanging bag. They were attractive enough in a homespun way. With Emily's help, I moved to a four-color process, turning my work from homespun to professional.

The one thing Emily asked in return was to join me in Houston. I was allowed to bring two people to help with my booth; one spot was spoken for by a friend who would be my companion on the show floor, helping to answer questions and hopefully take orders. Emily would be taking the other spot. She'd be free to roam the show and enjoy herself and would enter with me on a vendor badge, which allowed early and behind-the-scenes access. She'd be available if I needed her for anything, but she'd also be on her own.

A couple of times I brought up what I believed I owed her for her help. She would tell me stories about her life when she was first divorced, when she had young kids, and how friends helped buoy her and her children. She said that she considered helping me payback and that I wasn't to worry too much about it because someday I would be able to lift another woman up the same way.

Emily's office was my next stop after retaining Mr. Stenzel.

We had printed hundreds of copies of one of my smaller patterns and planned to give them away as samples. I wanted my work to stand on its own, and I knew that my directions were good. There were plenty of cute designs, but not everyone could write clear, accurate directions. I wanted anyone who could sew a straight line to be able to make one of my patterns, and I was willing to give them away to prove my point.

Emily met me with the box of freshly printed patterns along with a huge stack of carbonless order forms, decorated with my name and logo, which she had created as a surprise. I looked professional and businesslike. As long as I didn't break down and cry on the floor of the show, I was ready.

I was hauling my suitcases up from the basement when my brother called. They were at our aunt's house in California, only a few hours from home. The drive was taking longer than it typically would because Bean's autism mandated more frequent stops and extra patience. They were going to stay the night with our aunt and then finish the drive fresh in the morning. My brother assured me things were going pretty well and that, other than a few necessary interventions, all three kids were doing okay.

I got to talk to the kids, putting on my brave voice as I sat at the top of my basement stairs, suitcases strewn where I had dropped them. My gratitude that they were away, safe, and protected, was immense. I knew that in a few days, after the show when I flew from Houston to San Francisco, I would have to tell them the truth, but for the time being they were happy. I had no idea if I was doing the right thing by not telling them, but it seemed like the kind thing. I did not want the messiness of adult agency spilling over onto them more than it already had, and at least they could have a few simple days of fun at Grandma's house before everything changed.

"Mama loves you. I'll see you soon." The little voices giggled over the long-distance line, clear and bright. My aunt had a dog and lots of books. They were happy.

The suitcases were in a disjointed, unzipped pile near my desk. It wasn't so much an office as a pass-through space between the living and dining rooms, but it served as my staging area. Patterns were piled everywhere along with colorful banners I had sewn together at the last minute to in an attempt to make my booth look more friendly. Having no idea what I was walking into helped because I didn't know where to be intimidated or what to fear. I did the best I could with what I had, and I worked that night until I was exhausted. It was easier that way, and it kept me from thinking too much. And exhaustion at least shoved me toward dreamless sleep.

I woke Wednesday morning on the couch, which felt safer than the stark emptiness of my bedroom and was much more comfortable than my daughter's tiny bed. I spent the day running last-minute errands and shifting around my airline reservations. Originally I had been flying on a round-trip ticket between Washington and Texas. Now I had a new stop in San Francisco to plan and three children's tickets to book.

Wednesday night the doorbell rang. I was ragged and disheveled, and my house was a disaster. When I opened the door, I was struggling to keep my two free bags each under fifty pounds, and I was an absolutely scowling and red-eyed mess.

On my porch were Emily and two other friends from quilt group, smiling and chipper and ready to roll up their sleeves and help. They had brought additional suitcases and hot food, and they tumbled in my front door with hugs and love. Emily assured me that we could transfer some of the printed materials to her suitcases and easily make the weight restrictions for the airline, and she got to work.

The other women opened the food containers on the kitchen counter and set to work preparing the first warm meal I had eaten in days. I sat down at my worn farmhouse table and cried into my hot food.

The ladies stayed with me late into the night, packing, repacking, and weighing each bag. They fed me, cleaned up the house, cleaned up the dishes from the delicious dinner they had made, and took turns hugging me and assuring me that, while life was going to be different now, it was also going to be okay. I wasn't sure I believed them, but when they left, the bags were all packed by the door, the house was clean, and everything was ready for morning when Emily would be by at zero-dark-thirty to pick me up for the airport. Through sheer force of will and carried by the love of dozens of women, I was headed to Houston.

2008

Just back from running errands, I kicked my shoes into the basket by the door and dropped my keys on the piano. Hollering a greeting to David, I ran upstairs to my bathroom, grabbed some clean folded clothes from the basket he had left on the bed, and turned on the hot water. After my scalding shower, the kids came to greet me and we played for a few minutes before a phone call pulled me away.

Heading downstairs, I found David standing at the kitchen sink with suds on his muscular forearms. I kissed his cheek. "How was your day?"

He frowned. "Abby's pooped three times. Did you notice the bathroom?"

In the eighteen months since David lost his job, we had tried a lot of things. He was on an upswing, and clean and sober again. I'm not even sure which relapse we were between, but we were both feeling like we had our family back on track.

As part of his recovery process and as a place to funnel his energy while looking for work, David had decided to serve our family more fully. He took up a lot of new chores around the house—chores that had traditionally been mine. He was always an involved and loving father, but until he lost his job, I was the stay-at-home parent, and much of the domestic work had been mine.

When I started picking up freelance jobs and taking commission work, David started cleaning the kitchen, doing the dishes, and mopping the floors. I still cooked dinner, but that was because I enjoyed it, and then he cleaned up. When I protested, he gently placed his finger on my lips and teased, "Shhhut up." We both laughed.

He started doing the laundry and vacuuming and the general constant pickup that is part of a family with three little kids. He changed diapers and still took care of the garage and yard work. Each night before bed, he did scripture study with the boys, and I was free to work on commissions or write.

At first I felt a heavy guilt about how much he was doing, but he continued to insist that not only did he want it that way, but that he needed to do it. For me, it was eye-opening. When someone else is making the way smooth, it's easy not to notice the work they put in—housework really is invisible work, even for someone who's done it for years. You quickly forget and just enjoy the clean towels, the fresh bathroom, and the folded clothes, but not the work it takes to provide those things. I quickly found that I liked my kids better when I didn't have to deal with every squabble, every diaper, and every mess. I liked my husband again, and some of the knots of worry around my stomach and heart started to relax.

He was still looking for full-time employment and working the twelve steps, but it felt like we were heading toward being whole again. I suddenly knew how easy it is not to notice the little things; he found out how important it was to be noticed. I knew how nice it was to have a clean, orderly home; he knew how much work a clean and orderly home takes. I knew the self-esteem and value of paid work; he knew the frustration and humility of house work. I knew the unexpected joy of coming home to my kids and a husband I loved; he knew the relief and happiness when I walked through the door and it was no longer just him.

The phone rang again and I whispered "I love you" as I took the call, phone cradled on my shoulder, riffling through the papers on the counter for a pen.

I was running behind for a meeting with a cabinet maker who had hired me to paint for him, and I hated to pop home and run again, but I was going to be late. I grabbed my purse, blew kisses, headed toward the garage, and hit the opener.

David stuck his head out the garage door from the kitchen. "What time will you be back? Don't forget family night tonight..."

He stood a moment in the doorway, wiping his sudsy hands on a kitchen towel, watching me back out of the driveway, while Abby hugged his leg and the boys wrestled behind him.

4

Admission

OCTOBER 18, 2009

So. Perhaps I'm more poetic, more heroic, when I'm also being vague and cryptic. Perhaps reading Dandelion is more fun when you don't know the names of the demons that are haunting me. Perhaps. While I've held my cards close to my chest for a while now, I've also made it no secret that my heart was breaking.

Three days before I left for Houston, I filed for divorce.

There is a lot of personal pain that will remain just that—personal. This was not a step I took lightly or with anything but the most serious gravity. I tried everything humanly possible to keep from taking this step, but once the time came, I knew what I had to do. Publicly, all I will say is that sometimes the agency of others really sucks.

Right now, I am protecting my children. I am trying to keep our lives as normal as possible; we are all tender and raw around the edges. The kids spent the time I was in Houston down in California with my family, and I flew to the Bay Area to pick them up straight from Texas.

Now. I turn my weary, red eyes to the horizon, and I can see tiny glimmers of light. I don't want to get too excited too soon, but I really, really think things may be looking up. The road is hard and there will be bumps, I am well aware. I know there are hurdles I cannot yet see; being a single-mama is nothing I ever planned to try. But I'm going to make it. I really, really am.

WHEN I LANDED IN CALIFORNIA to pick up my children I had secured everything I needed for the immediate financial future from my three days at the Quilt Market. The show had gone better than I had dared hope. It had been overwhelming, intimidating, and scary as hell to step out onto an international stage, and I felt like an imposter. *At first.*

The vendors around me were kind and helpful, and they offered tips and tricks to help set up a beautiful booth. All of my neighbors had been to the show before and were generous with their advice and encouragement, going so far as to help me pin my wares up and arrange my tables. As the show progressed and I found my stride, and the orders started flowing in. I moved from apprehension and nervous fear toward tentative hope.

The Quilt Market is a trade show for textile manufacturers, vendors, and wholesale companies who sell to stores, and it's also for publishers, magazines, and fabric companies looking for new talent. On the first day of the show, two women dropped by my booth to chat, asking about my designs and my background. I'd had many similar conversations that morning, so I didn't assign them any particular significance. My booth was full, so they gave me their card and I added it to the growing pile in my apron pocket. They waved cheerfully and said they'd stop back by when I wasn't so busy.

During a lull, my neighbors and I were flipping through the cards we'd collected, and they saw the card from the cheerful women. "Wait. Leisure Arts? Leisure Arts came to you?! Are you kidding?! Do you know who they are?" one of the women exclaimed.

Clearly I did not. This is where my naiveté saved me. I didn't know enough to be nervous when Leisure Arts, one of the largest publishers of art and quilting books in the United States, sought me out. My booth neighbors were delighted to fill me in on the textile publishing world and were positively gleeful when I wondered aloud if perhaps they were visiting everyone. Apparently, Leisure Arts was a big deal. A very big deal.

Later that afternoon I had a short meeting with their representatives, and when I left Houston I had a book proposal in my hands.

I also had orders from stores all over the United States, an offer from a European magazine interested in licensing some of my designs, and a major fabric company that wanted to talk with me about creating kits from my work with their textiles. I had walked right into the quilting world's version of a Triple Crown.

On Monday morning, exactly one week from the worst day of my entire life, I left Houston for California to retrieve my children.

Before I left for Houston, I had given my attorney a short written statement on why I was filing for divorce. I tried to provide a high-level review of the past three years as I described David's relapses and his stints in rehab. I was honest, but I wasn't interested in inflicting further pain or punishment. I wanted him to get better. I still hoped he could heal and be a father even if our marriage was over.

While I was in California with my family, a judge read the papers my attorney had submitted and placed a temporary restraining order on David. I didn't ask for it, but I learned that when someone does really scary things, judges can and do intercede on behalf of you and your minor children.

The drugs and guns were a matter of court record. David lost his right to have a firearm, and he lost the ability to visit his children without court-approved supervision. He had to remove himself from the family residence, and he could not come within a specified distance of me. He also had to start another 12-step program for narcotics. All before I returned from California with the children.

I protested weakly. David had never hurt me, but even as I said it I heard the eerily familiar cadence of the abused woman—even though I wasn't, I insisted—and how sadly inadequate my words were in the face of the awful choices he had made. It was an ironically terrible situation where my own protestations made it seem worse, and his own actions were damning. There was nothing to be done but be still, accept the court orders, and move forward.

1983

I was around eleven years old when I found the court papers. My mother's name was listed, but the man named as my father was not who I knew and called "Dad." I remember ice water flooding my veins as I sat on the floor holding the official pink papers with familiar signatures at the bottom. *Why didn't they tell me?* There were pictures of me, a cherubic two-year-old, at their wedding reception. I knew I had been there, but I had never considered *why*. My parents were hippies and had been married on the cliffs of Mendocino. My mom wore a sun dress with embroidered blue daisies, and my dad wore brown corduroy pants. It was as fancy as they got. The reception had been held in his parents' backyard, their younger faces carefully preserved in the family photo albums.

With my hands shaking I shoved the pink papers back in the filing cabinet and went to my room. I said nothing to anyone until later in the week, when I was at my grandma's house. We were playing Monopoly at her dining room table when I couldn't hold it in anymore.

"Why was I born before Mom and Dad got married?" I blurted out. I was too afraid to mention the pink papers.

She set her tall glass of Coke down gently and was quiet. Crushed ice clinked against the glass, and I focused on the fizzing carbonation backlit against the window because I couldn't bear to look directly at her. My heart thumped wildly.

She reached across and laid her warm hand gently on mine. "I'm going to call your mama. It's going to be okay." I kept staring at the tiny bubbles popping above the rim of her glass and nodded.

I slid down from the green-padded chair and hid under the dining room table as she dialed my mom. I could see her permanent-press white trousers and matching shoes as she leaned against her desk—*it would have been sometime after Memorial Day but before Labor Day.* She was proper like that. I fidgeted with the cheery yellow fringe on the linen tablecloth from my hiding spot under the table. I caught snippets of her short conversation with my mother as my heart drummed in my ears.

"It's time…waited too long…she's scared…I'm bringing her back…you have to." I think there was a hint of anger in her voice, a note of frustration with her youngest daughter for not taking care of something so clearly important. But I was a kid, I don't really know how she felt. *She's gone now.*

Grandma returned the yellow phone to its cradle and pulled back the chair where I was crouched under the table. "Come on out, babe. It's going to be okay, but your mama needs to talk to you. Get your things."

I spent so many weekends at my grandma's house that I had my own room, though I never slept in there. I slept with her, in her giant king-sized bed with its soft percale sheets and satin pillowcases to keep her hair tidy. Grandma was a reader, and we read our respective books in silence, side by side until we fell asleep. I would take her glasses off and carefully place them on her nightstand next to her Big Ben wind-up clock when she occasionally fell asleep before me.

More often than not she'd still be reading late into the night, long after I nodded off.

I gathered my belongings from the needlepoint chair in her bedroom while she waited by her back door, white handbag over her arm, to drive me back to my house.

The official story goes like this:

My mother got pregnant with me at nineteen. Back then, being a single mother was not an option people smiled on, and there was pressure to get married—from both sides. It didn't matter how mismatched they were; there was a baby on the way, and that meant getting married. She wore an empire-waist dress to fit her visible belly. He was trailing ghosts and nightmares from his first tour in Vietnam.

It didn't work out. I was less than a year old when he took off; my mom filed for divorce and moved in with my grandma.

Looking back, it makes sense. They were too young. He was really messed up. My mom met a very nice, very decent man who was not only willing, but happy to take on a small daughter with a new wife. They had the best of intentions, but time moved on and the right moment to tell me just never came up. *No one meant to hurt anyone.*

But what also makes sense is that when you find out your parents—and your entire extended family, and all of their friends—knew something so fundamental about *who you are*, and they all kept it a secret, it changes you.

Trust evaporates. In the blink of a yellow handset being placed on its cradle, no one is safe, and innocence is gone.

When you're a kid you think adults know stuff. You think being an adult means you have answers, that you will understand things and people and mysteries. You think life will be clear, and right must be right, and wrong is always wrong. Being an actual adult lets you in on the big secret: there are no answers. None at all.

There is no big book of knowledge they give you when you are officially a grown up—there is no "they" at all. It's all you. How do you handle difficult questions, answers that suck, days that grind you down like a steel rasp, and dawns that take too long to come? Sometimes you don't. Sometimes, things are just hard.

I gathered my children around me on the floor in my mother's living room. My mom and I had talked privately about how to do this, but the best that either of us or our collective ghosts could come up with was to be honest without giving them more information than they needed. It was impossible to know where that line was, especially when they were eight, six, and three and a half.

I pulled Abby into my lap and wrapped my arms around the boys. I simply told them that when we got home Daddy wouldn't be living with us anymore. Daddy had to move out, and he was going to live with Nana.

"Do you know what divorce means?" I asked quietly.

Jeffrey scowled hard at me, his eyes narrowing, "Yes. I know what that means. I don't want that! I don't like that!" And he burst into tears.

I tried to keep my voice calm and low, and I pulled him into my crowded lap as my own resolve faltered. I hoped telling them how much I loved them was enough. I hoped telling them Daddy still loved them and that it wasn't their fault was enough. I said all the things the books and psychologists tell you to say to children when you are breaking apart the only lives they have known.

My mother stood quietly in the doorway, present if I needed her, but allowing me space. Yet we remained close in our generational powerlessness.

Three little faces looked at me and pleaded for answers I didn't have. Their eyes filled and overflowed, and we all sobbed, our tears mixing in a vortex of loss.

"I want Dad!" Bean cried and smashed his face into my shoulder.

"I know." My heart broke again with them. "I do too."

I held them close, unable to fix anything. There was no balm I could offer, no way I could make their world the way it was ever again.

In my mind, over and over I kept telling myself: *I am the mama. I am the buoy. I am who will keep this fractured boat afloat.* And I had no idea how.

1995

I was working in the design department of a marine supply company, and one day a client donated a blow-up raft—the yellow kind, made for two people. According to the box, one could mount a small outboard motor on it, but it came with two oars. It was free, and I thought it would be fun.

When I pushed open the sliding-glass door to my apartment, David was sitting on the couch, elbows on his knees, staring at the parrot I was bird-sitting for my mom. The bird's cage was in the corner, but the bird itself was perched on the back of a wooden chair near the door.

"Hey!" I said, "Guess what I got!" I dropped the heavy box on the floor, and the bird squawked loudly.

"Nice boat." He gestured toward the parrot. "Guess what the bird did."

"Dunno—what did you do today?" I opened the fridge. He'd been asleep on the couch when I'd left for work—he was working swing shifts and keeping weird hours. I had asked him to uncover the bird when he woke up.

"Get this—I'm going to see if I can get him to do it again. Watch!" He started talking to the bird and moved his hand toward him.

"He's going to bite the crap out of you," I laughed. The bird was mean. It had bitten my landlord's dog and chased my mom's cat. If you kept him shut in his cage, he'd squawk loudly until he was let out to sit on the perch on top of his cage, preening his feather/s and mumbling mostly unintelligible bird-words to himself.

David moved his hand closer, and the bird stopped grooming his bright green feathers and twisted his head to the left, giving David the parrot side-eye.

"*Asshole!!*" the bird shrieked loudly and clearly, and David roared with laughter. The bird shook and fluffed his feathers and went back to preening, keeping one eye on David.

"Can you believe it?" He was still laughing.

"You taught him that?!" I had to give the bird back eventually, and this was the only word he'd ever properly enunciated.

"Not on purpose. I overslept, and by the time I uncovered him he was totally peeved and lunged to bite me. I might have muttered something about my opinion of loud, bad birds, and then he repeated it!"

I looked askance at him across the kitchen. "Great. Now we need a pirate friend."

"Well, you got the boat already. Is this yours?" He picked up the heavy box with ease and started to read. "Let's go!"

"Right now?" I asked. I was still in my work clothes. "It's mine, got it from a client. Will it hold both of us?" I headed into the bathroom to change.

"We should blow it up here, though. We can toss it in my truck and take it out to the dam." He started unrolling the thick yellow vinyl.

There was a puny foot pump in the box, but after half an hour of taking turns, the boat was still a mostly-deflated yellow blob.

"Oh, screw this. Let's go to the gas station and fill it up with the tire air," he said as he scooped up the yellow vinyl boat and headed out the door.

I grabbed my keys and the oars and enticed the parrot back into his cage with a peanut.

David was in his truck already, and we headed to the gas station. A few quarters later and the boat was filled and looking suitable for Greenpeace—with ropes running through grommets on the sides and the nose curved up.

It was a beautiful afternoon, and we rolled the windows down as we headed toward the reservoir. David belted out B-52s lyrics with the radio as we zig-zagged in the dappled sunlight up the mountain road. His beautiful voice made me happy.

We parked at the dam and I grabbed the oars while he marched down the boat ramp, big yellow raft held high over his head, singing the whole way.

At the bottom, he flopped the raft into the water. *You'd think getting in a boat would be easy. We did. We were wrong.* The raft immediately started to drift away, and David had to grab for it, reaching for one of the grommets and rope and jumping knee-deep into the murky ramp water.

I yelled, grabbing for him and dropping the oars. He had the boat, but the oars splashed into the water and started to float away. He shoved the boat toward me, still dry, and lunged for the oars.

I yanked the boat up on the ramp. Some elderly men were fishing and turned to watch the novice comedy playing out.

We decided we needed a plan. We left our shoes and socks on the spillway, keys tucked into them, my backpack carefully over the top. We could see our belongings, and the fishermen were close by.

Getting in the boat was tricky. We tried several ways, and settled on me getting in first with the oars, then him jumping in as he pushed us away from the ramp. It was inelegant, but it worked. We were both in the boat, facing each other.

I passed his oars to him, and fastened my own in the grommet rings on the sides, and we started to paddle. The boat went in a circle.

"What are you doing? No, you have to push this way…" and he mimed the other direction from the way I was pushing.

"Wait wait wait!" My oars hit his.

"Stop! Okay, wait, this isn't working. We have to cooperate." He was looking at the oars and trying to figure out what we were doing wrong. "Okay, if we want to go that way, this side needs to go this way," he pointed to the west, "and these oars have to go that way." He gestured to the dam.

"Fine." We had drifted toward the middle of the reservoir, and I looked behind me, trying to situate my oars with his. "One, two, three.."

Our oars bashed into each other again.

The afternoon light was still golden, the water was inky black, and the fishermen were still watching us and smiling.

I laughed, letting go of my oars. "Let's just drift. It's pretty out here."

"No, we can do this." He was frowning. "Come on, work with me."

"Okay…" I picked up my oars. "I think it's like backing up a trailer, and you go the opposite way you think you're going."

We spent the better part of an hour trying to find a rhythm and get the boat headed in a predetermined direction. The sun moved behind the trees and the mountain, and it started getting cold.

I finally pulled in my oars and let David row. It worked much better with only one of us paddling. When we both tried, we seemed to go nowhere, no matter how we tried to time it.

He was happy rowing on his own. I can see him, smiling as we moved across the lake under his power, my oars impotent in my lap.

Then the boat started to deflate.

He rowed furiously, trying to get us to the ramp, while the yellow vinyl slowly reverted to its blob-like shape beneath us. I don't remember how we got out of the damned thing, but we were both soaked and cold walking back to the car.

We were *terrible* at boating.

5

Bravery

OCTOBER 23, 2009

But… but… but nothing. I can do whatever I want. Scary things don't scare me anymore.

WHEN I GOT HOME FROM California, the pressure holding the tidal wave of emotions at bay finally equalized, and everything crashed in. I knew it would, but knowing something in theory and being in the middle of it—submerged and swimming hard for the surface to take a gasping, panicked breath—is very different. I suspect we often agree to things in theory, things that don't seem so hard as mere ideas. It's like looking at a topographical map from space. The closer you get the more those little lines mean and the less confident you are in the terrain. By the time your boots are on the ground you can barely remember what things looked like from the sky and you wonder how you will ever get from where you are to where you planned to be.

As required by the judge, David moved out while we were away. It was a tidy idea from a distance, but we came home to freshly emptied rooms. Each missing thing the kids discovered felt like a hot poker in a fresh wound. I leaned against the closet door in our master bedroom and stared through a veil of hot tears at the abandoned hangers on the empty poles. Empty. Everywhere. He was gone.

I asked for this. It was a strange place to inhabit, aware of my own responsibility but not seeing any other option. Damned if I did, damned if I didn't.

The kids kept asking when they could see Daddy. David's mother had applied to be a court-approved supervisor, which would allow him to see the children at her home instead of at a state-run facility, as long as I agreed to the arrangement. I trusted his mother and supported her plan. I wanted to keep things as normal as possible, which meant setting aside my own frustration and anger. Nana's house was safe, and she loved the children. It was a good choice for a bad situation. It took ten days after we got home for everything to be arranged and cleared.

I was taking things day by day, but even that was laughable sometimes. Really it was hour by hour, sometimes even minute by minute. I'd be cruising along, working on pattern orders, stuffing envelopes, packing boxes of Houston orders. Then five minutes later I would be a wreck sitting on the floor of my office. Lather, rinse, repeat.

There were moments of renewed conviction, short bursts of feeling invincible—that no matter how hard it was, I could do it. Then the sun would set, the kids would go to sleep, and all the scary emotional demons would crawl out from under the bed with their unanswerable questions and their demands over a future I could not see, didn't want, and had never planned for.

It was overwhelming. On top of the daily logistics of suddenly being a single parent, I found myself embarrassed at the number of decisions and responsibilities that I didn't realize I had outsourced to David. I considered myself a feminist, but truthfully I had fallen into typical gendered roles in my marriage. I took care of the house and children; he earned and managed the money. I felt foolish. I knew better. Again, in theory. And yet on the ground, standing in the smoldering wreckage I helped create, I had to sort through all the shrapnel and figure out how to salvage a life.

The first thing I needed was to open a bank account in my name. In one particularly delightful afternoon at the bank I found out, not only that my credit was ruined, but also that David had taken out a second mortgage on our home. That was how he bought opiates from China, Russia, and India. My cheeks stung with shame as I thanked the helpless customer service agent who had to tell me the news.

It was so enormous, so vast a failure, I couldn't even figure out where to begin.

But I had to.

It was not going to be a typical divorce. I knew child support would be sparse, and spousal support wasn't reality. David hadn't worked in over two years, and I didn't know if he would ever work a steady job again. The safest route for me was to assume nothing, and to rely on myself. There was no hiding or hoping for a miracle. There were only three small, precious people looking to me. I couldn't opt out because it was hard.

There is a Shel Silverstein poem about a girl who eats a whale. I decided that, just like Melinda Mae, I didn't need to worry about the bites I would have to take next week, or even tomorrow. If I could just worry about the bites on my plate that day I could get through it. I could do that much. It was a way to manage the task and also to be kind to myself. I would figure out what things were on my plate for the day and do my best to swallow them down. What bites are on my plate today? It became my mantra.

Three banks turned me away before a local credit union was willing to give me a checking account. It was the very first thing I did in my own name, not my married name. My attorney asked if I was going to change back to my maiden name. I wished aloud that we all just kept our names and moved past the tradition of losing our identity when we got married (I might have been projecting). I told him that it didn't feel right, and he said I could pick any name. *Wait. Any name?* I didn't want to pick a name out of a hat, but there was a family name I had always loved and felt tied to. My mother's family name—my maternal grandparents' name. It meant satin pillowcases, reading books late into the night, cold Coke over crushed ice, and rooms the color of marigolds. Safety of my own.

"Would that be possible?" I asked.

And so my name legally became McKay. It felt like a righting of something that should never have been wrong. *I chose my new name.*

There's this very odd sensation when you are going through trauma: while you may be doing your best to keep from floating off the earth, preoccupied with your personal demons and feeling like the world is ending, regular life goes on.

Your bills need to be paid. Your kids get hungry and need food. Again. And again. There are birthday parties and special meetings with teachers, and you run out of pull-ups for your three-year-old who really shouldn't need them anymore—but what the hell, her dad disappeared and it's probably not the time to force a potty training issue. You look in the mirror as you are rushing the kids out the door to get them to a church ice cream social (*what even is that?*), and you see a haunted face with wild hair coming loose from its bun, and some new stress lines punctuating the eyes, but who otherwise looks the same as she ever did. It's shocking in its normalcy. Heartbreak and sorrow must surely be written across your forehead like a news feed, but no…really you just look like every other tired mom with little kids.

I sighed and tucked my unruly hair behind my ears and told the kids to buckle up. I didn't want to go. I couldn't think of anything I wanted to do less than going to an ice cream social (*whatever that was*). But the kids were excited—even Bean, who hated crowds and did not eat ice cream—and they were all smiling as they got in the car.

It had already been a terrible day. My computer, Bessie, had crashed that morning. When your life is in your computer, and that computer crashes, it is definitely time to panic. All my invoices from Houston, all my patterns, all my family and professional photos, my websites…everything was in Bessie. I had a couple of guys working on a new website for me, but we only communicated through email. I didn't even have their phone numbers. The server I used was in Arizona, and I couldn't tell them my computer had crashed because I didn't have a computer. It was a uniquely modern and perfectly impossible situation.

That day I made several trips to the garage to cry. A guy from church was coming by to see if he could salvage anything, and while I was at the ice cream social he worked on retrieving files. Through some crazy magic entirely lost on me, he retrieved all my photos, my invoices, and a good chunk of my data. But he was sad to inform me that Bessie was truly dead.

It was a long, sleepless night without Bessie and the doors she opened for me.

The next morning was our children's program at church. Most people loved that day and looked forward to it. Even before my life blew apart, I hated it. I hated parading kids before the congregation and having them repeat what grownups told them to say. Having the kids sing cute songs about loving their families and being kind to each other was great, but the pageantry never sat well with me. It felt wrong. I always squirmed under the social pressure to make kids appear a certain way, and I never felt like children's behavior in unusual circumstances (like singing in front of the entire congregation)

reflected parenting skills. I didn't take pride in their being "good" any more than I blamed myself when they acted out. They're kids. They do weird things.

That particular morning my boys were in fine form, picking their noses in front of everyone and waving their arms in giant flapping arcs just in case I was looking elsewhere while Jeffrey sang his off-key heart out. Bean never sang and refused to cooperate, but he would stand next to his brother. Abby was not old enough to take part in the program, so she rolled around on the floor while I tried to keep her quiet. I briefly considered the wisdom of animals who eat their young.

After church, the guy who had been helping with my computer stopped by with a small computer he had built from spare parts in his garage. It wasn't much, he apologized, but I was welcome to use it until I could find a more permanent solution. Words failed me. What a tremendous act of kindness.

My dining room table was sagging under the weight of patterns waiting to be packed and shipped. There were boxes stacked everywhere, and I tried to put a handwritten thank-you note into shipments to new stores.

I was frazzled, attempting to give Abby small tasks so she could feel helpful while really trying to keep her busy enough for me to get actual work done. I had to get to the post office, as I hadn't yet figured out the ship-from-home option. It took more trips than it should have with Abby's help, but the car was loaded, and I headed out.

Wearing a Snow White dress I had made her during a bout of insomnia, Abby skipped ahead into the post office while I tried to balance the boxes, my keys, my phone, and the diaper bag that had become my purse. My arms were full when Abby started pulling me. "I have to potty." *Of course.*

As I was wrangling my boxes, she peed. Right there. Peed on the post office floor. I pulled wipes out of my bag and attempted to mop up the urine, keep her from dragging her dress through it, and simultaneously shove my carefully-packed boxes out of the way with my foot. It was a fine moment—performance art for the line of postal customers who stood and watched in horror. For my encore, I dumped my entire purse on the floor when I fished for my debit card to pay for the packages. Unfortunately, I would be back.

I pulled into the driveway and rested my head on the steering wheel. I was exhausted. This business thing was nonstop, and being an even passable mother to three little kids was nonstop, and dealing with a terrible divorce was nonstop, and the holidays were approaching, and I just needed a moment to catch my breath. Abby was asleep in the back seat, but she never transferred well, so for her to get any nap at all meant leaving her in her car seat. That particular day I was perfectly fine sitting in the quiet car. The boys were not due home yet; I could just sit and be still.

I rested my cheek on my hands and looked idly at my house. Something looked different. I scowled, momentarily puzzled. My yard looked … nice. It took a second to register. Everything was raked and tidy. *How odd.* When Abby woke and we went inside, I looked out the back door and saw a dozen piles of neatly raked leaves and my emerald grass peeking out again. I hadn't seen green grass for weeks.

I wondered who it might have been. Friends? People from church? Neighbors who got sick of my yard? A Scout project?

The next morning the doorbell rang. In my driveway were my friend Mo and her entire family, with gloves, rakes, and leaf bags, ready to work. They had come back to finish the job.

Mo was a real-life friend who had entered my life through my computer years earlier. She read my blog and one day cautiously commented that she thought, based on a few details, that we might be neighbors. We were both hilariously cautious at first. In public writing, I was careful to not use our last names or mention our specific town. She was the same. We emailed each other and realized that we lived a few miles apart. We agreed to meet—in a public place, of course.

We met at a taco stand and talked for hours. We moved from the taco stand to the shopping center, where we let our kids feed quarters into the arcade games so we could keep talking. We loved each other immediately. That had been several years earlier, and we still hadn't run out of things to talk about or stopped finding things to love about each other.

David canceled his next scheduled visit with the kids. And then the next. He had excuses—he wasn't feeling well, his mom was busy—but it always fell on me to tell the kids and watch their faces fall. And then it fell on me to help them navigate their disappointment and sadness.

I had known he was going to have a nearly impossible time staying sober and dealing with the reality of parenting. I knew it was going to be hard and that I was going to be fielding it alone. It was just so much easier in theory, when I didn't have to hold my disappointed, crying children, doing my inadequate best to catch and absorb their grief. There in the trenches, my boots were saturated with tears.

6

Gathering Rocks

NOVEMBER 29, 2009

I'll be cruising along, thinking I'm doing fine, and then BLAM! right into the brick wall of what being a single mama means. Tonight, while trying to handle a boy with the stomach flu who barfed all over my bed, I hit that wall. Stripping a king comforter, six pillows, sheets, and blankets, for some reason was the trip-wire today.

I am fighting back tears, but they are winning. I have a sick child, and he needs me. I have two other kids who also need me. There is no "divide and conquer" anymore. It's me. All me, all the time. Lugging the dripping laundry downstairs, my child starts to barf again, and I have to leave the laundry to attend him, wipe his brow, and give him comfort. And clean up Barf Part II.

I got the first batch of laundry going when I realized I have no bleach. I am out. I cannot send someone to the store. I cannot run to the store. For some reason, the lack of bleach is cataclysmic to me, and standing amid the pile of towels and pillowcases, I burst into tears.

They are hot tears of frustration, fear, anger, and aching sadness churned together with a fair dose rage and a dash of self-pity. Cursing my soon-to-be ex under my breath, I climb the stairs and begin putting my room back together. I had to dig to the back of the linen closet to find a sheet, and wrestled the thing onto my bed, crying the whole time.

Then I get to explain to my children why Mama is crying. This is just so damn much fun. This is not what I signed up for. This is not what was supposed to happen. And yet, here I stand. Now what am I going to do with it? I suppose that's the true test. Life sucks sometimes. It's hard, and it's not fair. At all. But... What am I going to do with it? What are you going to do with it?

And so I pick myself up again, wipe my tears, kiss my kids, say a prayer, and carry on...

I WAS ANGRY. I WAS so damn angry. The permeating sadness was being brutally shoved aside by anger. Deep, abiding, furious anger. I knew it would happen but, as with everything else, I was unprepared when it finally hit.

Because of David's choices I looked in my kids' faces and tried to answer their unanswerable questions. *No, I don't know why Daddy didn't call. No, sweetie, it wasn't your fault. Because he was sick, and he's trying to get better. No, I don't know when you can go to Nana's again to see him. No, I don't know why he canceled the visit; I wish I knew. I am so sorry. No, baby, he's really not coming back, and I am so sorry.* I tried to parse together answers that were neither all truth, because they didn't need and weren't prepared for that ugliness, nor all lies, because they at least deserved my best attempts at honesty. I picked up the emotional and physical wreckage left behind because David found it too hard to deal with life. I did it because I had to.

I had no way to carve out time to feel my own feelings, so the anger just bulldozed me. It was all I could do each day to keep bailing out the boat to keep us afloat.

The kids took out their emotions on me. The counselor we'd visited told me to expect them to act out. In situations where one parent basically bails, children tend to fear that they will lose everyone, and they tiptoe around the negligent parent hoping that they can fix things by being really good. They then act out against the stable parent because they know they are safe, and those emotions have to come out somewhere. The counselor told me that it would be hard but that it was perfectly normal and meant I was making them feel safe and loved. *It sucked.* It was another thing I expected intellectually but was unprepared for when it happened.

What I wanted more than anything was to be a good mother. I wanted to be stable and keep my kids' lives steady through this nightmare. I wanted to hold onto my home, and to hope, and not allow bitterness to take root and grow in my heart. I was in a constant struggle with my own fury, but I refused to give up on the idea of something better. I refused to fail my children.

I hadn't yet realized the importance of including myself on the list of people who mattered.

The holidays were upon us. I knew that the *firsts* as a changed family were going to be tough—first Thanksgiving, first Christmas, first birthday—but I was also learning that we could do hard things. I knew that I could help the kids through those first bumps. Doing so meant learning to let go of preconceived notions and consciously deciding what mattered to me, not to some ideal I once held. I also had to completely abandon the notion that I could manage everything myself. I couldn't. I needed my friends, and my children needed people besides me in their lives who loved them. I simply could not do everything.

To help manage this process, I developed a coping mechanism: when I was getting emotional about something I would ask myself, "What are the rocks?" By that I meant, what were the facts? What were the things I could absolutely count on, and what were the things that depended on other people, or were hopes and wishes? There were places for hopes and wishes, but finding my "rocks" was the first and most important step in deciding which path to choose.

This meant looking at the holidays with new eyes. As much as I wanted to do a Norman Rockwell Thanksgiving, I couldn't afford it, and my kids didn't really like Thanksgiving food anyway. Neither did I. That was a rock. So, plan something different. Have Mo and her family over for a Mexican dinner; it would be fun, a change, and not stressful. It was amazing how liberating it was to consider doing things differently. We didn't have to be sad about not meeting an imaginary ideal.

I wanted a real Christmas tree, but they were expensive, and we had a perfectly fine fake one in the basement—*rock*. Give up the notion of an idyllic Christmas and embrace what we had. I wasn't going to have much money for presents—*rock*. Turn it into a crafting Christmas with the kids and make presents for our family. Involve the kids and ignore the voice telling me what was lacking, because the kids didn't have my expectations. It wasn't perfect, but it was a plan.

I started applying it to bigger issues. David had established a pattern of canceling visits and not calling—*rock*. It didn't matter that it sucked, and getting mad didn't change anything—*rock*. What could I do? I stopped telling the kids when he was supposed to call or when they were supposed to see him. I would wait and see what happened. Then they weren't disappointed if he didn't show, and if a visit actually happened they could just be happy. If I needed to talk about my anger and frustration with him, I did so with friends, away from where the kids might overhear.

It didn't matter that life wasn't fair, or that I wanted things to be a certain way. Welcome to the big leagues, baby girl. What are the rocks? *Look for the rocks*. This coping mechanism helped release me from the clutches of debilitating anger. I was no longer constantly in fight-or-flight tension about nursing the kids through another emotional breakdown. Holding onto my rocks kept me sane and allowed the kids to be happier and more stable. It removed them, to some extent, from the adult effluvia. Finding my rocks was the first solid step I took away from anger and helplessness and toward a new life.

By the end of November, David had managed to show up twice for visitations. I drove the kids to his mother's house and dropped them off. They were overflowing with excitement and burst from the car before I turned off the engine, throwing themselves into his waiting arms on the porch. I watched from the driveway, my throat tightening as Abby nestled herself in the hollow under his chin, wrapping her small arms around his neck. *Those arms once meant safety to me, too.* And now I stood back and watched, over the minefield of broken dreams between me standing at my car and him standing on his mother's porch.

Each visit was supposed to be three hours. It broke my heart that he'd only managed to see them twice. They needed him. Whatever happened between us, whatever mistakes he had made—we had made—no one could replace him. I would have driven them to his mother's house several times a week if he'd allowed it—not for him, but because it was the right thing to do for them.

Seeing him even briefly was hard. Seeing him smiling and hugging our laughing children was a gut-punch. Instead of driving home while the kids were with him, I headed to the craft store and wandered aimlessly. I felt like a second-day party balloon—without enough oomph to reach the ceiling, but with just enough gas to linger in between ceiling and floor. I was not really married anymore, but I didn't feel like I would ever be single again. I couldn't see what came next, and I couldn't really make sense of what was behind me yet. I shook the malaise away—what bites were on my plate that day? Where were my rocks?

I left my cart by a register, one lonely skein of yarn in the basket, and walked out into the clear cold twilight.

I could barely even think about Christmas. I knew we would get through it. I knew it would happen. I would get the decorations up, I would celebrate with the kids, and when the lights were all out and I knew no one was looking, I would be utterly swallowed up by the aching loneliness and the chasm of loss hiding behind my heart.

1991

I moved to Seattle for art school on Thanksgiving Day. I had been on my own for nearly a year. I had managed to find a room-mate, get a job, and attend college part time. I was feeling restless, and scraping by in my little seaside town wasn't terribly satisfying. *I wish I had known to apply to a real college.*

Just before Christmas I got a phone call. David was driving up to Seattle, and he was bringing our mutual friend, Danny. Around midnight, they pulled up in a shiny new beautiful blue truck David had bought before they'd left for the trip.

I was over the moon to see David. I had missed him so much, and ran out of my building in my stocking feet to exuberantly embrace him. He picked me up in his giant arms and I squealed with happiness.

"How long are you here for!?" I rushed to hug Danny too, who was pulling bags from the under the tarp on the back of the pickup. "Nice new truck!"

Danny, who had grown up with David and had twice the charm of a normal human, looked surprised and then laughed. "Wait, you didn't tell her, Dave?"

I spun around "Tell me what?!"

"We're here to stay!" Danny exclaimed.

There was a flurry of hugs and exclamations and a shuttling of bags and boxes into the building. Two days before Christmas, and I suddenly had room-mates.

I folded out the couch, made space on the floor, and was generally just overjoyed to have friends close. I had no idea what would happen with the landlord, or how we could manage with us all in such a little apartment, or if they were really truly staying. But I was so happy to see friendly faces.

"Wait, so tell me what happened! How are you here? What about your job? And that new truck!" I peppered David with questions.

He looked at me, his familiar face so warm and missed. "If you can pull up stakes and leave, so can I." He grinned. "I bought the truck because my old one was dying, and I loved the color. Then I quit my job at Apple, paid off my credit cards, and I told Danny I was going to Seattle. He decided he could use a change of scenery too. It really wasn't any more complicated than that—except I guess we did forget to tell you."

It was a good Christmas.

The boxes started arriving in the weeks before Christmas. My mom always sent boxes of presents, but these were different. These weren't from my mom. They were from California, Utah, Virginia, and even from overseas APO addresses. They were from places I had never been, and in some cases, from people I had never met. Some were anonymous, but some had lovely little notes of support and encouragement from people all over the country who had been reading my story in real time on *Dandelion Mama*.

There were people who had never commented but who knew someone who knew me and wanted to do something kind. There was a gift card or two for a grocery store, and there were Christmas gifts for my children. Years later, I still choke up at the generosity that so many kind people showed toward my family. A woman I had never met, and who was deployed to Afghanistan, contacted me and asked if I would let her be Santa Claus to my children that year. She told me I would be doing her a favor by allowing her that joy, and I found myself again weeping.

For the twelve nights before Christmas, we found a gift on our front porch every evening. The doorbell would ring, and we would open it to find a beautifully wrapped present—things like new coats for all three kids, winter boots for everyone, Christmas pajamas, baking dishes and kitchen towels, LEGOs—beautiful and thoughtful gifts which someone had clearly taken a lot of time and thought to put together. All those perfect holiday expectations I had jettisoned actually paled in comparison to reality. I'm not sure that could have happened if I hadn't let go.

One particularly difficult day, David had been two hours late for his visit with the kids, and everyone was a little emotional. I was sitting at my desk, fighting with the loaner computer. My patterns were selling well, but as we approached the holidays things were naturally slowing down. I was trying to stay on top of my invoices, but I didn't have a bookkeeping program on the loaner computer, so I had to manage my billing with hard copies and paper clips. It was a bit of a mess, but it was happening.

The boys dragged a box in from the porch addressed to me from California. My whole family lived there, so I finished my invoicing and made some phone calls before I turned to open the box. I sliced the tape, and opened the box to find an Apple MacBook. My brows knit in confusion and disbelief.

Lifting it from the box, I gingerly opened the screen. I had never even held an Apple before. It was fully charged, and a little window opened on the glossy screen, "Hi Tracy!" it said. It had been loaded with MS Office, Word, PowerPoint, Excel—all the programs I knew, along with all the happy new Apple stuff I didn't yet understand.

I burst into tears. I gently ran my hand over the top of its pretty, smooth surface—yep, it's still real—and then cried some more. I riffled through the box, looking for some clue about who it was from.

There was a note in the box. It was a gift from a man I went to high school with—we hadn't seen each other in years, but his wife was a reader of my blog, and they worked for Apple. *They wanted me to have this gift....*

My pride wanted to protest, "I cannot possibly accept it!" And yet, I could not afford that kind of pride. The last few months had been a lesson in humility, and in the fact that gracefully accepting desperately needed help is as much a necessity as is generously giving help when possible. It was hard to be in the position of being the receiver—it was much more fun to be the giver. But at that time I didn't have much to give. But I was learning how to behave toward others, so when the wheel in the sky someday clicked around to my turn I would be ready.

౪

My children will never know how little I was able to provide for them that Christmas. Through the kindness and generosity of so many, they were blessed with an abundance of love. Jeffrey had been questioning me on Santa and I had shrugged it off, explaining that Santa was about the spirit of giving and loving other people. But on Christmas morning he stopped playing for a while and came and sat on my lap.

"Mom?" he said, slinging his arm over my shoulder. "I think I was wrong about Santa. No way could you have done all this. I think maybe Santa is real."

The lump in my throat kept me from answering. Yes, my sweet child, the Spirit of giving and love is very real.

It was the best Christmas.

1992

After Christmas, I started school and everyone got serious about finding work. Danny had worked for moving companies for years and managed to charm his way into an interview at a furniture warehouse, where he got both himself and David jobs. The woman who owned the company was elderly, and she kept a dress code. If the boys wanted the jobs, they needed to clean up. They had to cut their hair.

I had just gotten home from classes when David and Danny walked in. Danny had a military cut and a clean shave, and he could have batted his eyelashes at any girl and made her blush. But David was a different man. He'd kept his sun-streaked hair long and in a ponytail the entire time I had known him. He also wore a full, neatly trimmed beard. But when he opted to cut it, he wasn't kidding.

His head was shaved bald, and his beard was trimmed into a goatee. His gold-flecked eyes and long lashes stood out. He'd bought a black bowler hat to keep his newly shorn head warm, and he was wearing a parka and work boots as they tromped toward me, both grinning as I took in their new looks.

My mouth hung open. "Holy…! I can't even believe that's you!"

David grabbed me and flung me around, and we all laughed. I rubbed his head for good luck and tried on his hat. Danny did too, but it really looked best on him.

"You like it? It feels weird." He rubbed his naked head.

"Yeah, I really like it—it's so different, but you look great." I smiled at him.

He stopped at the landing as we trailed behind Danny, and he peered hard at me. "I don't know what to do with it, but just now is the first time you looked at me like a man instead of like a friend."

Surprise rolled over me. "I…" I didn't know what to say. I wanted to say I didn't understand, but that would have been a lie. I did know. I did look at him differently for the first time, and it had happened right then. I couldn't lie to him. That's not how we worked. But I couldn't admit it, either. There had never been even the slightest hint of romance between us—and I needed it to stay that way. He was my best friend. But I also knew that something had changed. I pushed it away.

"You're beautiful, David. You're my best friend." I looked at the floor. *Coward.*

I screwed up every romantic relationship. Romance was impermanent, transient, fickle. I needed David to stay in my life, not be another boy who disappeared someday or who I had to push away. It was unconscious, but it was safer for me to keep him close in the big picture and not mess it up with romance. It was safer for me, but it was unfair. I did it anyway. And he let me.

I leaned against him briefly, inhaling the scent of his warm amber and sandalwood incense. Safety. I couldn't afford to risk him. He hugged me tightly for just a moment, and then turned and walked after Danny.

Interlude
One Saturday Morning

THE SNOW CRUNCHES UNDER HER tires as she pulls into the Grandmother's driveway, and the children are out of their seat belts before she has turned off the engine. The Grandmother has volunteered to host a supervised visit so her children could see their father, and they are excited. The woman is fishing in her pocket for her keys and watching her footing on the icy walk as the children tumble ahead, a flurry of boots, scarves, and dropped mittens.

The Grandmother flings open the door, and her flushed face and wide eyes show panic as she calls out to the woman over the heads of the boisterous children. "Something's wrong! Come, I don't know what…he's fallen… in the hallway…!"

"What? What? Where? Keep the kids here…" The woman pushes past the children and runs toward the back of the house. In the back hallway, her ex-husband is on the floor, trembling and spasming in the throes of what looks like a grand mal seizure. His mouth and face are bloody and his eyes are rolled back in his head. His body convulses over and over.

"Keep the kids away! Call 911!" she cries over her shoulder, adrenaline now coursing through her body.

Somewhere over her right shoulder the Grandmother thrusts an iPhone. She has misdialed and cannot figure out how to erase the numbers. The woman fumbles in her coat pocket to find her own phone and punches the numbers in with shaking fingers. The children are crowding behind the Grandmother, wanting to see. "Keep them in the living room! Please!" she cries. The man keeps thrashing, and she doesn't want this image burnt into her children's memories.

"911 Operator, what's your emergency?" the official voice comes on the line.

They exchange information and within minutes the sirens are outside. Four firemen burst into the small house. The woman can step back and let professionals take over, and she is relieved and terrified. One fireman asks her questions about the man; she answers as best she can, then excuses herself to check on her children.

They are in the front room and ask if their dad is going to die.

"No, I don't think so. The firemen and ambulance are going to drive him to the hospital now, and they'll make sure to take care of him." The words are bitter for her. She's had to pretty up too many things for them lately, and she hates it. They are so innocent, and she balances being truthful with protecting them from things that only hurt.

The paramedics move the man to a rolling gurney and ask the woman to accompany them to the hospital. The man has stopped seizing, but he is unconscious, and they need her to give his medical history to the doctors at the hospital. Her children watch, wide-eyed, as the paramedics roll the man out of the house and into the waiting ambulance. She wishes she could hide their eyes. She tries to explain that she isn't his wife any longer, but they insist, and the Grandmother offers to keep the children so the woman can go to the hospital.

Kneeling down to hug her children, the woman explains that she must leave, but that she'll return shortly to pick them up and that the Grandmother will make them lunch while she is gone. Grabbing her coat and keys, she declines the offer to ride in the ambulance and follows in her own car to the hospital.

The man is gradually regaining consciousness. He is confused and has no memory of what has happened or why they are at the hospital. The triage nurse takes the woman in a cubicle in the ER and begins gathering the man's medical history.

No, no history of seizure. No. No. Addict. Yes. Hospitalized for prescription drug addiction two years ago. No. Prescription painkillers. Online. Yes. Yes. No. Started two years ago. Charts were marked. Yes. No. Divorce in process. Not final. Three.

The nurse thanks the woman, and leaves her standing in the hallway outside the man's room while the medical staff works on him. They get an IV drip going, and he starts to come around and can begin to answer basic questions like his name. This is good, the nurses say. A male doctor approaches the woman and extends his hand. She shakes it and looks at him quizzically. "You're doing the right thing. If this doesn't scare him, nothing will, and next time he will be dead." She doesn't speak. She can't.

A nurse notes that the man had ingested eight times the suggested dosage of a particular painkiller that morning, along with a handful of other pills they don't recognize. The woman feels her knees go weak, and she sits in the flimsy metal chair in the hallway as the nurses hurry in and out. The man had told her he was clean. She allowed him to see their children. She had hoped he was telling the truth and was sober. And then this.

She gets up and gathers her things. She enters the small ER room and sees the man hooked up to machines that softly beep and hum. He looks at her. She stands at the foot of the bed. He doesn't remember what happened, so she tells him. She tells him his kids got to see him convulsing on the floor, bloodied from clamping down on his own tongue during a seizure, and that she needs to go get them now from his mother's house so she can try and explain their fears away. The room is cold, the silence punctuated by the soft whir of the blood pressure cuff on the man's arm.

She is hard. She does not make any effort to comfort him this time. She wants him to feel the weight of what he has done. What if he'd been driving? What if she'd not been there? What if he'd had the kids alone? What if…what if…what if….

She cannot breathe. She tells him his mother will be up to stay with him, and that she is leaving.

The icy January air hits her like a clenched fist as she exits the sliding vestibule of the ER. The cold is welcome—bracing—and reminds her she is alive, and that there are three children waiting for their mother. A fierceness rises in her chest, thinking about her children. She will protect them. She will not allow this to happen again. This will never happen again.

7

Heart on Pyre

The inky words swim before my filling eyes: I am losing my home.

How long now have I told myself it was all going to work out? How long have I clung to fragile bubbles of hope? Does it get so bad that thinking "at least my kids aren't terminally ill." is the best I can come up with? Because at this point, if it's really going to suck more, please just get it over with. Please....

I am not a victim. I am not powerless. But none of this is my fault. I realize I sound like a petulant child, but now, my home is going to be taken from me.

What am I supposed to do? What am I supposed to do? And how do I tell my children? How do I tell them without my anger and sadness spilling over? How do I do this? I am finally, utterly, at a loss.

ROCKY GOT THE SNOT BEAT out of him. He got knocked down, knocked out, bloodied, bruised, and humiliated. And he kept getting back up. Sometimes it took longer than others. Sometimes he had to cling to the ropes; sometimes his trainer had to peel him off the mat. But he got back up.

I got back up.

I had been flattened like a boxer and was seeing stars. The life I had planned and worked for was a smoldering wreck. The house I was losing held the fragrant cedar chest of my hopes—it was where I had imagined raising my children, growing older and gentler, and becoming a grandmother. Another casualty of agency and addiction.

It hurt. I was not grieving for a structure, but for the hopes, for the million futures that were no longer mine. It felt like being kicked in the chest, shock waves rippling out from my heart. And I couldn't do a damn thing except wait for it to pass. I welcomed the numbness that I hoped would follow.

But a strange thing happened....

The worst had come to pass. I lost my marriage. I lost my best friend. I lost the promises and dreams of the future I wanted. I lost my co-parent and my love. I lost financial security, savings, retirement, my good credit, and my health insurance. Now I was going to have to let the house go, too. I felt like stupid Rose when she watched frozen Jack sink into the icy north Atlantic blackness. (*There was room on that piece of wood, that's all I'm saying.*) Perhaps for me to live, I had to let it all go.

It was curious to find my future before me in wide, uncharted waves. When you lose everything, when you are stripped of artifice and pride, you realize that only a few things truly matter. It's oddly freeing. I walked out of the smoldering wreckage of my marriage with nothing but my children and my own resolve.

My legs were shaking as I grabbed the ropes and pulled myself up yet again—but I could already feel the flame of hope kindled, strong, still, calm, and safe deep inside.

David was not allowed to see our children anymore.

When I told my lawyer what had happened at the last visitation, he asked for a hearing, and members of David's own family appeared before the judge to testify and confirm the worst. Mercifully, I was not required to appear.

The original protective order was only for thirty days. The new protective order was for a full year. David could not see our children at all for six months. He was allowed one phone call each week. During that six months he was required to enter a drug treatment program, not miss a single meeting, and submit to weekly and random drug testing. If all tests were clean after six months he could resume supervised visits with our children, times and locations subject to my approval and ongoing drug testing. His parental rights were terminated—I was granted full legal and physical custody of our children. If he wanted to reinstate his parental rights he could petition the court to do so after one calendar year and a completed drug rehabilitation program.

As with the first protective order issued when I filed for divorce, this wasn't about me. When the judge read what had happened, he invoked all available legal protections from the bench. The court documents I received had hand-written notes from the judge as he listened to my attorney and heard the testimony of people who loved David, but who also loved me and the children.

There was nothing conventional about our divorce.

There would be no shared time. There would be no financial support. There would be no alternating weekends. There would be no weeknights spent laughing around a different dinner table. I had wanted those potentially joyful things for my children. I had given up any hope for us, but I wanted him to find a way to turn himself around for their sakes.

All the courts could offer me was freedom and protection—for myself and for our children—from further damage. May it be enough.

※

We were moving.

Before me was the task of packing up the house where I had planned to spend the rest of my life, and sorting, dividing, donating or selling what I couldn't take or didn't need. We were moving from a neighborhood of landscape lighting and security systems to a tiny house in an older neighborhood. We were moving from gleaming hardwood floors, toile wallpaper, and curving staircases to linoleum, outside parking, and one bathroom. And I was grateful.

The bank told me that I could stay in the house during the foreclosure. But we wouldn't know when it would sell, and we would have to let real estate agents stop by at any time. The situation was beyond my control. Coming to terms with that was a bed of hard, sharp rocks. The idea of sitting there waiting for everything to die was more than I could stand. I could not keep the house—*rock*. It didn't matter that it was sad or that I was hurt—*rock*.

The only thing I could control was my own response. When the tiny rental was mentioned by a friend at church, I only paused for a moment before saying yes. Her eyes lit up and she said she would take care of everything—she knew the man who owned it and would let me know what he needed. I waited to hear back from her.

Mo went with me and the kids to see what I had decided to call "Little House." I hoped that giving it a charming name would help. It was a tiny, post-war bungalow on a busy street with a big picture window. It had a small galley kitchen with a gas stove, original cupboards, and a tiny breakfast nook. There was nowhere for my farmhouse table. The basement had a laundry room, and there was a small detached garage that leaned slightly to the left. There was no fence, and I worried about the busy street but shoved that thought away. The kids don't notice things like linoleum floors, and they thought that sharing a bathroom would make Saturday chores go faster. Cleaning four bathrooms does take time, and who needs two walk-in master closets anyway? My cheeks stung with humiliation at my pride, and I was filled with shame that I was not immediately more grateful for Little House.

While the kids checked out the closets and ran from empty room to empty room, Mo and I stood in the kitchen leaning against the laminate counters. I fidgeted with my keys, and she let me be quiet for a moment. "Hey," she said, "Craigslist has tables. I bet we can find one to fit in that tiny nook." I looked out the window, afraid that if I looked at her I would cry. I was so tired of crying.

She rested her head against me, as close as she came to a hug, and quietly said, "I know, sweetie. I know. It's alright. It's going to be okay."

I told my kids that it didn't matter where we lived, that it was our family that mattered. I told them that houses were like clothes—a house may change, but it was the family on the inside that mattered. A house was just a house. My pride had taken a good, solid—but clearly necessary—beating. I finally started to listen to and believe myself.

Packing my house felt like undressing the dead. Removing the pictures from the walls, clearing the mantle, disrobing my home and making her a blank canvas swelled all the sediment from the bottom of the sea. All the hopes and joy that I felt while unpacking and set-ting up my beautiful home rose on the gentle swirl of sorrow in the tide. It wasn't cruel or malicious. It just was, and it seemed almost gently mindful of my sorrow as it rose up and broke the surface of the water, to float away in the cool winter sunlight. My tears dried into tight trails on my cheeks, and time rolled on.

Five different women from church showed up, arms laden with boxes, packing tape, and bubble wrap. In two hours, my entire kitchen was packed and they were working on the living room.

Meanwhile over at Little House, the landlord had given the green light to my friend, and a crew of volunteers were painting the whole house. I had been told not to come by—not to even drive by—until evening. They wanted to surprise me.

The flurry of activity over the next few days was exactly what I needed. I had been drowning in my own sorrow, getting stuck in the sap of packing memories; having my house flooded with busy, helpful hands kept me focused and distracted all at once. It was perfect, and I suspect that the women who kept showing up knew it.

Whenever I got to a box that made me cry, somebody laid soft hands on my shoulders and steered me to another room, to another task, and the stacks of neatly labeled brown boxes grew while other hands gently wrapped, boxed, taped, and labeled. These were acts of pure love.

Every night someone brought dinner for everyone—including paper plates, plastic forks, and disposable cups—and they even thought to bring Jell-O for Bean, who did not eat regular food.

My printer and Houston companion Emily brought special boxes and bubble wrap and spent the entire afternoon carefully wrapping up my wedding china, so that someday my kids could fight over who gets a lovely service for ten of Lenox Federal Platinum.

Mo packed the linen closets and then helped me get my Craigslist kitchen table over to Little House, where the fresh paint was clean and bright, the carpets were shampooed, and everything looked sparkling and new. It took several tries to get the old round oak table through the small door, but we finally turned it on its side and rolled it into the nook. There were no chairs yet, but it was the first piece of me to come home to in Little House.

Saturday morning was moving day. All the pieces were in place.

ル

1990

David was crushed into the tiny kitchen of my first apartment, watching with interest as I pulled a soufflé from the oven. The windows were flung open and the sounds of the ocean, the gulls, and the piano shop next door floated up, mixing with the Santana playing on the stereo. My roommate was gone for the night, and I was cooking my very first impromptu dinner, using a recipe I had found in *Sunset* magazine.

I sat and looked out the window, smiling, while David scooped another serving of soufflé onto his plate and proceeded to shower me with ridiculous compliments.

I balled my napkin up and threw it at him across the table. You could see the train trestle over the rooftops outside of my second-story apartment window. It had been months since our first conversation on the trestle, but it had become one of our favorite places to meet and talk. I was taking classes at the community college and waiting tables at a restaurant down on the esplanade.

David would often wait for me after my shift ended, and we'd grab an ice cream and wind our way up the now-familiar pathway to the trestle. It was a stellar place to watch the sunset, and we spent dozens of nights up there watching the sky turn violet and the sun sink and burn.

"Do you believe in Jesus?" I asked him over the soufflé. "I mean, do you believe what Christianity teaches about him? Do you think he was the son of God?"

We came at life from wildly different formative experiences—my childhood was idyllic, with a loving and close atheist family, which left me with a million unformed questions. His childhood was lonely, with a distant, much older family where church was mandatory but he had no love for it.

"I don't know. But one thing is for sure, you cannot avoid the hourglass effect Jesus had on history. I mean, think about it—maybe he was just a dude in Palestine who said some wise things. Maybe he was the son of God, maybe he was God incarnate. I don't know. But the truth is, when we consider the world there is Before Jesus, and there is After Jesus. So whatever anyone wants to think or believe about him, his existence changed the world. That means something. That matters."

I studied him in the dimming twilight. "That's actually a more satisfying answer than I have ever received from anyone. Thank you."

"Anytime." He looked at his watch. It was time for him to go. He had to be at work early, and he still had to recite evening prayers. His routine and self-discipline mattered tremendously, and he was meticulous about his prayers.

I curled up on the futon with a book and watched out the window as he walked down the street to his white Victorian.

Interlude
Moving Day

WHEN SHE REALIZED SHE WAS going to lose the house, she practiced moving in private. Before she could muster the courage to tell anyone, she took a single picture off the wall and placed it gently in a box. It was a hard thing, but she no longer used bombastic words like "hardest." She knew better.

Days later she sat looking at the bare spot on the wall, a lump in her throat and the tears threatening to come again. Taking that picture down was acknowledging the inevitable, and she kept forgetting to breathe. It didn't matter how much she wanted to stay there; it was time to move forward.

Kindness began showing up on her doorstep. The doorbell would ring, and she never knew how many faces would be gathered there, smiling gently, holding packing paper and boxes. But every day they came like the sun. Her shoulders were bowed under the weight of a life imploding, and those hands held up more than packing supplies that week.

Divorce ripples out and changes people who thought they were far enough from the ragged epicenter to be safe. No one is safe. Divorce, while at first a deeply private and painful rending, surprised her in also being a communal sorrow. She did not anticipate—could not have anticipated—the families affected by, touched by, and changed by the private hell that had turned into the public loss of her marriage.

During the last night in her house sleep eluded her, and she paced the smooth wooden floors, navigating the labyrinth of carefully labeled boxes. She was alone. Her children were spending the night and the next day with beloved friends where they could be protected from the emptying-out to come. She allowed the memories and plans for the life she had wanted to wash over her as she wept, and then she gently and quietly bid them goodbye.

At seven the next morning there was a knock on the door.

Her friend stood smiling on her porch with three teenage boys while her husband backed a large truck into the drive. They stepped over the threshold and asked where to start. Trucks started arriving, and by eight o'clock there were busy people running in and out of the house with boxes and furniture. She was trying to stay out of the way, trying to be helpful, but as the rooms began to empty she felt the panic and sadness start to rise and grow like a monster.

She stood still in her foyer, teens and boxes whirring past her, utterly incapacitated. She felt like she couldn't remember how to move her feet, and her hands were shaking as uncontrolled tears rolled down her face. Her friend found her standing there amid the chaos, gently put her arms around her, and steered her toward the door. Tenderness was in her voice, and she said simply and clearly, "You need to leave. You do not need to stay and see this happen; I want you to go to Little House and wait. We will take care of everything. Go."

Nodding like a child, she grabbed her keys and purse and stepped outside.

She was not prepared for what she saw. Lining her street, on both sides, were pickup trucks and trailers. Whole families had shown up to help and were waiting their turn to pull into her driveway. There were people everywhere. Large parts of her house, furniture, and piles of boxes were already stacked and tied neatly in the backs of trucks. Young men and women rushed in and out of the garage and front door carrying big boxes to appointed staging areas, and people called out cheerful greetings.

She stood there, afraid to move lest she break apart, perplexed by an odd mix of gratitude and awe. *She didn't deserve this*, she thought, and she waved meekly to her friends as she found her Suburban that someone had moved down the street to make room for the trucks.

She followed her friend's directions and headed to Little House. She didn't know what else to do, and allowing someone else to call the shots felt like a beautiful mercy.

At Little House it was only a few minutes before the first trailers began to arrive and the same hive of activity began unloading and reassembling her life. By lunchtime, her kids' beds were assembled, the washer and dryer were hooked up and running, and the living room was entirely unpacked. Even her piano was in place and being played by a talented young man. Her own bed was being assembled, and someone brought a drill to hang curtain rods and new curtains. Someone unpacked and put together her entire kitchen and hung a new shower curtain in the bathroom. Someone hooked up the TV and the video game system, imagining that when the kids arrived that night it would help it feel like home. This bustling activity continued until every truck was unloaded, and almost every box was unpacked.

Early that evening, her friend who had told her to leave came by Little House. She reached out and placed the keys to the old house in her hand. She hugged her tightly and said, "It's done. You don't have to go back there." Confused, she looked at her friend.

Everything was done. Not only were all of her and her children's belongings moved, but a group of friends had shown up after the movers and cleaned the empty house. They had mopped, vacuumed, and scoured the bathrooms and kitchen. The only things left belonged to her ex-husband, and they were stacked neatly in the garage should he wish to retrieve them. She never had to walk through those empty rooms and could instead remember it when it was full of happiness. Done.

That night in Little House, her children tucked in and dreaming, she looked around. Her entire life had been picked up, and in one fell swoop—like transplanting an orchid—had been moved to a new home. It might not have been as big or as fancy, but it was a very good home.

When her kids had been dropped off earlier it looked and felt like their home. They ran through the rooms, opening closets and drawers, finding familiar belongings and safety. Their beds were made, their photographs were on the walls, even their books and reading lights were all in place. Everything that meant home to them was now in Little House. They never looked back.

A day overflowing with the potential for sorrow ended up being one of the most beautiful days of her life.

She later found out the teenage boys on her porch at dawn had canceled a high school ski-trip—of their own volition—to serve her family. Who does that kind of thing? She knew.

8

The New Normal

FEBRUARY 15, 2010

It's strange around here. I keep catching myself in little moments holding my breath—pausing and waiting for something—noticing the absence of tension, and wanting to call it something else... and then feeling off-kilter because of the quiet... normalcy. I'm not so dramatic as to think I've got post-traumatic stress disorder. Yet, when someone lives in a pressure-cooker for almost three years, and suddenly the steam-release valve is thrown, it may take some time to trust the new normal.

It's hardly eloquent to think of myself bumbling around the house, trying to figure out What's' Next...but that's exactly what I'm doing. I have a list as long as my arm of things that need my attention. Maybe they've been there for a long time—I don't know. It was hard to notice the match under my foot when my whole life was on fire.

What a blessing to have plain, old, normal problems again. Hello, life. Nice to see you again—it's been a while. Yes, we look a little different, but oh, how I've missed you.

"Wonder" by Natalie Merchant was blaring on my computer speakers while I unpacked and sorted another box. Slowly, order was emerging from the wreckage and chaos. (Has there ever been more of an understatement?) The kids were laughing and playing. Bean was attempting to teach Jeffrey to skip rope, which he had just learned how to do that day. Abby was giggling, watching them get tangled up. A friend dropped off a pizza on his way home from work, just because, and my mentor from church came by to measure a coat closet that he had offered to turn into a shelved pantry.

I stopped, a bolt of fabric in my arms. I was perplexed for a moment as I listened to my children giggling and felt the warmth of the furnace quietly clicking on to heat Little House. A stray lock of hair tickled my neck, blown by the warm air from the vent, and I realized that I was holding my breath. What was that feeling? What was it? My heart raced, and my muscles started to tense. *What's wrong?*

I stood perfectly still, like a doe in a glen. Alert, wary. And then realization rolled over me in shivering, hot waves. Nothing was wrong. *Nothing was wrong.* We simply were not living in fear anymore. I realized that moment that I was exhaling for the first time in three years. I was relaxed, humming to myself even, and my children were laughing and playing. That feeling, that tiny whispering thing I could not even recognize? It was the still, hopeful, deep stirrings of… happiness.

I met with my attorney to go over the final papers. Ten years of marriage, nearly twenty years of my life, distilled down to a small stack of clean white paper. It was shocking in its legal simplicity. In a divorce only tangibles matter: one house, two vehicles, three children. Sort, divide, and sign.

My attorney showed me the stack of papers and indicated where I should sign, and I took out my pen. Before we'd gotten married I managed a successful campaign launch for my company, and as a reward I bought myself a beautiful fountain pen. I used it to write and to sign important things. I signed our marriage certificate with it. I signed our first mortgage papers with it. I signed Jeffrey's birth certificate with it. My lawyer waited with kind patience while I fought back tears, one hand gently touching the paper, the other wavering over it with the pen.

Even when you know that divorce is the right thing, even when you know that there isn't any other way, the moment you sign those papers is horrible. Sitting in this warm, tastefully decorated office near the courthouse, my signature would dissolve the one bond I had hoped would last forever. It was all so very civil.

I placed my pen on the paper, watching the ink puddle slightly in the way I loved so much, and I wrote my new name.

1999

The week before David and I got married, my friend Maggie held a small dinner party for our closest friends. It was the middle of September, and the doors and windows were open to the deep blue late summer night. Sprigs of jasmine spilled from small vases, gardenias floated in white bowls on the linen-covered table in her dining room, and candles cast twinkling pools of warm light. There was nowhere I felt safer.

Maggie was standing next to me the following afternoon, and our dresses hung in her room, draped in protective cotton and waiting patiently. We had gone shopping for dresses together and had each chosen the only dress we tried on. I wasn't a conventional bride. My mother had made most of the decisions regarding the wedding and reception, and that was fine. I cared about the vows and the people; getting caught up in the color of the napkins was baffling to me.

I sat looking across the beautiful table at my cousin Michael, who had gently pushed me into David's arms months before. He smiled at me in the warm light, his love shining on his face but mingling with the edges of sorrow just beneath the surface. The night before, he'd come to my house unexpectedly.

"Don't do it. Tracy, please, I don't know why, but don't do it." He had stood in the middle of my living room, hands open.

"What the hell, Michael?" I was shocked. He was David's best man, and the wedding was in a matter of days. "I don't...what? How can you do this? Why?"

His eyes were openly pained. "I don't know, but please, just... don't do it..." he trailed off.

I didn't know what to do. I trusted his sincerity, but I couldn't fathom calling things off a week before the wedding.

It would have been easier to dismiss him had I not been having similar feelings. I had been on a walk with Michael's sister earlier in the week and was talking with her about normal wedding jitters. She empathized, and shared some of her own reservations from before she got married.

I don't remember the details of that conversation, but I do remember very clearly a juniper bush on a busy street corner near her house where we stopped to catch our breath. I had been saying prayers in my head for calmness and clarity. Our staccato footsteps on the pavement created a cadence I found soothing, and I allowed my mind to wander.

As we stopped at the corner, a thought came lucidly clear to my mind: *You can do this. It's not going to go the way you hope, but you can do it if you want to.*

As Michael stood in my living room, achingly vulnerable, those are the words that again sprung forward. *"You can do this. It's not going to go the way you hope, but you can do it if you want to."*

Instead of confessing my fears to Michael, I gave him all the platitudes about cold feet and expected hesitations. We sat down, and I told him how much I loved David and how right we were for each other. We laughed, and he nodded.

"Do you think you can still stand with him next week?" I was afraid; everything was already in place, and I think he could feel my anxiety.

"Of course. I will be there for you. And I love David, that's not it at all…" he trailed off again.

One of the non-negotiable conditions David had set for moving back to California was that he would not have any contact with people from his drug years. That meant shutting out old and dear friends like Danny, and it was why Michael was his best man. It was a hard line he'd chosen to draw himself. When I suggested perhaps inviting old friends to the wedding, he strongly objected, and we never talked about it again.

Michael knew he was a placeholder, but it was about him loving and supporting me, and my entire family had lined up to do their parts.

My brothers were both ushers, Michael was the best man, Maggie was the matron of honor, and my two cousins were bridesmaids. My parents had rented a beautiful park and reception site, and we'd been through pre-marriage counseling with the minister we'd hired. We'd known each other for a decade, and David had almost two years clean and sober. All the proverbial ducks were in their rows.

Back at Maggie's table that beautiful evening, surrounded by laughter and good food and candlelight, I looked across at Michael. He smiled again, gently. I knew he would be there for me come hell or high water.

The morning of the wedding was sunny and warm with that golden light so typical of the San Francisco Peninsula. We all met at my mom's house. She and my step-dad had hosted a lovely rehearsal dinner barbecue the night before for David's family, who had come into town from the four winds. David's uncle Courtney had knelt down in the shadow of the ancient redwood in the corner and earnestly sung a beautiful hymn to us over dinner, immediately endearing him to my heart.

My mom had been to the flower market early to pick up the bundles and buckets of flowers she had ordered the week before, and my cousins, brothers, and friends gathered around the picnic table to make their own bouquets and boutonnières. In the middle of the piles of pink and yellow flowers, Maggie was making my bouquet, winding a white silk ribbon around a spray of white roses and gardenias while everyone chatted and laughed. The boutonnières were imperfect, the table vases were wildflowers, and my friends all made their own bouquets—imperfection was the theme of the day, and everyone embraced the relaxed and easy atmosphere.

Once the flowers were done we all dressed in my mom's bedroom, and the photographer, who I had hired from the tiny local paper, snapped candid black and white shots of us as we goofed around. I had asked her to capture things as they happened, and not to have us stop and pose—*I would not be pretending to throw the bouquet or to cut the cake*—I was just going to do it, and if she got a picture, great. For me, the day was entirely about celebrating our family and friends, and the joining of our lives. It wasn't about perfectly posed photographs.

Those decisions to discard the stress of perfection contributed to the lasting beauty of the day.

Michael arrived at my mom's house to load up the flowers and headed off to the hall to set the tables and decorate with his mom and sisters. He also had a full bar stashed in the back of his Tahoe, which he would later stealthily back up to the catering kitchen and liberally toast to the happiness of everyone present.

From the bride's room at the venue, with my family gathered around and waiting for all the guests to arrive, I could peek out between the sheer curtains and see the photographer snapping pictures of David and his family. All the men were wearing classic black tuxedos, and they made a striking image against the fountains and lakes of the park. I covertly watched David smiling and hamming it up with my brothers and Michael, and when he spied me peeking out of the curtains, he pointed and let loose with his rich baritone laugh.

The photographer captured that moment of perfect happiness in one candid shot.

It was to Celtic harp music provided by another cousin, and not to the Wedding March, that my dad walked me out to the edge of the water where our minister and David stood surrounded by our families. My dad and step-dad, long-time friends and co-coaches of my brother's baseball teams, sat on either side of my mom, providing the example I took for granted and giving me a perfect model of the co-parenting that I would later try to adopt.

David and I wrote our own vows, and waiting to the side for our signatures was our Ketubah. In my ongoing search for God, I had been investigating Judaism. I had taken some Hebrew classes and attended temple at my local synagogue, and I found the traditions and history especially rich and fascinating. The Ketubah was traditionally a marriage contract, but modern versions reflected the tastes of the married couple and could be as elaborate or simple as one liked.

Painting the Ketubah had been a sacrament for me, and I had carefully researched and prepared before beginning. I had gathered supplies, ordered the best thick cotton paper, new sable brushes, watercolors from England, and I made a vial of strong walnut ink. At the antique oak dining table of my childhood, I had laid out my compass, triangle, and square. After saying a prayer for guidance, I set my tools to paper.

Two days later, I had created a piece of art that was deeply personal, yet beautiful enough that I would want to display it in my home. With great care, I had laid out a perfect square on my paper, and within the square, using compasses and 24k gold ink, a perfect circle. Within the circle was a smaller circle, and between the two was a string of moons, depicting the phases from full to new and back again. Around the outside were stars, illustrating the constellations as they would be in a corresponding phase of the year. In the middle was the sun.

After the ceremony, using the beautiful fountain pen I had recently bought, David and I carefully signed our names under our walnut-ink vows, which said, in part, "nor shall death part us, for in the fullness of time we shall meet and know and remember and love again."

Long before we joined our church, we were already using the symbols that spoke to our souls.

Years later, during the bad years, I would be in Nauvoo, Illinois with some friends for a conference. In a somewhat spontaneous decision, some of us decided to go to the rebuilt LDS temple. It was my first time in that temple, and the architecture and beauty of the building, even from the outside, is splendid. From the inside it defies description.

Dressed in white, we made our way toward the spiral staircase, and I found myself near the back, able to watch the procession as my friends ascended. Through the western windows, the late afternoon sunlight landed on glowing faces, on friends nodding and talking softly to one another, joyous to be together. Unexpectedly I blinked back tears. A friend put her arm around me, squeezed, and we walked up together.

After our ordinance work, we were able to rejoin and quietly visit in the celestial room. Entering the grand room, my eyes were drawn upwards—in the middle of the ceiling, a beautiful stained-glass medallion window commands attention. As I looked up, my breath caught in my chest.

There, next to the Mississippi River, in a rebuilt holy building of my adopted faith, was a glowing window with a golden circle of moons through all its phases, surrounded by stars, with the glowing sun in the middle.

I would never feel more encircled in love, more beloved of God, than I would standing in that moment.

"Mom!" Jeffrey called down the hallway. "Have you seen the Calvin and Hobbes books?"

The week before I had found a box of old Calvin and Hobbes anthologies while cleaning out the garage. Jeffrey was all over them, and Calvin and Hobbes quickly became his new heroes. He'd been devouring them, and after days of solid reading he came bounding excitedly into my room holding the book. "Mom! Hobbes is a *stuffed* tiger! Did you know that?! It's all Calvin's IMAGINATION!!" Seeing him figure this out on his own had been a singular delight.

I was sorting through another box when the phone rang. "Did you check your backpack?" I asked, reaching for the phone. I was starting to appreciate the "little" in Little House; I never had to go looking for anyone. The rooms were small, and I could see into the boys' bedroom from the kitchen. It made keeping track of everyone easy.

"Hello?"

"I signed the papers this morning. I thought you should know." David's familiar voice cracked as I spun around and jammed the handset further into my shoulder.

Bean ran into the kitchen chasing Abby with a moving box that had transmogrified into a monster. Hot tears sprang up, and I couldn't speak, choking on my words. I swallowed hard; when I opened my mouth to say something, a sob escaped. It's done. It's over. Ten years of marriage and almost two decades of him being my best friend, and in that moment it was over.

My vision swam, the emotional condensing to visceral. It was hard to breathe as the room swirled around my drowning eyes, and

I sat down hard on the box closest to me. I leaned my head between my knees while flashes of a life imagined and scenes from happier times fired rapidly on the screen of my mind—like a cruel awards show retrospective of those who had died.

There I was in my wedding dress, peeking through the curtains when he spied me and burst out laughing, on the happiest day of my life. There he was holding my hand at the top of Vernal Falls on our honeymoon in Yosemite. There we were in the hallway of our tiny rental house as we inspected the stick with two pink lines on New Year's Eve. There we were crying with joy as our first baby slid from my body, making us parents. There he was standing on the porch of our first house, so proud, holding a chubby copper-haired toddler. There we were welcoming another baby, another copper-haired boy. There he was carrying my fainted, limp body from the floor of the bathroom, so ill, and then there was the surprise baby girl. There we were buying our dream house, and then there we were in the dimming light. There was the sadness permeating years, there were more tears than the oceans, and then there was this.

His soft, sad voice on the end of a phone line, saying that, out of respect for me, he had signed the papers. It was over.

There was nothing else to say.

When I was a child we had some poppies in our yard. I loved the beautiful curling pods that would arc up in delicate fronds, their fuzzy sepals covering the furled petals. It was magic to me how they would unfold, crumpled like tissue, and open to magnificent orange and black flowers.

One year I was so impatient for the glory of the flowers that I decided to help them by peeling back the sepals before they natural-ly burst. I tried to be gentle, but every flower I assisted was damaged, and the beautiful petals were bent, bruised, and in some cases, never opened at all. I never forced another flower.

I felt like a poppy gardener. I had a growing awareness of being at a particular place and time in history, in personal growth, in my development as a soul. Others had been there before me, and others would stand there after me. I was a steward of that garden at that moment, but there was nothing new under the sun. We all sang the same earthbound song.

Someday I hoped to tend another garden, to sing another song, but for the moment I was exactly where I had to be, and I knew I wasn't allowed to help the poppies. I had things to learn there, before I could move on. I had to hold onto faith. Faith that it was possible that the beauty of the song was its entire purpose. Faith that the wheel would turn. The faith of bone as the infant metamorphoses into the woman.

In time, the sap would run, the bulbs would pop, the sun would shine, and hearts would mend. In time. Only in time. There was no helping it.

9

Facing Forward

FEBRUARY 9, 2010

The wagons have been circled, and I and my children are safely in the middle of that tight, loving, organized, closely bound company.

Of one thing I am certain; there is no earthly way for me to ever repay the people who have given me shelter in the storm, who have loved me and my children. Indeed, no repayment is humanly possible.

Miracles happen as normal everyday people reach out to others in their hour of need. Hands that wipe the brow, sop the tears, hold the weeping and grieving, and hands that guide the traces of the wagons into that tight, loving, circle. Those hands are working miracles. Those hands are the hands of God.

IT FELT LIKE THE EYE of a hurricane. I still didn't really trust the calm. It would be years before I would start to trust any calm. I knew there was more hard work coming, but I had been granted a brief respite—a place to catch my breath before the winds picked up again from a new direction. I wasn't sure yet what that would mean, but I hoped the new storm would at least be mine and not one thrust upon me by someone else.

In the basement of Little House was a low-ceilinged room where I set up shop. My farm table may have been too big for the tiny breakfast nook upstairs, but it ended up making a great work table in the center of my new basement sewing room. The heavy benches were unnecessary around a work table, so I stacked them against the wall and turned them into shelves for fabric. My sewing machines formed a bank along the windowless wall, and I got back to work.

Orders were coming in, and I was working with Leisure Arts on a book of my best patterns. I sent my samples to them to be professionally photographed, measured, and double checked against my patterns, and then I waited. While I waited, I continued to fill orders, print new patterns, and slowly generate a little income.

Living on a tight budget was nothing new—two years of unemployment had taught me a lot. At first we'd had our savings, and that lasted a little while. We cashed out our 401K, and that helped us hobble along for a little while too. I had qualified for WIC when Abby was a baby, and the boys received free lunches at their schools. Our church was able to help with food when we needed it, and David's mother tried to help where she could.

Many women in my situation have a co-parent still in the picture. They might not like that person, there might be bad blood, or anger, or whatever—but that person is still present and invested with the kids, still seeing them on some schedule, and most likely providing some sort of financial support for the family, even if it's modest.

Not me.

Most days I did just fine. Really. The kids were happier, and we all laughed a little more often and more easily at Little House. I was learning to let go of a lot of control—it's just not possible to do it all and do it well when you're doing it alone. Most days we were fine. Most days I was fine.

Then, some days. . . . Some days would bring me to my knees, and you could follow my path through the thorns by the drops of blood I left behind. The fact that I was one person trying to meet the needs of three little human beings was never far from the surface. But it wasn't just trying to meet their needs—which were deep and real. I had to manage all the parts of a regular life too. Bills, insurance, rent, gas in the car, the garbage, Scouts, homework, baths, laundry, meals, bedtimes, IEP meetings for Bean, dentist and doctor appointments, church . . . and that didn't even begin to touch on anything personal. We were all still grieving. The kids didn't fully understand why they couldn't see their dad, and that loss was always just below the surface. More nights than not a child would crawl into bed with me and weep into my shoulder, our tears mingling on the pillow. My daughter would tell her dolls, in her sweet little voice, that she didn't have a daddy anymore.

I didn't feel special. I didn't feel cut out to handle this mess, and I knew that other women had really hard rows too. Most of the items on my lists were on the lists of every other woman. The only difference was that there was no one else to share the weight. If a child was sick? I had to take all of them with me to the doctor. Out of milk? Everyone in the car. Need the prescription filled for the ear infection? *Let's go, buckle up, buckaroos.* It was all me, all the time. There was no "divide and conquer" anywhere anymore.

There was one particularly awful day when the brambles broke my skin and tore my feet, and I left crimson footprints all over my life. By dusk I had put all the kids in their rooms while I stood in the kitchen with a broom I had just broken while trying to fish a LEGO out from under the stove. I stood holding the two pieces, crying in the middle of the floor, and let the waves of sadness roll over me. So many things had gone wrong that day, I figured that sending the kids to bed to read was the best thing for everyone. We all had days like that sometimes. Days when your kids were monsters, you hadn't slept, your spouse was on a business trip, and you were counting the hours until they got home because you were so exhausted. I had been there. I remembered that feeling. I would have loved that feeling again—the anxiety coupled with the anticipation that surely you could make it to Friday—what a relief Friday would be when he got home!

Only now, Friday was never coming.

⚘

"I have a proposal for you, and I want you to really think about it. The church will be helping you, and that's okay. I figure we can do one of two things: we can help you with childcare while you try and find decent work. That's one possibility. Or—and this is a different option—we can pay your rent—IF you go to school full time."

My bishop sat on my couch in front of the big picture window at Little House, looking at me earnestly. He was a kind man with a blue-collar job; his wife was a teacher. His words fell on my surprised ears with a little disbelief. He'd been counseling me through the move and the tail end of the divorce, and he knew my situation better than most.

I hadn't thought seriously about school in years. After things started falling apart, my thoughts about school consisted mostly of wishing that I had done it when I was younger and imagining I was too old to start now. I had been writing regularly for several years at different websites and had become friends with professors and other very educated people through those channels, but I knew that I was a misfit. Because I could write, I was able to navigate conversations that required a dictionary, but my cleverness didn't alleviate the truth that I was the only one in my group of friends without at least an undergraduate degree. It was my professor friends who really encouraged me to consider going back to school.

I always loved school. I loved being in a classroom. I loved the first day of school like I loved Christmas morning—it was pregnant

110

with anticipation, laden with sharp new pencils and clean stacks of neatly lined paper with all the potential it contained. I was weird that way, at least in my family.

Neither of my parents went to college, though they both did well enough. My dad was a civil employee in the city that we lived in for his entire career. He worked for the parks department and spent the majority of his time outside and very little time behind a desk. He was happiest outside, and his job suited him perfectly. It also provided a comfortable, middle-class California life. He was able to own a home and raise his family before the tech industry blew up and chased people with modest incomes from our Bay Area neighborhoods.

My mom graduated from high school and then had me. She was a stay-at-home parent for most of my childhood. She baked bread, made preserves from the apricots and plums growing in our yard, and made fruit leather in our dehydrator. She ran a food co-op with the other women in our sunny Peninsula neighborhood, weighing and portioning out giant wheels of natural cheese and sacks of whole grains. She kept chickens in our large yard and one of my jobs was to collect the eggs every day that we sold to the neighbors. We had a vegetable garden with zucchini the size of my thighs and more tomatoes than we could eat. We even had a milkman—a real milkman who would deliver milk to our door when I was small.

When my parents divorced, my mom started a small sports clothing company with her portion of the equity from our house. At first she ran it from home, and as my younger brothers grew so did her company. When she retired years later, she had outgrown two different storefronts and turned her home-based idea into a successful business. She didn't go to college, but she was resourceful, creative, and she worked hard.

When I graduated from high school, no one even suggested that I should apply for college. Working full time to support myself was a necessity. Looking back, I find it ridiculous that I didn't prioritize education—I was smart enough, and I could have done it. But

I didn't have any models. Instead, when I moved to the beach and worked as a waitress, I continued to take a few courses at the community college, and I supplemented my income with art and design work. It seemed good enough, I was young, and time was long. Then suddenly it was fifteen years later, and I was a shell-shocked single mother with three children. What a series of catastrophic decisions I had made. So many things to regret and absolutely no time to spend wallowing in that regret.

I snapped back to the present, and the bishop was explaining that the family who owned Little House was willing to work with him. It was a mutually beneficial arrangement for everyone: we got a place to live, and the landlord got a good tenant and guaranteed rent. The bishop was fulfilling his responsibility to help me while ultimately helping me help myself by providing the means for me to get an education. I could go to school! Well, if I agreed, I would actually *have* to go to school.

Was I ready? It didn't matter. I had never even applied to an actual university—never seriously considered it as an option. I knew I could do what my mom had done and work hard to grow an independent business. I already had the seeds for such a business in my patterns, and they were selling well. But I also knew the risk and lack of security of being a small business owner, and I craved security for myself and the kids. There were a million roadblocks in my mind, but one thing kept rising to the surface: Education was the way to move forward.

"Yes." I said, nodding, and I felt the smile overtake my whole body. "Yes!"

꙳

Walking onto the campus of the state university was an act of validation and rebellion, of radical self-respect and personal hubris.

It was the best decision I could have made. In that simple act, I proclaimed that I believed I could do something I had never even tried, and that I was worth their time and money and classroom space. My old story had been that I was a half-hearted student who would fit classes in as I could around other more important things. I feared I would continue to identify myself this way if I again chose to go to a community college. I needed to grind that narrative into dust. It was time for something new, something better.

It felt so good.

I had called and made an appointment with an academic counselor to see what my options were, and I filled out the application in the admissions office while Abby rolled around on the floor playing with wooden farm animals. I had been able to fill out a FAFSA application from home and get started on the daunting prospect of gathering my spotty transcripts. I didn't know if there would even be anything useful or transferable, but in my mid-thirties, anything that saved me a class or two was worth trying. The counselor informed me that the university also had a program for people in my situation—those returning to school as "mature" students. And there was support for single mothers returning to complete their education. The depth of their resources surprised me. It meant that, with some work, I might qualify for some credits for my independent professional experience. I would have to submit a detailed written portfolio with supporting documents. I left the admission counselor's office with my wiggly preschooler and more hope than I had felt in years.

I wanted my kids to see their mom work hard for something, to see me study and succeed. I wanted them to see in my actions that I loved and respected myself and that I valued education. I wanted them to know I was brave and I could do things that were scary and hard, and that they could be brave and do hard things, too.

I just had to wait and see if the school accepted me.

Interlude
At the Car Wash

SHE HAD JUST LEFT THE dentist. Her face was numb to her eyeballs because of the massive amount of work her friendly dentist had to undertake. He was trading dental care for a painting for his wife, and she knew she was getting the better, if not the less painful, end of the deal. It was cold and clear outside, but the car was warm in the sunlight, and her nose and hands began to tingle and thaw as she started the car and flipped on the heater. It felt so good not to hurt—even if the temporary credit went to Novocain. Her teeth had ached for more than a year, and she had grown accustomed to the pain. The right side of her face sagged as she tried to smile in the rearview mirror and slather some lip balm onto her numb mouth. Such a strange sensation, she thought. It was after noon, and her stomach was gurgling and complaining. But with half her face not cooperating, food would have to wait. The dental hygienist said feeling would return in an hour or two.

She had grown accustomed to too many things that hurt. She had a lot to unlearn.

She had twenty minutes before she needed to pick up her kids, just enough time to tidy up the vehicle. No matter how hard she tried, her car was always a disaster. In grade school, she would sit at her desk idly chewing on her Ticonderoga and stare wistfully at the spotless white sneakers of the girl one desk over. That girl played on the playground, ran around, and did flips on the rings like she did—and yet her shoes were always gleaming white. Despite her best efforts, her shoes were always scuffed, the laces were always frayed, and she could not keep them clean. It baffled her. It still baffled her. Her car was the same way. She was mystified when mothers had clean cars like she was when girls had white sneakers. *How did that happen?*

She headed to the car wash, poking and pulling on her floppy lips as she drove in silence. Her radio had broken months ago, and all she could get was a thin, tinny sound on a few stations. Sometimes it sucked and she missed music, but sometimes she relished the quiet. This was a day for quiet.

The cold was brisk and startling as she stepped out of the car. The yellow sunlight and her warm car had fooled her, and she had forgotten about the bitter cold. Her ears were full of silence, and her face hung slack as she pushed the silver button to activate the car wash vacuum that would swallow up at least a Jackson worth of LEGO pieces in her backseat before she was finished. Sometimes, she would carefully collect all the loose LEGO pieces, but not this time. The constant roar of the giant vacuum was almost as good as the quiet.

She swore off drive-through fast food and wondered how one mother with three little children could generate so much stuff. There were papers, homework, socks, gloves, mittens, a rabbit-fur-lined hat thing her dad had sent her son, more LEGO bricks, shoes, fruit snacks, water bottles, junk mail, and maps shoved in the door pocket. She silently gathered it all up and placed it in the trash bin. She meticulously vacuumed the mats, the seats, and the bland beige carpeting.

The hose curled up compliantly on its arm when she finished, and she drove around the half-loop toward the yawning opening of the car wash. It dawned on her that she may never before have done this alone—it was usually a family affair anticipated with great glee and rejoicing. She enjoyed the quiet. She didn't even chitchat with the wash attendant. She just handed him her money, checked the windows, and nodded as he waved her forward. The little light turned red, and she slipped the car into neutral.

The car wash took over.

Somewhere underground, she imagined, giant wheels turned, and the car moved forward into the great wet tunnel. She rested her numb chin on her hands and peered into the jets of water cascading over the hood. With her hand, she could feel the softness of her lip, the curve of her cheek, and even the curve of her cheekbone meeting her eye, yet she had no sensation of her own touch. Disconnected.

The giant wheels drew her deeper into the car wash, and the fluffy foam soap squirted and sputtered as huge drum rollers spun and swirled over the sheet metal and glass. It was oddly soothing. The white noise, the darkness, the foamy colors, and the water. Being pulled forward with nothing required of her.

She had grown accustomed to pushing and to struggle, to immense effort to get anywhere. She had grown accustomed to constant hurt and living with pain. She wished the carwash were five miles long and she could just sit there for an hour, numb, protected, warm and gliding through the outside storm.

She was grateful for the brief respite. She was grateful for car washes, dentists, and Novocain. She was grateful that eventually, no matter how bad things hurt, numbness wore off and feeling came back. She was grateful for rainbow soap, giant vacuums, and odd moments of peace amid white noise.

She was grateful for the tingling that meant life was returning.

10

Saddle Up, Buttercup

MARCH 23, 2010

Lately, as I plow through what must be done, people have been making what I know are meant as kind comments about how amazing or strong I seem. At first, this felt kind of nice. But as they've become more frequent, I'm becoming perplexed. I'm confused—I am no more or less strong than anyone—I get up each morning and do what has to be done. Sometimes it's harder than others, sometimes I cry and yell, sometimes I laugh and dance. Sometimes the weight feels crushing, sometimes I feel invincible.

It's not "strong" or "amazing" to take care of your children—it's simply what a mother does. Some days I rock, other days I crash and burn— just ask my kids. Hopefully when it all shakes out, the rocking-days will outnumber the fireballs, but who knows yet. The fact that there is no one else to share this task doesn't make me strong or a hero. It just makes it part of life.

THERE WERE SO MANY THINGS during the burning years that I let slide. Like a parent trying to get the oxygen mask on herself first in a depressurized plane, I was finally in a place where I could breathe and get my bearings. The decision to go back to school was the first and biggest step in looking ahead instead of back, but it was time to sift through more ashes for precious things lost.

I had to consider my kids' welfare in new ways. David had no legal or custodial rights any longer, so, if something happened to me, I needed to make sure that they would be taken care of in the future. It's an awful thing to contemplate, but defaulting to doing nothing felt irresponsible.

I couldn't hide from the fact that I was the only thing standing between my kids and the unknown. I had neglected myself for a long time, the way that so many women do: by making everyone else's needs so important there was no room for me to exist as a person. My own needs were easy—and sometimes necessary—to shove to the bottom of the pile. It's easier to focus on the kids, especially when their needs are so immediate and never-ending. Kids are a great way to lose yourself as a woman. It's a slippery slope because what starts out as altruistic love for your family can quickly become martyrdom seasoned with resentment. We cannot shove ourselves out of existence and then expect to have a life worth living. We cannot allow "mother" to be the only thing that defines our existence.

I was someone before I became a mother. The truth was, I was able to become a mother through a series of happy circumstances, most of which required me to be an interesting and valuable person on my own. I needed to remember who I was and decide what parts of that to incorporate in the future I wanted.

Childbirth changed my body. I gave birth to three nearly nine-pound babies in four and a half years. That is a lot of intense strain on your reserves, and a lot of lost sleep. I also suffered from *hyperemesis gravidarum*—severe pregnancy sickness—with all three babies. The nausea and vomiting lasted all day, sometimes accompanied by fainting. I had the severe kind—where I couldn't keep water down,

I couldn't drive (in case I lost consciousness behind the wheel), and I needed IV hydration. When you vomit constantly with a nine-pound baby in your abdomen, there is nowhere for the pressure to go but out. I broke my water vomiting at 38 weeks. My body had been through a lot.

I also had to come to terms with another truth: I moved to my own rhythms. Oh, I got a lot done. I was creative to a fault and had a million projects and ideas in the air at any given time, but...things happened in their own time. When I tried to force creative projects, they were often disasters.

Inspiration came in fits and starts. I would usually let things go until I was swamped and then open up a can of crazy and run like a madwoman. I did that with little things like housekeeping and chores, but also with the bigger things in life—like waiting until I was twenty-nine to have kids and then having three in a row. Feast or famine.

My struggle to take care of myself fit the same pattern.

For a spell I would float along, sitting in a comfortable inner-tube floating down a plus-sized lazy river. Then one day something would click and I would decide it was time to do something. That something could be weekly weigh-in meetings or any new diet. I would join a gym or go to aerobics at the community center, beat my brains out, and get praise from people. And that felt good, but it also felt kind of terrible. It was a constant, daily effort to resist gravity and keep myself moving in ways that did not feel natural.

Struggling with my weight felt like pushing an enormous boulder up a mountain. I kept waiting for the point where "exercising" would become a happy part of my identity—the way I enjoyed being an "artist" or a "good cook" or even "Mom." It just never happened. It always felt like pushing that boulder was something I was doing while waiting to get back to the life I enjoyed—my real life. I was strong, and I could muscle that boulder a long way up the hill, but there was no place to pause, set the boulder aside, and enjoy life before resuming the push up the mountain. It didn't work that way.

I wanted to pay attention to something besides pushing the boulder—frankly, the view wasn't great. There were people who seemed happy, whose whole lives were about pushing that boulder. How could I push the boulder and still stop and take some snapshots of the beautiful flowers on the side of the mountain? What if I wanted to have a campfire, and maybe swim in a sparkling mountain stream? Because the mountain was sure pretty when I peeked around the side of the boulder

Life was full of such amazing things. I got really tired, really quickly, of looking at the ass-end of a rock. I needed to figure out what taking care of myself meant to me in crafting a life I wanted, away from external validation.

One of the things I did know was that spending my life behind a boulder was not in the plan.

I was really lucky. When considering potential guardianship for my children, I had a whole host of people who loved us and could be trusted, if necessary, with the children's well-being. It's not a decision that's fun to contemplate, but it is necessary one.

The obvious choice is usually one's parents. My mom and step-dad were retired and lived in California, and they were busy going on cruises and trips to Alaska and visiting all the baseball parks in the Western United States. I knew that my mother would not hesitate to take on the responsibility. They would certainly be a logical choice, but they were also enjoying retirement.

David's mother was alone and much older than my own parents. She loved the kids without question, but I knew they would be too heavy a burden for her.

One of the most touching moments during this time came from my uncle. He and his partner were neck-deep in restoring a historic Southern California bungalow, including period-piece antique furnishings with names like Stickley and Frank Lloyd Wright. Their home was a magnificent, beautiful showpiece. My uncle's heart was plainly on his face when he said that he and Mark would be honored to love and raise my kids for me. I will love him forever for that.

Choosing someone to raise your children in the event of your death is at once a ghastly and a beautiful thing. There were friends who were willing, and extended family too, but I ultimately decided on my brother and his wife—the same brother who had been there that awful day in October and who had taken them to safety when I went to Houston. They had two young boys already, they lived near our parents, and my kids would be close to many people who loved them.

I drew up the papers, and I crossed that difficult task off my list.

While I was waiting to hear back from the university on my application, I had to take a hard look at my finances. I hated thinking about money, and I really didn't want to know how badly David had left things. I steeled myself and started digging.

It turned out I didn't have to panic. When there is literally nothing left, the mess isn't actually that big.

I had nothing. I knew that in theory, but seeing it all spread out on the round kitchen table before me was pretty stark. The one bright spot, if you could call it that, was that David had assumed responsibility for the house in the divorce, and I was insulated from the foreclosure process.

If I got into the university, the church would be managing my rent. I needed to come up with enough money to pay the rest of my household bills on my own—food, heat, gas, water, garbage, and whatever various sundries arose. I knew that the church would help with food if I asked—we ran an efficient food charity that helped many in our community—but I didn't want to ask for more if I could help myself. I was making enough on patterns that I believed I could manage my bills as long as nothing major happened. *Please, paid-for trusty Suburban, continue to be the bulletproof reliable vehicle you've always been!*

We didn't have medical insurance, but someone had told me that the kids would qualify for state insurance. I wouldn't have insurance, but at least they would. That meant a trip down to the welfare office to apply for aid.

Looking back, it's silly how busted up my pride was over this fact.

I had paid into the system for years, but the stigma against being a "welfare mother" was so strong that I fought it. I tried ten ways from Sunday to keep from going to that office.

I was a fool.

*

Instead of pushing the boulder further up the hill, I decided I was going to revamp how I looked at things. I wanted to be comfortable in my skin, not necessarily thin. That wasn't going to happen at the gym; it was work I had to do inside of myself.

I wanted to be healthy. I wanted to be strong. I wanted to move away from equating either of those things to a number on the scale or a tag in my pants. Since I was the only parent, I felt keenly the responsibility to be as healthy and as strong as I could be—both physically and mentally.

I had been on every program in the world. None of them had fixed me, and it was because I hadn't yet realized I didn't need fixing. Diet plans are about food. Writing down and weighing every morsel I ate wasn't something that I wanted to do again. I didn't want to think about food all the time. Doing that only worked for short periods, with external results. But none of them got to the *why*.

That's what I was interested in—*why*. I never wanted to yo-yo again. I wanted to be healthy and strong, not starve myself down, feeding on praise, only to recoil after a short, exhilarating fall. That wasn't about me; that was about someone outside of me approving of my appearance, and that wasn't healthy either.

It wasn't about the food.

Weighing myself every week at a meeting didn't fix the loneliness of three years of free fall. Counting points didn't fix the fear of raising my children alone. Keeping a list of food didn't make it easier to walk into the welfare office. Neither did eating a whole bag of potato chips. It was about so much more than the food. Until I solved that problem, everything else was just a bungee jump—good for a cheap thrill, but not taking me anywhere at all.

I started by throwing out the scale—literally taking it out to the trash on garbage day and tossing it into the bin. I promised myself that I would never again tie my self-esteem to those numbers, regardless of which direction they went.

I decided food was just food. There was no moral value to food—it was neither good nor bad, it was simply food. Some of it was really tasty and some of it wasn't. It's amazing what happens when a potato chip isn't a "bad" food and instead is just a piece of potato. You can have it or not. A salad wasn't "good," it was just a bowl of vegetables. Maybe they would taste good and make my body feel stronger. Maybe I would choose to eat them, maybe not. It was liberating.

There were no more lists, no more calorie counting, no more documenting every bite. I needed to eat to live, to be strong, and to have a clear mind. My muscles needed protein so they could be strong. I liked food that tasted good, but there was no taste that would make my feelings go away. Separating out my feelings and letting them just be feelings allowed me to feel them instead of eat them.

Was I hungry? If so, I ate. Was I angry? Or afraid? Or lonely? Those answers required different things from me—and were much harder—but I stopped trying to fill those voids with Cherry Garcia.

Being strong also meant that I needed to use my muscles. I needed to not just heal my emotional heart, but also to take care of my physical heart. When I was no longer focused on what the scale said, no longer focused on wanting attention for being pretty or whatever was considered acceptable, perhaps using my muscles and working my heart could be just a pleasure instead of another way to push a boulder.

I was going to try and find out.

✍

I walked across the street to Little House's mailbox. All of the mailboxes were on the south side of the busy street we now lived on, so I couldn't send the kids to get the mail anymore. It was a two-lane road with a double-yellow turn lane in the middle, and it made me nervous to see how fast people drove even though it was a mostly residential area.

I opened the mailbox, and right on top of the pile there was a thick, creamy envelope with a crimson return address. I stood staring at it for a moment, afraid to touch it. My hand was jittery as I picked it up and shoved the other mail under my arm. I looked around, and took a deep breath.

I slipped my finger under the flap and pulled out the heavy sheet of paper. *On behalf of the staff and faculty of the university, we would like to congratulate you on your acceptance....*

Yes!!

I exhaled in a great happy rush, relief mixed with joy mixed with hope, my hand clutching the letter to my chest. It was still just me standing alone on the empty twilit street, but now I felt triumphant. I got in. A real university wanted me, believed in me, and was inviting me to attend. I did it.

11

Heart Mind Body Spirit

MARCH 31, 2010

Bean worked so hard today, and for the first time managed to climb thirty feet up the rock wall at the YMCA and ring the brass bell at the top. He harnessed himself up, and despite not having the right shoes, he still did it. He did so well, the woman managing the belay rope offered him a pair of climbing shoes, and he made it up a second time. He says his legs hurt but he really liked doing it, and seeing him accomplish a goal he wanted made me tear up.

All three kids are signed up for swim lessons, and Jeffrey wants to take a kickboxing class. That might be more his strength than rock-climbing. He's more of a bison, not a mountain goat. It's fun finding fitness-y things they each like to do. Abby can't wait to try the kids' climbing wall when she turns four next month.

I DECIDED PART OF TAKING care of my heart meant using it. But I hated gyms and aerobics classes, and I had vowed to not beat myself up anymore. So what could I do? I needed something that wasn't about conforming to an outside ideal. I needed somewhere I felt sort of safe, and where there was no end result in mind besides being healthier and stronger. I wanted activity to be fun—something the kids could do with me that wasn't numbingly repetitive. I knew I would quit anything that seemed to require perfection. I found the local YMCA.

There was a new Y near where I lived, nestled up against the mountains, not far from Little House. A fitter, more energetic person might have jogged there, but I remembered Melinda Mae—one bite at a time. This was about taking care of myself, not about having stupid expectations that I had no ability to meet. I could drive.

The Y made me feel safe because it was for families. It had two indoor pools: one lap pool and one kids' pool with a water slide where they could take swimming lessons. There was a giant rock wall, basketball and handball courts, yoga classes, a playground, and a child-care center, plus all the usual gym things. I liked the options, and I loved the fact that the kids could be more active with me. I could swim with them. They needed swimming lessons anyway. Rock climbing actually looked fun. It seemed like something we could do that was geared toward us enjoying each other, not my beating myself into a smaller box where I didn't really fit. They also offered sliding-scale fees, so poorer people could have access to these good things. All of this checked my boxes.

David's mother offered to help with the membership, and we joined. The first thing I did was sign the kids up for swimming lessons. The second thing I did was make an appointment for myself.

Skinny people will never know how hard it is for a big woman to walk into a gym the first time—even a kinder, family-centered place like the YMCA. It's like being dropped at a train station in a foreign country—you don't speak the language, and you don't have any friends.

Just so I couldn't change my mind, I put it on my calendar. Between 9:30 and 11:00, I was going to the Y. Other than taking the kids swimming now and then, I had not set foot in a gym in a decade. I could write a thesis about why, but I also decided it didn't matter anymore.

All the planning in the world cannot get you through the door. I was ready to turn around by the time I got there. I was dragging two little kids behind me with my cell phone wedged between my ear and one shoulder as I took a call. The school nurse had phoned right as I was parking to tell me that Jeffrey was on the cot in her office complaining of a sore throat. When we entered the gym, Bean ran one way, Abby ran the other, and I dropped my phone as the door slammed me in my ample butt. Off to an excellent start.

The school nurse suggested a vitamin C drop for Jeffrey's throat and said she would call me if anything changed. I rounded the kids back up and made my way through the line and scanned our little plastic cards. I signed Bean and Abby in at the kids' zone, giving the worker a quick-and-dirty primer on autism, and they ran off happily.

I went to find the locker room. Standing around looking clueless also means standing around feeling very vulnerable. The anxiety at the back of my mind started to whisper that I didn't belong. *Shut up. I'm here. I am going to take up space, and I belong.*

In the locker room, I hadn't expected to see so many naked people. A lot of naked people. Not that I mind naked people. I just hadn't thought of it. As a totally out of shape mother, getting naked in front of strangers was a level of vulnerable I wasn't quite prepared to conquer yet. I was glad I wore my new stretchy pants and a white t-shirt. I only had to find a locker, throw my bag in, and fasten the little clip to my shirt naming me the claimant to two smallish children in the play zone.

Okay, deep breath, and I am ready. Eating the whale. One bite. Maybe food metaphors aren't helpful? I decided to check out the place and get my bearings. I didn't like standing around wondering where to go, so exploring seemed like a good start.

There was a large gymnasium next to the rock climbing walls where many women were bouncing all over the place with half-balls stuck to the floor, while someone who seemed a little crazy was yelling at them. *Not for me. Not today. Maybe not ever. That's okay.*

There were some lonely stationary bikes, mats, and climbing equipment outside the basketball courts. I really liked the idea of rock climbing, but there was no way I was ready to get into a climbing harness. *Maybe that could be a goal.* Maybe.

Making my way upstairs, I came to a large circular room with windows overlooking the pools on one side and the basketball courts on the other. Nearly every inch of floor space was filled with machines. *It looks like that medieval torture room I saw at the Tower of London, and I know I'm not the first one to make that comparison.* I had no idea how any of the equipment worked, and I was feeling self-conscious and a little embarrassed. There was no way I was going to step onto a machine when I didn't know how to work it.

I found the information desk and waited for someone to notice me.

It was a lonely place to stand. There was activity all around, and I felt so unsure of myself. The doubts and unkind voices in my head got louder the longer I stood there. As a plus-sized woman, I already felt invisible a lot of the time. Humiliation crawled up my back and started to burn my shoulders. *Someone, please notice me....*

A woman finally asked what I needed.

That's the thing. *I don't know. I'm new. I think I need someone to show me what to do. But I don't know.* People offering to help usually assume that the recipient will know what they need. I didn't. I felt awkward and masked my fear with wisecracks and bravado. *Help me. I am here, and that is more than half the battle. You don't even know. Tell me what to do, how to carry me from here to a stronger heart and a longer life.*

"I'm new, and I need a consultation—I am unsure how to use the equipment or where I should even be." I hoped my smile hid the glazing of tears in my eyes.

She saw me. "Come with me. Didn't anyone give you a tour when you signed up? No? I'm so sorry—it gets hectic. Let me introduce you to Heather, and she can help." *Oh thank you Lord. I like Heathers.*

Heather was older than me and dressed in a tracksuit, and she invited me into her office. I felt the color come back to my face. I was so afraid. I was so out of my comfort zone. She told me how to sign up for a personal health session—I received two free with my new membership—and then she showed me a list of classes. She offered to walk me around the facility and show me how the machines worked, how to turn them on and off, and what I might expect from my consultation. *Yes, yes please. ...if someone would just tell me what to do, show me where to put my feet, give me a plan, I will conquer my demons and just do it.*

She left me on a machine that I think was usually for the geriatric crowd, but I needed a win, so I got on and kept going until my legs were shaking and my shoulders were hot—not from humiliation, but from use. *Take that, voices. Shut up. I don't have to listen to you anymore. Go away. I'm the boss now.*

Making my way downstairs to the locker room, my legs felt how they did when I was a child and took off my roller skates after a day at the rink. Wobbly and numb. The next day I would hurt, I knew. *But nothing hurt as much as being scared and invisible.* I could do it. I could do hard things.

The emotional work of taking care of my body was so much harder than the physical work. It wasn't my muscles that were the problem; it was my mind.

Overcoming years of shame at being big, of feeling like I didn't belong, of feeling like my value was somehow tied to my appearance, was far harder than swimming a lap or punching the heavy bag—which I found that I really, deeply enjoyed! *Punch! Punch! PUNCH!*

In taking care of myself, I made the conscious choice to be kind in how I spoke about my body. Just like there was no moral value in a slice of potato, there was no moral value to "fat" or "thin." They were simply words, neither inherently good or bad. Uncoupling those terms took vigilance. I had previously made a decision to never speak poorly of my body in front of my children—and while that was simple, I had continued to let the disparity run rampant internally. I realized the kindest and healthiest thing I could do was ask myself, "Would I say that to someone I love?" If the answer was no, I had to cut those words from my personal narrative.

An amazing thing started to happen. I started to find joy in my body. I stopped worrying how my butt looked and instead enjoyed the feel of the rocks on the climbing wall under my hands. My legs were strong, and they could push me up the wall. My lungs were amazing, and it felt great to reach the end of a lap in the pool and take great gulps of air. I had to guard that new joy from years of conditioning, but I discovered I could change the way I experienced embodiment.

And I never once stepped on a scale.

Interlude
Welfare

"What we do is nothing but a drop in the ocean, but if we didn't do it, the ocean would be one drop less than it is."—Mother Teresa of Calcutta

We are imperfect, and there is grace in our imperfection. —Me

SHE PARKED IN THE LOT outside of an unassuming glass office building. She was grateful that the offices were in a nondescript complex, where she could have been for any reason. She felt shame again at her stubborn pride. She had done as much of the work possible prior to actually visiting the offices; this was the last step in qualifying for assistance. Next to her was the necessary paperwork, and in the backseat were the three squirming children she was also required to bring. She understood why—DSHS wanted to ensure not only that they were real, but that they were being cared for and were not visibly abused. More humiliation. In asking for help, there were a million unanticipated but unsurprising indignities.

She got the kids out of the car and hoped that her son with autism would manage to hold it together under the stress of unfamiliar surroundings and strange smells while also picking up on her own anxiety, as always. Her youngest was still struggling (with limited

131

success) to master her bladder, so she shoved an extra set of pink clothes and a pull-up in her bag. Her oldest helped herd the younger kids toward the reflective doors that slid open as they approached.

Inside it felt a lot like the DMV, only with more crying children and tired women filling the seats. There was a kiosk where you entered your case number and waited for your number to be called. She appreciated that they didn't need to queue up. Lines and close personal proximity to strangers were not good for her son with autism.

There were some baskets of neglected-looking toys and torn books, but she'd brought things to occupy her kids. She didn't want them getting sick, so she steered them to a corner where she hoped it would be easier to contain and entertain them. She knew the wait was going to be unpleasantly long.

When her number was called, she gathered her papers and nervously approached the window. The social worker greeted her with a friendly smile. She seemed well versed in calming nervous mothers and generously explained the process as she double-checked the paperwork against what she had in her computer. This small human kindness might have seemed irrelevant in other circumstances, but finding it in a welfare office while applying for assistance renewed her faith in humanity.

"Here are your papers. Your caseworker will call you in a few minutes." The kind woman smiled and pointed her and the children back to their corner seats.

After an hour, she'd gone through all of the snacks and toys in her bag; out of desperation she resorted to letting the kids play with the basket of neglected toys.

The caseworker finally called her number and led them all back to a small cubicle, where there was another basket of somewhat less neglected toys. The kids sat on the floor and dumped them out. The caseworker began by going over the basic information she'd already provided and then began to ask more in-depth questions. She was asked about David, about child support or spousal support. She was asked about any bank accounts, savings accounts, or retirement accounts. She was asked about cars, boats, assets, homes, or other places money might be tied up, and she was asked to provide documentation on the value of her vehicle, on any bank accounts, and on the foreclosure of her home.

She had all the paperwork in her folder.

Had her car not been already paid for, she would have had to sell it. Had her car been worth over a certain amount, she would have had to sell it. Had she had any assets, she would have to liquidate them or she would not qualify. For the first time ever, she was glad her car was older and paid off. *Please please please just keep working.*

She told the caseworker that she did not need to apply for housing aid and then had to explain how her church was helping with her rent. She was only applying for state medical coverage for the kids. The caseworker explained that it was procedure to submit the application for all available services and see what came back, but that they would need written verification regarding the rent on official letterhead.

She added another item to her list. *Call church.*

Her bishop had counseled her to apply for whatever aid the state could offer. Her situation was pretty bad on paper—displaced homemaker, three children, addict ex-husband not paying support, foreclosed home. She wanted to protest, to explain that she wasn't *that person.* But she was. And she was so keenly aware, now stripped of artifice, of how easily anyone—and so many women with young children—could become *that person.*

The caseworker thanked her for being so organized and complimented the children on being well-behaved. She'd be hearing back from DSHS regarding her application in a week or so; if she had any questions there was a number to call.

She gathered the kids and walked out the shiny sliding doors into the cold. They skipped ahead to the car, unaware of anything except their happiness to be back outside. Lost in her own thoughts, the woman opened the door of her paid-for car and the children buckled themselves into their seats. *That's one good thing about them getting older*, she thought idly, *they can buckle themselves.*

She felt confused, conflicted. She didn't want to be a "welfare mother." She didn't want any of this. She didn't want to lay bare her personal and financial dire straits to strangers, and she didn't want to need help. But she couldn't pretend she didn't need it.

She found herself oddly impressed by the safety system in place. Previously, welfare had only been an idea to her, something she heard about on the news or that people talked about with derision. She hadn't necessarily shared the derision, but she had absolutely internalized the stigma, and her pride had made her resist help longer than she should have.

The people at the welfare office had been professional, kind, and very thorough. The offices were not lavish, but they had been clean and efficient and were staffed by people who devoted themselves and their careers to helping others. Her impression of what *welfare* meant was changing in real time as she leaned against the car that chilly morning.

The enormity of what it had meant to think of a class of sisters and brothers as a monolith hit her. Labeling people who qualified for public assistance as "them" had allowed her—and allowed society—to distance themselves, believing *they* could never be *them*.

The humiliation she felt earlier returned, but it had shifted and was no longer about personal pride for her situation. She felt a deeper shame for failing to understand what it meant to actually love and serve her brothers and sisters.

Realization washed over her in a giant wave. Despite the sometimes-catastrophic consequences of agency, there were mechanisms and safety nets and hands outstretched waiting to help. She lost her home, but because of the legal system she was able to protect herself and her kids. Her children's father was swallowed by addiction, but there were laws, judges, and courts to ensure that her children were protected and that their father was protected too—from himself and from doing further damage. Addiction was a nasty, slouching beast, but there were programs and therapies everywhere dedicated to slaying it. She may have been suddenly impoverished and without child support or hope of receiving any, but there were welfare programs in place for people just like her.

It was hard to navigate, and it was difficult to prove qualification, but there were people who dedicated their lives to protecting the poor and needy and did so without huge salaries. She couldn't provide gifts for her children at the holidays, but people cared enough to make sure that children like hers were not forgotten. She was in the process of trying to qualify for low-interest student loans to get an education, to lift herself out of need. This would require work, but it was work she could not have done had there not been aid available. Her pride? Obliterated. But also obliterated was any lingering notion that life's blessings were somehow owed or earned.

There but for the grace of God go I was tattooed on her heart, right in the parking lot of a nondescript office building while her kids finished strapping themselves in the car and started yelling that they were hungry.

12

Mothering Bean

10 APRIL 2012

"MOM! Meteorologists call big clumps of air 'masses' or 'fronts' and today the warm front is winning. I'm going to go outside until the cold front moves in when the sun sets!"

"MOM! It's nice the people at Target leave crawling holes in the stacks of paper towels. They must have autistic kids who like to hide, too!"

"MOM! Did you know the sun rises in the east EVERY SINGLE DAY?!!"

"MOM! Abby actually thinks there is a fairy who comes and takes her teeth. Can you believe that? I told her that was illogical and she's dumb."

"MOM! Sometimes I like to use my imagination, but Abby doesn't do it right."

"MOM! Look! I made a bracelet out of explosive caps from my cap-gun. I'm wearing it to church in case I hate the songs in Primary."

"MOM! I think I'll eat toast now instead of English muffins. See, I do like new food!"

"MOM! I need a new hammock so I can watch the sunset properly."

"MOM! Did you know that cuttlefish are by far the smartest invertebrates? Octopus like to think they are, but they're wrong. It's cuttlefish."

Sometimes I feel like Calvin's mom.

AS I WAS SORTING THROUGH my financial papers in hopes of going back to school, a friend asked me about motherhood. She was a brilliant grad student who was contemplating having children but was concerned about her ability to deal with being a parent. She said she didn't want a "defective" child. She kept talking, but I was suddenly outside of time, everything floating unnaturally and disjointed, and I stared at that ticking, dangerous bomb in my mind. The hardest part, even in my horror: I knew that feeling.

I had a defective child. An amazing boy who, within days of his birth disabused me of my previous notions of motherhood. He stripped me of my carapace, my pride, and my preconceived ideas of what being a good mother meant. In the natural storm of his childlike, all-consuming needs, there was no room for holding onto anything nonessential. Worrying about convention and caring what the neighbors thought were the first casualties.

Like all growth and stretching, it was painful. We cut our teeth on each other, and I was not immune from moments of despair and frustration. But because of my "defective" child who lives purely without guile or artifice, our family became more fully human. My neurotypical children were laden with compassion and kindness, and I was confident in my ability to meet challenges.

Before I became a mother I knew exactly what kind of mother I would be. What an astounding combination of hubris and naiveté. I consider my beautiful, defective child and his inimitable spirit, his amazing way of looking at the world, and the priceless joy he's brought to our family and think, *Not everyone is lucky enough to get a Bean.*

When I came back to the present, I swallowed hard and said to my friend, "Then you probably shouldn't have children."

Bean came into the world screaming bloody murder. His little shoulders weren't even pushed from my body, but his face was torqued with pain and what I can only imagine was intense confusion over the sensory chaos of being born. Of course that's hindsight, but given what I've learned about my child since then, I suspect that it might be close to accurate. I remember holding him as I had held Jeffrey and wanting nothing more than to comfort him. It was a work in progress. It still is.

Within days of his birth I knew that he was different. All the things I had done with my first baby were futile with Bean. He seemed to be in a constant state of panic—muscles tense, back arched, wailing until exhaustion. When he was three weeks old I called our pediatrician to ask what might be wrong. He dispensed the usual advice about breast milk, colic, gas, and letting him "cry it out." I tried everything, and I still had a baby who never stopped crying.

If he was awake, he was purple-faced, back-arched, lungs-burning, screaming. Getting him to eat was a herculean effort. He had trouble latching, and his sucking was uncoordinated and weak. I moved him to a bottle in a desperate attempt to get more calories into him with less effort. He would eventually fall asleep from the sheer exhaustion of crying so hard, and quiet would descend for a short interlude. As soon as he awoke, it started all over.

All the things that helped calm other babies did nothing for him. Rocking, bouncing, warm baths, patting his back, driving in the car, the swing, a sling—all only seemed to make him panic and scream harder. It was hell. And no one seemed to have any answers. I changed my diet. I stopped feeding him breast milk because I was worried about allergies. We tried gripe water and special formulas, but nothing seemed to calm or soothe him. Kind people at church would take him from me—assuring me that they could help, that they could calm any baby—and inevitably they would return confused, frustrated, and shaking their heads in resignation as they passed him back to me.

He didn't stop screaming until around his first birthday.

There are swaths of time in that first year that are completely lost to me. I know that Jeffrey moved from two to three. I know that my parents came to visit once, but all of my recollections are clouded by intense sleep deprivation and constant worry.

He was ten months old when I first asked the pediatrician about autism. The doctor brushed me off, explaining that autism seldom presented in children before eighteen months. Looking back, he's got some ignorance to answer for—and some continuing education to catch up on. Bean was smaller than Jeffrey, but he was growing and, except for the unending screaming, was meeting the expected developmental milestones only slightly behind schedule. I tried to explain to the doctors how he cried in the bath, how he wouldn't get food on his hands, how he hated his feet being bare, how he panicked when I changed his diaper. But no one listened.

Around his first birthday we also got a computer with an internet connection. One day I Googled "my baby cries all the time" and I started reading. I read everything I could find. I recognized my son in the stories of others. I recognized and learned about other kids who hated food, who banged their heads, who reacted with alarm to gentle touch, who couldn't stand being set down on the lawn, who hated riding in the car, and for whom bubbles in the bath were a reason to panic.

I got mad. I dumped that first pediatrician and found another. Then another. I found a pediatrician who listened to me, who believed me when I explained Bean's life, and who started testing him. I had one perfectly typical child, and I wasn't an over-reactive new mother—I knew that something was different, and someone was finally listening to me.

I became my son's advocate. It's often one of the first and most powerful lessons that parents of special-needs children have to learn. But we all get it eventually.

When the tests and assessments came back, the autism specialist called me. She asked me to meet her at her office and to bring Bean. His scores for sensory processing were in the < 15% range. He showed impairment in vestibular, auditory, verbal, and proprioceptive processing. His adrenal levels were through the roof. The doctor explained that the adrenal medulla produces a hormonal cascade in response to acute stress—what we commonly call the "fight or flight" reflex. In layman's terms, Bean was stuck in "panic" in his brain, and he experienced everything without filters. Imagine even the most benign input feeling like a ball was being hurled toward your face. We need that flood of hormones to react and duck from the ball, but we don't need it when our mother is trying to rock us to sleep. I cried with a mixture of relief to finally have some answers and grief for what his little body had been going through.

It was during this first diagnosis that David stood in the kitchen and quizzically rattled the pills from my dentist. I've been told that the stress on parents from a child with autism has torn apart many marriages. I'll never know how much that stress factored into David's decision to reach for those pills. But the why is irrelevant; he reached for them. I enrolled Bean in early-intervention therapy. After three years in a special pre-school, with occupational therapists, physical therapists, sensory therapy, swings, slings, pressure suits, weighted blankets, lap pads and vests, jaw pressure sticks, skin-brushing, a special autism-immersion kindergarten, more OT, more PT, typical school classrooms with immersion IEPs, BIPs . . . what happened?

Things got better.

While some parents grieve an autism diagnosis, I only ever felt immense relief. I had a child who was so clearly developing differently than his peers, and finding out why lifted a massive psychological and personal weight from my shoulders. It perplexed me when other parents resisted the "label." With the label came the help! With the label came the specialists, the therapists, the professionals trained in exactly what to do to help my child! I would wonder at parents who resisted, wondering why they were putting their own preconceived notions of who their child should be above who their child actually was. By every metric available, early intervention worked.

Young brains are super plastic. They accept input and feedback, and the synapses and dendrites will grow and branch with therapy, sensation, and stimulation. Bean learned to hold a pencil, to manage the complicated process (you don't think it is, but it is!) of squeezing the instrument, pressing down to achieve a mark, and then moving his hand while maintaining both downward and forward pressure. It took months. He learned to cope with sounds by using noise-canceling ear protection. He used swings to help his vestibular processing. He learned where his body was in relation to other people and things. It was hard work. It was daily work. It still is.

The thing about autism that first cracks your heart is that there is no cure.

It's never going away. He will never be "normal," whatever that means. I no longer thought of his autism as something that needed fixing. It was just a part of him. It *is* just a part of him.

Then you realize it isn't your child who needed a cure—it is your heart that needs to change.

My two typical kids didn't know life without Bean. What we kindly referred to as his "quirky" behavior was just a part of our lives. He would rock and hit his head, two things that many people recognize as autistic behavior, but there were so many more symptoms that are not as easily understood. He would make a honking noise when something stressed him; we learned to get him to someplace quiet. He would hide or run away when sounds, colors, smells, or touch overwhelmed him; we learned to find exits and knew which places were safe and where he liked to hide. This happened more often than any of us liked. Jeffrey carried the weight of explaining his brother to his peers and curious classmates, and most children were naturally empathetic.

Bean ate the exact same food for breakfast, lunch, and dinner every single day. New tastes and particularly new textures were extremely hard for him, and he avoided them at all costs. I learned that I had to pack for his needs whenever we went out or we would all suffer the consequences. It just became a part of my life—there was always a peanut butter English muffin in my purse. Sometimes peanut butter Ritz crackers were okay. Often we had to leave a party, play, park, or social event early because he couldn't process the chaos of a lot of people and noise. People generally have very little tolerance for a child who appears "normal" but who cannot control his limbs, his voice, or his behavior. We all felt the sting of the comments.

There were times I wanted to hand out little cards that said, "This is what autism looks like" to the cowardly people who muttered about discipline and control.

At night, he would crawl into my lap. I wanted to brush his red hair back from his forehead in the timeless gesture of motherly love, but I stayed my hand, holding back so he would continue to relax and talk. If I touched him, he would pull away and the moment would be over. It was a constant balancing act, finding ways to show love that he could understand and that were never going to be about what I wanted.

2006

"This is so weird. I think this might apply to me, too." David was flipping through the charts and doctor's reports from Bean's assessments and tests over the previous weeks. The diagnosis had just come back: high-functioning autism with an array of sensory processing issues.

We didn't know yet what most of the report meant, but there was hope in having specialists and doctors finally give us some answers.

"How so?" I asked, sitting down in the sunny window with him. Abby was sleeping in her bassinet, and the boys were downstairs.

"I was like this. It fits. Only when I was a little kid, they didn't know what to call it. Think about it." He shuffled through the papers and pulled out a chart that measured Bean's adrenal levels.

"Look, he's in a state of anxiety and panic a lot of the time, over basic stuff. I felt that way too, but no one understood. My teachers just thought I was a bad kid."

It seemed to fit, I agreed.

He'd told me stories of when he was little. He had a fascination with electronics and math, and was very bright, but he wanted to be left alone most of the time. He figured out how to build a forge in his backyard and smelt metal when he was about ten years old. He was great at chess and logic problems, but he was kicked out of two elementary schools for being 'disruptive." He had the hallmarks of a child with a learning disability, at the very least. But in the 1970's, they didn't have the vocabulary for it.

He told me that when he discovered drugs it was revelatory— not because he wanted to get high, but because it made him feel normal. Just normal. Drugs took the edge off his overactive mind, his highly sensitive nervous system, and allowed him to process touch and light and color in a more modulated way.

He looked at me, his eyes full of emotion. "This is going to change everything for Bean. He's not going to have the demons I had, because he's going to get the help I never got. This is..." his voice was thick with emotion. "This means my boy has a chance."

"Where's Bean?!"

I don't think any words have passed my lips with more frequency and fervency than those.

In our big house before the divorce we had to alarm the windows because he figured out how to open the screens, and he would take off running down the street. I introduced him to all the neighbors and asked them to please not try and grab him, but to call me immediately. I had to repeat the same process when we moved to Little House, though he was better by that point about not running out naked.

It's very common for kids with autism to run.

Taking him to Costco was always a bad idea, but sometimes I had to. He was an escape artist and would weasel away and squeeze into small places. He thought it was very funny to be quiet and watch while we frantically looked for him. He once tried to scale the orange racks to better see the giant fans near the ceiling. I managed to coax him down and ease the panic of the people gathering around and pointing up at him.

It's very common for kids with autism to hide.

I usually had Bean in a harness, because he was a master at silent escape. He was clever, and he loved solving puzzles, even when he was very young. He could solve a complicated spatial problem at five. Just don't touch him.

It's very common for kids with autism to have logically oriented brains.

He took to music like nothing I had ever seen. He picked up the cello, and then the trumpet, with almost no training or practice. He would hear a piece of music and ask me if I had heard a particular note and then he would play it. He doesn't have perfect pitch, but his ear is uncanny.

It's very common for kids with autism to be musically gifted.

Because of his propensity to slip away, and because he grew too big for the tether, I started dressing him in very bright colors—safety vest orange, neon yellow, and tie-dyed things. He adored flamboyant clothes as long as they were a fabric and fit he required. That meant no flappy pants (anything loose around his legs) and no tags or scratchy fabrics. If it was soft, snug, and colorful, he was happy. It made finding him in crowds much easier. And frankly, it still does.

This is all very common.

Bean will continue to bound through his life, secure in the knowledge that he is loved and that he always has a soft place to land. Someday he may or may not understand how much he has done for his family, but that's not the point. He's busy being who he is—it's for the rest of us to make sense of it.

We are who we are because of each other.

2014

"Hey there. What's up?" I was neck-deep in an editing job, but I never let David's calls go to voicemail. I glanced at the clock. The kids would be home from school soon, but it was not quite noon in David's time zone.

"Hi. How's it going? I was just looking at pictures of the kids. I miss them. I think this is a parenting call." His familiar voice greeted me, rougher around the edges than it had been when we were younger, but still him.

We talked about Jeffrey and Abby and circled around to Bean. Earlier in the year I had pulled him from his elementary school because they weren't following his IEP, and then I spent days reading up on IDEA (Individuals with Disabilities Education Act) case law before requesting a meeting with the school district. It had been an exhausting ordeal, but I was able to get him placed in a new school with a wonderful autism program where he was thriving.

It had been emotional for David, watching me battle so hard for Bean. It dredged up a lot of sad memories of himself at age ten, when he really started to fail at school and was expelled the first time. We talked about it a lot. He'd been sober again for a few years, and the filters around what his drug use had cost him were low and thin.

"You're saving him, you know that?" he said.

"No." It scared me to think about the genes the kids had inherited, and what that could mean for them. "No," I said again, "I'm doing the best I can to give him tools so that he can save himself."

He laughed softly. "Yeah, call it whatever you want. You're teaching him that he's valuable and important and worth fighting for. That changes everything."

Years and miles and silence and space and fractured dreams and briars of thorns and everything that couldn't be mended lay in the field between us, but the line of sight was clear and open.

"I'm sorry." I said sadly.

"Nah, don't be," he said with characteristic frankness. "You did the right thing. He's what matters. He's the future."

13

He's Not Heavy, He's My Brother

APRIL 16, 2010

My house is quiet. Surprisingly, deeply quiet. I can hear the washer churning away on Abby's sheets, the water clicking on in great whooshes, then clamping down. The computer is humming, and my own fingers are clicking, but the rest is... quiet.

My good friend swung by on her way to the park and swooped my kids up, giving me a morning alone at home. I've gotten breaks from my kids here and there, but it requires me setting up a sitter, and I always spend that valuable time running errands or taking care of things outside the home. This might be the very first time I am utterly alone in Little House.

It's... a balm. Quiet is so underrated. Solitude is something I need to feel whole. All I have this morning is waiting on the University to schedule a placement test, and changing the laundry over. Peace. Peace and quiet. Be still my soul.

THE STORM CLOUDS BLEW IN, obscuring any stray bands of yellow sunlight that might have fallen on the grey couch. My fingers were cool on my chin as I gazed idly out the large picture window at the passing cars, which made an odd whistling sound as they approached and then faded gradually into the distance. I drew a blank on the physics principle it demonstrated—something about an oncoming train? I couldn't remember. *Was the heater even on?* I wondered, as I pulled my slippers back on my feet and wandered down the hall to check the thermostat. *I'm cold.*

Little House was starting to feel like home. I'd finally found almost everything, and we'd settled into a new routine. We had celebrated our first holiday there and it helped make it feel more like ours, though I had fallen asleep and forgotten to be the Easter Bunny until Abby woke me up at 1:00 in the morning needing to pee. I threw some eggs around the living room, put their baskets on the couch, and I fell back into bed. We could totally call that good. Mo and her family came for an Easter dinner of cold cereal and candy. All six of our combined kids were over the moon. *Parents of the year.* It was amazing how much fun it was sometimes to just let go and enjoy the moment.

The kids were watching *Star Wars* downstairs. Jeffrey was obliviously engrossed in the movie while Bean coached Abby on the proper way to wield her foam light-saber. She was being non-compliant, and he was getting frustrated, but I could hear him breathing deeply and trying to be patient. *Atta boy.* Progress.

Nothing was wrong. I was still trying to get used to that, and still trying to learn to trust that it was real. For days, a tiny nagging somewhere deep wouldn't stop, but I couldn't pinpoint where or to what it was pointing. Was it real? Or was it muscle memory, residual sensations of when things were really not okay? It was like the itch in the center of your back that is just beyond the tips of your fingers. Like a dog-whistle, it was making me feel a little crazy.

I was misunderstanding friends, misreading emails, mistyping letters, asking the wrong questions, and guessing at things I should have known. I was messing up pattern orders and having to triple check my work. I was plagued by doubts and worrying over imagined slights and conversational miscues. I wondered at my own intellect and doubted my own validity as a contributor to anything meaningful. *What was going on?* I knew better than this.

Yet the malaise hung close. Narcissus beckoned. The siren's song was powerful. Persephone was stolen. *No. Go away.* I would not fall into the pond. I knew better. Self-loathing and doubt were really no different than self-aggrandizement and ego in the underworld. Both amplified and elevated the importance of self to the exclusion of reality. I had long ago learned they were backed faces of the same shiny but meaningless coin. *Snap out of it.* What was going on?

I was like this as a child, too, only I didn't have the words, myths, or experiences to calm the internal storm. The clouds would blow in, the wind would kick up, and I would be drawn outside, the skies mirroring my mind. Disquiet. I was perhaps seven or eight, and I would sit on the edge of our crabgrass, my feet in the gravelly pebbles near the street while I leaned on the crooked redwood fence marking our property. My sketchbook would be open in my lap as I wrote terribly bad poems trying to capture the elusive wistfulness in my mind. I felt like the only weird kid in the world.

You're okay, kid. Your spirit is big, your mind is strong, and you will understand more someday. Just ride it out. It's not as big as you think it is, and yet it's so very much more than you can imagine.

Shaking my head to clear the cobwebs, I knew the best step was to immerse myself in something physical, to get out of my own mind. Sometimes, corralling the intellect and stepping fully into the physical was the best path away from the pond. I headed downstairs to join the foam swordfight.

It was early spring when we pulled into the driveway after morning swim lessons, and our front yard was teeming with people. We saw a large truck with a trailer and a small backhoe being driven by Dale from church. Men with tape measures and shovels were milling around a large pile of planks and posts. I got out of the car slowly, amazed.

My friend Mike grinned as he walked up. "I hope you don't mind, but we were worried about Bean and the busy street, so we're building you a fence. While we were at it, we figured it would help to put in sprinklers. We cleared it with the landlord already, and Dale and Roger volunteered the materials." My mouth was slack as I tried to stammer something grateful.

The kids were jumping for joy in the driveway. Since we'd moved, they hadn't been able to play outside. The street was too busy for it to be safe. Fencing the yard was going to open up their world in the happiest of ways, and I couldn't even find words to express my joy. I plopped down on the concrete stoop, unsure what to say or do, while men smiled and waved as they transformed Little House's yard.

Another truck pulled up towing a trailer, and in the back was the dismantled Rainbow Play Fort we had to leave at the big house when we moved. I had imagined it would just be part of the foreclosure, but more volunteers from church had gone and dismantled it and brought it to Little House. They hopped off the trailer and cheerfully asked me where I wanted it. I burst into tears.

Mike put his arm around me while I cried. He and his wife Nancy lived up the street. Their kids were grown, and they had sort of adopted us. They stopped by to check on us frequently. Mike did little repairs for me, and Nancy would stop by to see how we were doing or drop off a little treat on her way home from work. The kids loved them.

Mike let me cry for a moment, gave me a squeeze and a smile, then invited Jeffrey to help him with a post-hole driller. Jeffrey's eyes lit up, and he was immediately on the trailer with Mike getting a safety lesson and donning a pair of too-big leather gloves.

The activity continued for several days.

When they were done, we had a sprinkler system so the grass would stay green and lush all summer, and I could plant flowers in the beds under the windows. Someone had put in some roses. The kids' wooden fort was reassembled under the large maple tree shading the front yard. Mike had hung climbing ropes from the highest boughs for Bean and added a hammock for proper sunset watching. The entire yard was fenced, and the charming little gate had a safety latch in hopes of keeping Bean from escaping.

My kids had a yard, their own fort, and a small garden, and we had a community beyond belief.

Bean running away was just part of our lives. It was one of his coping mechanisms, and we all knew it. At home it wasn't such a big deal—he would hide, and in a few minutes he was usually centered again, and life went on.

His hiding and running in public places was a lot harder to manage. Outside it could be dangerous. He didn't really understand *dangerous* though. Giving him a fair amount of latitude was the best way to cope. If I could see him, I tried to roll with it.

We met some friends at the park on an unseasonably warm spring night, and Bean took off running. The park was big and open, and he kept going. He ran from the playground where we were preparing a picnic dinner—which contained smells he couldn't manage—all the way across the baseball diamond toward the bleachers behind home plate. It was further than I was comfortable with, and I attempted to coax him back. This made him retreat further, as it usually did.

I left Abby with my friends, and Jeffrey and I got in the car, hoping that he would see us preparing to leave and come back. Nope. We sat in the car for a few minutes as I contemplated strategies. I knew if I walked toward the diamond he would run. I rested my chin on the steering wheel and watched his tiny form on the bleachers.

"Hey Jeff, why don't you take a walk over there and tell him we need to go." He hopped out of the car and began to jog across the field. Sometimes Jeffrey was less threatening than Mom. It wasn't necessarily fair, but it was our reality.

They were far enough away that I couldn't hear anything. I could only guess from the pantomime of their gestures what was happening. Jeff approached and pointed, and Bean climbed higher up the bleachers. Jeff shrugged and started back toward the car. I was trying to formulate a plan to retrieve Bean before he ran into the stand of trees. That would be bad.

Jeffrey was halfway back across the field when he suddenly turned around. Bean was still sitting on the bleachers. Jeff tromped, there was gesturing, then Bean climbed down. As they came from behind the backstop, I could see that Jeffrey had Bean on his shoulders and was carrying him. My eight-year-old son had gently coaxed his brother into trusting him and headed back to the car. He did it by offering his own back.

My hands knotted over my heart. What a tender kindness from my son—and what an amazing heart that he didn't give up. He got an idea, trusted himself, and then turned back to get his brother.

Jeffrey carried Bean across the entire field, easily a hundred yards. By the time he set him down, Jeffrey's face was flushed and sweaty, and Bean was delighted by the piggyback ride, oblivious to the ruckus he'd caused.

Sometimes we just have to throw out the playbook and let our kids write new rules. My eldest son taught me a powerful lesson about his abilities and tipped his hand to the big heart inside of him.

Few things rankle me like being late. I hate being late. Fabric scraps three inches deep in my sewing room and a play room that needs a snow shovel? Meh, whatever. But being late? When I am late I can feel my temples start to throb and my blood pressure soar.

But I am not a good planner, so I end up being my own worst enemy.

I tried to plan my day. I really did: breakfast, school, YMCA, grocery store, lunch, bus for Bean, school prep for me, birthday prep for Abby, carpool, chaperone school fundraiser at a trampoline place, home for dinner, baths, bed, done. Of course, this must all be done with three kids, one of whom has autism and another who was trying to master her bladder. It sounded like fun.

The train jumped the tracks right out of the station. I woke up with a sore throat. By the time I got Jeffrey out the door to school, I had a ninety minute window to get to the Y and back. Bean decided that he suddenly hated going to the gym and playing on the rock wall, he hated the playground, and he hated playing. Nope. He was not going. It went downhill; it was 9:40 by the time he was calm. Time to reassess.

Okay, I thought. *I can be flexible.* I rearranged the puzzle pieces of my day, and we all jumped in the car.

I went to the doctor, and we had to wait longer than I planned, but the kids were surprisingly good. Bean liked the doctor, which helped things go smoothly. By the time we were done, I had to scrap the grocery store; we had just enough time to run to the produce stand, then zoom home for lunch before Bean's bus got there.

Bean made his bus, and I changed Abby into dry clothes because eating lunch was too important to stop and use the potty. We were out of milk, bread, peanut butter, and popsicles—items not available at the produce stand. I had two hours before carpool. I threw Abby in the car and headed toward the grocery store, completely forgetting about Bean's fundraiser.

The grocery store took five times longer than it should have because Abby had to pee every five minutes, and I couldn't assume that any of them were false alarms. She also enjoyed the hand-dryer in the bathroom. I tried to be patient, but I had to get to Jeffrey's school, and we weren't even out of the dairy aisle.

I was two minutes late pulling into the carpool lane at Jeffrey's school. I had forgotten that I had volunteered to take another child home, and I suddenly remembered that Bean's field trip meant he wasn't taking the bus—so my window was tighter than I thought. I would never make it to Bean's school across town before he got on the bus. Time to reassess again.

Executive decision: Let Bean take the bus, and then head to the fundraiser. I called the school and told them the change of plans, put the groceries away, and waited on his bus. It was almost fifteen minutes late. Jeffrey and Abby were loaded in the car waiting when it finally pulled up. Our time slot for the fundraiser was from 3:30 to 4:30, but it was already 3:45. I could have still salvaged it, though, until I got caught in a construction zone detour and had to back-track.

When we finally got to the fundraiser, I apologized for missing our time slot, and an obnoxiously perky PTA mom used a sing-song voice to tell me how sad it was that we were late. She chewed on her pencil as she conferred *in actual whispers* with the other PTA lady about whether or not they should let us in.

I was not amused. I had paid; I planned on playing on the trampolines with my kids. She informed me that we could play in the next session, which started in forty-five minutes.

Dammit.

That meant I had to revamp dinner plans and get everyone something to eat because the later start meant missing dinner. For Bean, missing a meal was catastrophic. Routine was everything, and we were already way off schedule.

Bean was wound up and excited to play, and I explained that we were going to have to wait. Strike one. The only place that I could find open was a deli. Awesome. Determined to be flexible, I dragged everyone there and hoped against hope that they might be able to make a peanut butter and jelly sandwich.

The deli was cavernous and dimly lit, and we were the only customers. The kids noticed their voices echoing and made loud use of that information while I tried to find something on the menu they would eat.

While I was ordering, Jeffrey climbed over the metal railing of the queue and knocked the whole thing over. The insanely loud clatter of metal bars hitting the concrete floor sent Bean running and screaming, and Abby peed herself. I still hadn't ordered, and I wanted to cry. I left my bag on the counter and found Bean in a corner. I coaxed him out by telling him they would make him a peanut butter and jelly sandwich.

Two sandwiches, a cup of soup, and two pops cost me $22. Almost $10 for a cup of soup and half a PB&J?? But we were stuck. The food arrived, and lo! Bean's sandwich was on the wrong kind of bumpy bread (of course), the soup had celery and red peppers in it, Abby wanted ham not turkey, and no, they could not share drinks. I should have just thrown $22 out on the lawn.

Back at the fundraiser we took off our shoes, I put Abby in clean clothes, and we played. It was great.

When our hour was up the employees cleared out the kids and began to clean up. But I couldn't find Bean. The entire play area was empty, and the workers were beginning to clean up—but no Bean. I put Jeff and Abby in the car, where Abby burst into tears because she imagined that we were leaving Bean forever. I went back in to search. This was such a normal part of my life that I was utterly resigned. I knew he was there; I had been watching the door like a hawk. The employees helped, and we finally found him in a crevasse on a giant slide. He hid on purpose. He didn't want to leave. I had to drag him to the car, and he vocalized the whole way home—great keening honks of dismay and misery. *I was so mean.*

In our driveway, he locked himself in the car and refused to come inside until I took him back to the play place. *I'll bring you a blanket, buddy. Keep the doors locked.*

As I jammed my keys into the side door of Little House, I heard the phone ringing. I ran in, accidentally dumping everything on the counter, to hear Bean's dentist on the machine, and grabbed for the phone. His oral surgery, which was scheduled for June, could be moved to the next morning—did I want the spot? *Oh yes. Yes, I do.*

The dentist reminded me that siblings cannot accompany the patient and parent during anesthetized dental visits. This appointment was at seven in the morning, which meant I needed a babysitter at dawn. I stood at the back door while Jeffrey and Abby got their pajamas on, keeping an eye on Bean in the car, puzzling about a sitter.

The phone rang again. It was someone from church wanting me to supervise a potato sack race at the Family Fun Run early Saturday morning. I felt myself waver on the edge of breaking. I told her my kids might be there, but I didn't think I could help. The waves of desperation hit me, and I started to cry. I understood the importance of giving back. I knew full well the amazing things that had been done for me, but I still told the poor woman more than she ever bargained for in her simple phone call.

Meanwhile, the kids found the Nerf samurai swords in my closet and were beating the crap out of each other in my room, and the clean laundry that was previously on my bed was spread all over my floor.

Out of sheer exhaustion, I picked up the phone again and called the women's leader at church. I asked if I could temporarily be exempt from anything extra. Just for a little while. She totally understood and assured me that there would be a season for me to give back, but it wasn't now. She said there would be an invisible *hands-off* rope around me, and I sighed with relief as I hung up the phone.

It was bedtime, but surprise! Abby had peed all over her pajamas and on her blankets—the ones I had freshly stripped and laundered the day before. I stripped the bed again and heard Bean standing at the back door, wailing because he was hungry. Hungry? *Maybe that's because you didn't eat your $22 peanut butter and jelly sandwich!* I vigorously shoved the blankets in the washing machine while he waited in the kitchen.

While I was feeding Bean and getting him ready for bed, Jeffrey snuck off to my bed, and Abby spilled a cup of water on her new, dry bedding.

And then my period started.

14

One Step

MAY 4, 2010

The journey of a thousand miles begins with a single step.

Today, I became a college student. Classes don't start until next month, but today, I walked the cobblestone pathways and entered the beautiful brick buildings of academia. I picked my classes and I am officially enrolled.

Last time I went to college, Kurt Cobain was still alive, flannel was hot, and the first Gulf War was going on. Last time, I was a flighty, flaky kid with talent but no follow-through. I don't even remember what I thought, but it must have been self-centered and self-important—because aren't all twenty-year-olds? Today? Today I value myself. I value my talents and am going to use them. I am driven. I am motivated by my children, by being a good example, by studying hard, by getting good grades, and hopefully adding some pretty braids and cords to my graduation robes in a few short years.

I can do hard things. Bring it on.

PREPARING FOR SCHOOL AND JUGGLING the demands of regular life replaced the chaos and panic of a few months earlier. We celebrated Abby turning four by having a rainbow *Star Wars* party with Mo and her kids, after which we attended our local Comic-Con. Abby dressed in the Darth Vader costume that she received for her birthday. That year she wore her Darth Vader helmet everywhere, including to the grocery store, to church, and while reading on the potty.

David was still trying to earn back his right to contact the kids, so birthdays and other milestones passed without phone calls or visits. It was a double-edged sword. They asked about him less and less, but I worried about how they might be internalizing his loss and what would happen when or if he was finally well enough to come back into their lives. I talked about him in kind terms, stressing that his absence wasn't their fault, and reminded them that he was trying to get better and that he loved them. It was a hard line to walk, but I prayed that I was right to err toward kindness.

My business was thriving, and a national distributor had picked up a few of my patterns. I had solidified the contract with the fabric company for making kits, and I was working on a new design for them while I still filled orders from the stores I had picked up in Houston. The cash flow fluctuated, but each month I miraculously managed to pay all of my bills.

With my quilted-together income and no child support, we qualified for food stamps—officially known as the Supplemental Nutrition Assistance Program—and for medical assistance for the children. I was on my own should I fall ill, but the kids were covered. It was a huge relief knowing that I could take them to the doctor. The food benefits equaled about $4 per day for each of us. It was a modest amount, but it made all the difference. That assistance meant not having to decide between keeping our heat on or being able to eat. I could make that $4 stretch a long way.

At the gym one May morning I found myself swimming in tears. A song David loved had cycled through my iPod, and it brought me down. I knew the divorce had been inevitable. I absolutely knew that it was the right thing. I had waited until I knew beyond any doubt that I had to leave, and that certainty had been a merciful tenderness amid the pain and loss. I never once second-guessed the path I chose or what that choice meant for my children.

But that did not keep me from missing my best friend.

How was it possible for one vessel to hold so many complicated, swirling emotions? David had been my ally, my roommate, my daily companion, and my confidant. We spent years picking each other up from broken hearts caused by others, wiping tears, and being each other's shelter in the storm. When he asked me to marry him, part of my initial reluctance was that I loved him too much—that he was my best friend, and I couldn't bear to lose him like I had lost all of my other romantic relationships.

And yet there we were. Behind me was a blast crater and a trail of broken dreams, and while I was making good progress toward a new life, sorrow still snuck up on me unbidden and crawled inside my skin.

I missed him with a hollow, echoing ache. I missed our history. I missed sharing victories and little things the kids did. I missed the intuitive communication and having someone by my side. I missed our cheering for each other and telling stories with just a glance. I missed the shared experiences and inside jokes that only come from a lifetime of laughter and mistakes made together. I missed him. I missed him so much.

So when a guy at the gym smiled at me that morning, all I could think was, "No! Where is David?" He was gone. In more ways than I could ever express, he was gone. My heart broke into a million shards—but even so, I knew that I did the right thing. So I stood up, buried my face in my towel, and moved on. I didn't know what else to do.

ϗ

1994

We lasted about a year in Seattle, before deciding that we'd had enough of the grey skies and depressing weather. Back in California, I found a small backyard studio to rent in the neighborhood where I grew up. For the first time since I left home, I lived alone. Well, sort of alone. David divided his time between the couches of his friends, and he spent a fair amount of time on mine. He was working for another Silicon Valley company—his employment background and experience made it relatively easy for him to get hired. He would chip in for rent or groceries when he remembered. It was a sort of symbiotic relationship—I fed him and he had the couch, and he was there for me if I needed him. In the days before ubiquitous mobile phones, anyone who was looking for him, including his mother, would start by calling me. More often than not I knew where he was, though sometimes he would disappear for days.

I worried. But I would come back to that afternoon in the stairwell, when cowardice made me deny the space between us, and I knew I had no right to ask more of him.

Then he would reappear, bringing a brilliant friend or two from work, and my kitchen table would again be bursting with laughter and rambunctious stories. He boasted about my cooking to anyone who would listen, and I would happily gather apricots from the tree in the yard and whip up a pie.

One night after everyone else had left, it was just the two of us at the table. I had been painting earlier in the day, and the piece was leaning up against the kitchen wall. I was intent upon finding remnants of the divine feminine in Western religion, and I was exploring my frustration with God in my painting. Motifs of snakes and women and creation were recurring themes, and David was looking intently at the unfinished piece.

"You're painting more than you realize," he said as he picked at the crust of the most recent apricot pie.

I leaned back in my chair to see the painting, now hidden partly by late evening shadows. "Tell me what you see."

"Look, I know you're mad at God—and that's totally okay, by the way, God can take it—but he's talking to you in your paintings. You're asking questions, and he's answering you in the things you paint."

I frowned and looked harder at the half-finished woman standing in tall grass. "I don't understand."

He turned to look more fully at the painting. "Look...look carefully. She's standing in the grass, her feet are hidden, invisible, but you know they must be there. She's floating, but just because you can't see her roots doesn't mean they're gone. Doesn't that mimic your question?"

My eyebrows knit together tighter, and I didn't respond.

"There's a snake on her leg—where is it going? Obvious symbolism of the Christian world aside, it's also the symbol for wisdom and knowledge. She's pregnant, but her belly glows. Why? What is she growing inside of her? How does a goddess bring forth a world? Who is the consort of God? How can it be any other way? These are as much answers to your questions as they are your questions themselves."

I suddenly felt very small. He continued to speak animatedly about the symbols he saw in my work, but my head felt disconnected and far away, floating. I could hear him, see him, but there was a buzzing in my ears and I felt lightheaded, faint. My head tipped back as the roaring in my ears overwhelmed me.

"Hey! Hey! Are you okay? Come on, here...." His voice was far away. I could see his enormous eyes over me, full of worry. He half-carried, half-dragged me to the couch. "Take deep breaths. I think you fainted."

I was disoriented, but the look of concern on his face struck me as funny, and I laughed. "What happened? That was so weird. You didn't spike the pie, did you?" I joked weakly.

"You know I'd never do that." He was dead serious. He was right, I knew he'd never do that.

He brushed my hair back from my forehead and went to find a washcloth. "Stay sitting!" he yelled from the closet, his voice muffled by the door and the towels.

"What the hell was that?" I half-whispered.

He sat down next to me and pressed the cool washcloth to my forehead. "Sometimes, when we get close to what God is trying to tell us, things get weird. It happens." He said it matter-of-factly and shrugged, like it was common knowledge, as though we were talking about the weather.

"There are stories of it everywhere," he continued. "Do you think people fall on their knees before angels in art because they're all respectful? Heh. Nope. It's because you literally cannot stand before holy things. The presence of the divine brings us to our knees because there is no other option."

It felt surreal, outside of time, like we were in a bubble.

"You didn't see an angel or anything, but you brushed up against the reality of the divine, which is what you've been asking for. I always feel so small afterwards. Like, I thought I was the artist, but really I'm just the pencil…." He trailed off.

I pushed myself up. "Yes, that's it perfectly. I thought I was painting, but instead, I'm the brush." Glancing at the painting, it just looked like a painting again. But the memory of something more lingered in the air. I looked at David intently.

"This happens to you?"

His low laugh punctuated the dim light. "All the freaking time." He stood up and extended his hand. "Come on, let's go for a walk. A walk is always a good idea."

I felt very small beneath the dome of the sky. The sun had set and only the barest glimmer of pink remained on the horizon. The stars were as bright as they got under the light-filled Silicon Valley skies. We walked in silence for a few blocks.

There was a large empty field on the edge of my neighborhood. It's a community garden now, but then it was just acres of grassland. We squeezed through a hole someone had cut years earlier in the chain-link fence and set out across the grass.

As we walked, David pointed out constellations and explained how to tell the difference between a star and a planet. *Stars twinkle, planets do not and are usually brighter. Stars move, but do not rise and set like planets.* He pointed out Mars and Saturn on the darker horizon. He loved the math of astronomy and wandered a bit into esoteric musing as we walked through the tall grass.

I was quiet, enjoying the deep cadence of his voice and the comfort of his presence and willingness to share his knowledge. He was as comfortable talking about prayer as he was talking about microprocessors. He moved so easily between worlds.

We walked on in silence before he spoke again. "Tracy. You know I love you."

"Yes," I said simply. I felt oddly at peace, and safe. I wasn't going to deny it this time, and I was trying to be aware of the margins of my own fears. "I love you, too."

"I know you do." He laughed quietly. "But I mean, more than that. I mean I love you as a man loves a woman, and I want the same things you want. I want a family, I want a wife. I want children. I don't just want someone *like* you, I want *you*."

I didn't say anything. I couldn't. I didn't want to push him away this time, but the reality of my fears was pressing hard against me. Boyfriends were temporary. That kind of love was transitory. Romance disappeared. Marriages ended. *I can't lose you, too.*

He was never intimidated by silence, and he let it sit. He gave me all the space I needed while I wrestled with my own demons, and we kept walking.

"You are too important to me. I love you more than I love anyone. Maybe someday, but I just can't. Not now." I knew how weak it sounded, how unfair. But it was better than I had done before.

"I get it." He gently reassured me, "It doesn't change anything for me. You are the star, Tracy Leigh, and I can never change who you are to me."

Maybe that was a horrible moment for him. Maybe the rejection, no matter how gently I tried to couch it, pierced his heart. I will never know. But even then, if he was wounded, he still made himself a safe place for me and allowed me to be who I was. We kept walking, companions through the empty field, into the night.

Mo spent a lot of time at Little House. Her husband was deployed again—to Iraq for the first time—and she carried with her a life-sized cardboard photo cutout of him that her kids called Flat Daddy. It was a way for him to be present in the minds of their young children. Many military families use such creative tactics to manage the stress and sorrow of a missing parent.

My Craigslist kitchen table had become our meeting place—a safe spot for judgment-free support of each other through our worries and fixations. Mo had to navigate through the possibility of her husband never coming home, and I had to navigate my troops through another kind of paternal loss. We were each other's parenting life buoys in weirdly parallel worlds.

We'd talk with fizzing sodas poured over ice while the kids climbed the tree ropes in the front yard or beat each other with foam swords playing *Star Wars*. Our kids matched up in both age and gender, so everyone had a friend. One of her boys was also on the autism spectrum, though he didn't require a special school like Bean did. Her easy laughter was a balm and support.

Mo's hair color changed with the seasons. She was a military wife and mother, and also a member of my church, but she was utterly unconventional. She wore rockabilly blouses and military boots, and she painted her nails bright blue to match her new bangs. She might arrive with a giant pho pot, eager to show me how she learned to make the spicy Vietnamese soup from another Army wife, or she might call me up to help "decorate" the houses of friends the night before the Army/Navy football game.

One morning she walked through my kitchen door and dropped a large case on the round kitchen table. I looked at her quizzically while nursing a cup of lukewarm tea.

Her previously blue hair was now an adorable fuchsia pixie cut, and she was wearing a smart black turtleneck with jeans and lace-up boots. Her daughter was already dragging her blanket downstairs looking for Abby, as comfortable in my house as in her own.

"So," she started. "You're far too pretty to look the way you do."

I feigned shock and smiled over my cup. "Listen," she continued, "don't take that the wrong way—if you're happy with things the way they are, that's great. But you've spent the last few years taking care of everyone but you, and I can help with that."

Mo was a master at managing different looks; the extent of my personal care routine was to tie my naturally curly hair in a bun while it was still wet. "Go get your makeup and let me see what you've got."

I went to find my makeup "kit," which was a Ziploc bag containing some Chapstick, a nude lip gloss, a crumbling beige eyeshadow, and a tube of brown mascara for when I felt very fancy. It personified *sad* as I handed it over to Mo.

Her blue eyes sparkled with laughter under raised eyebrows, and she fought a smile as she examined my baggie. "Well. You know what this means? This means we can go any direction we want!" She crossed the kitchen and dropped the bag in the trash.

I was secretly thrilled. I wanted the *option* of being able to manipulate my appearance if the whim struck. From where I stood, women like Mo who could navigate dozens of looks were like magicians, and I hadn't the faintest idea where to start. I didn't want to wear heavy makeup, and I had no desire to make my appearance the center of my routine, but lacking the ability or know-how was completely different than being able to choose. Mo wanted to teach me some skills and give me options.

It was a gift of love, and of sharing herself.

We spent the afternoon with her magic kit, where she introduced me to brushes, creams, sparkly powders, and pretty colors—things that I used in my art and creative life but was always afraid to try on my body. Being a bigger woman had meant, at least in my mind, that I needed to stay neutral and not draw attention to myself.

Mo rolled her eyes and grabbed my hand. "Screw that, sweetie. You can be whatever you want to be."

She got out a bottle of bright red nail polish. I pulled my hand back instinctively. Bright red was for other people. My nails were short—I couldn't sew or use a thimble or type quickly with long nails. I never painted them. She reached back across and gently took my hand, talking soothingly like she would to a spooked animal.

"If you have something you don't like about yourself," she gently rubbed cream into the rough skin of my hands as she talked softly, "and you ignore it, it looks neglected, forgotten. If, instead of neglecting the parts you don't like, you give them attention, love, *polish*—it looks like you did it on purpose. You must own it. Claim all the parts of you. Own it."

While she was talking, she smoothed my nails with a file, pushed back my cuticles, and rubbed them with oil. She unscrewed the top of the polish and painted my short, neatly buffed nails a scandalous, deeply attention-grabbing ruby red.

"I can't wear that!" I protested. Holding my hand and brushing on the crimson anyway, she looked askance at me. "No one can see how you feel inside. Act as though this belongs to you, and it will. Own it."

I stopped protesting and watched the bold color cover my nails. Why did I believe I couldn't wear something so silly as nail polish?

Why did I think pretty things were for other people? Why did I believe *dull* was my color? The red was really beautiful.

What would happen if I started to embrace the pieces of myself that I had neglected? What if I stopped seeing myself in terms of my flaws and instead incorporated those flaws into part of a beautiful whole? What if all of me became something I owned? What would happen? My eyes swam with tears.

Mo sneered at me over the table with mock seriousness, still holding my hand. "Now don't mess it up!"

I was poor.

I was divorced.

I was a single mother.

I was a welfare mother.

I was heading back to college in my thirties.

I was learning to love and accept myself for the first time.

I was helping my children heal and grow after the trauma of losing their father.

Everything I had feared, every stigma I had hoped to avoid, had become part of my life. In the prevailing narrative distilled down, my ex-husband was a drug addict, and I was an uneducated single mother on welfare.

So what? What are you going to do about it?

I'm going to reject the pre-written script and write my own story from here on out. All of it.

I'm going to own it.

15

Deep End of the Pool

JUNE 11, 2010

My plate is very full, and I'm trying to walk the line between tackling things one at a time, not panicking, and actually accomplishing things. It feels like as long as I don't look down, I'll be fine, but it's really hard to keep my eyes trained on the horizon. Slippery. Dangerous. But at the same time, I feel like I have to look down, and maybe if I do, the ground really will be much closer than I think. I have to decide what's more scary— knowing, or not.

My textbooks are almost all here, and I get to print my syllabus on Monday and then I can get started on my reading. No idea how this is going to affect my blogging, writing, or creativity. But for better or worse, this is the new ride. Get in, and buckle up.

ABOUT A WEEK BEFORE SCHOOL started for me I had Bean's triennial IEP. An IEP is an Individual Education Plan, a legally binding contract in which the educators and parents create a plan to accommodate the needs of a student with disabilities. IEPs are not for children who are having a hard time or who are struggling in general—they are for children with verified diagnosed disabilities. Each year, parents and school officials meet to review a child's needs, but every three years there is a larger meeting in which a child's entire team of educators, therapists, and specialists come together to assess the child's progress and plan the future.

All children in the public education system with any disability—cognitive, physical, neurological, or emotional—are entitled to support under federal law, covered in the Individuals with Disabilities Education Act. Private schools are exempt and do not have to follow IDEA or IEPs.

I had been in dozens of these meetings over the years, and I no longer had the trepidation many parents felt when facing an IEP. At first it was scary—so many new words and acronyms. Because an IEP is a contract, it requires specific legal language. To understand, I read a lot. I asked a lot of questions. As the parent I had the right and obligation to give my input, and I had to remember that I knew Bean best. I also had the obligation, for his sake, to listen to what the specialists were saying and weigh that against my own instincts. It wasn't always easy, but Bean had been well served by many professional, competent therapists and teachers who had done tremendous work with him.

While I was waiting for my textbooks to arrive, I was prepping for the triennial meeting. Bean had been in a special school for children with autism for three years, and his teachers proposed that he be mainstreamed for first grade. He would spend part of the day in a typical classroom with an aide, and another part in a separate classroom where a special education teacher would further meet his therapeutic needs. The general trend in education is to mainstream kids with disabilities whenever possible.

It was scary to consider moving him from a highly successful and supportive environment into a typical classroom. But it was time to try. Add another acronym: LRE, or Least Restrictive Environment.

In order to further their education, children with disabilities should be in the least restrictive environment in which they can function. I weighed this against my fears. He was doing so well. Moving him to the LRE meant change and possible backsliding. But it was also the best way for him to grow.

Transitioning from safety and surety required courage; it was a risk. Staying where he was meant familiarity, but it also meant stasis. And there is no growth in stasis.

I thumbed through my syllabi, contemplating my own stasis. It would have been far more comfortable for me to avoid the challenges of moving into my own LRE. The idea of sitting in a college classroom with kids half my age was scary as hell. I had no idea if I was going to be able to manage a full course load with three kids. Since I was starting in the truncated summer quarter, and it was my first school experience in years, my counselor had suggested I begin with just three courses and see how it went. A three-course load was twelve units, making me a full-time student; I knew I was going to have to take more than twelve units if I wanted to finish in under four years. But I needed to succeed first and then up the stakes.

Bean and I stood at similar crossroads. We had outgrown the safe and dependable nests we'd built, and we needed to give ourselves room to unfurl. Ready or not, it was time to fly.

Mo was moving.

My track record with friends wasn't so hot. I didn't trust people easily and was always waiting for the other shoe to drop. It had happened enough in my life that I was cautious with new friends. Shortly after we met, I got a card in the mail that simply said, "Shoes are for wearing, not dropping. ~Mo."

We celebrated the births of two daughters and many birthdays, and we shared every Thanksgiving since we met, a couple of

Christmases, and countless ordinary days. We had moved each other's households, pulled through her husband's deployment to Iraq during much of her third pregnancy, weathered the diagnosis of two children with autism and the deaths of grandparents, celebrated the marriages of friends, and survived the crater blown into the center of my world by divorce. We'd attended church together, cooked holiday meals together, shared secrets, and wiped each other's tears. We cleaned up each other's messes, disciplined each other's kids, and did our best to put back the pieces of each other's broken hearts.

Mo taught me that I didn't have to fit any model or ideal to be who I wanted to be. I learned that I could take off the cultural shoe that was just too damn tight and still live the faithful life I wanted. I learned that a woman with pink hair and tattoos has as much claim to God as any person I have ever met. I learned I could be whoever I wanted to be and be really good at it. I also learned how to wield my makeup brushes like a pro.

Mo moving had always been a reality—it was just a fact of life for military families. I would be there to help pack and load the truck, and I would be there to help clean her house. They were only moving a few hours away to a new station on the west side of the state. Their new house had a yard and a basement, things she'd never had in base housing. I was happy for her.

But I couldn't pretend it wasn't really hard, too. In a year that had cost me so many things I loved, I was losing my best friend. I felt like a petulant kid staring out the back window as the station wagon drove away. My heart was aching. I knew I would see her again, but the days of hanging around the Craigslist kitchen table were ending. I was going to miss her so much.

I choked up a little, but shoved the tears away. There was work to do. I picked myself up, grabbed my cleaning things, and went to help her pack, then say goodbye.

My first philosophy textbook arrived as I was heading out to get the boys for an end-of-school party. I didn't have time to really look it over, but a quick glance had me marveling at the density of the material. I was taking philosophy, geography, and English. Textbooks were even more outrageously priced than I remembered, but having the ISBN and access to the internet made the used textbook market much more manageable. All my books were second-hand, sourced from used bookstores online, and I didn't even have to fight the crowds at the university bookstore.

We were heading to the house of Mike and Nancy, my friends from church, for a celebratory dinner and swimming party. It had been a rough week—along with Mo leaving and gearing up for my own school starting, I had also signed papers on the old house and attempted to work through some financial snarls tied to David. I was exhausted, but the kids were really looking forward to swimming and playing with friends. Mike and Nancy were godsends. They continued to care for us in a million small ways, and in some pretty big ones too—along with fencing the yard for the kids to play in, Mike had started a vegetable garden in the backyard with Bean and was teaching him about cultivation and water dynamics. They treated us with such tenderness.

Their house was piled high with visiting children and grandchildren when we pulled up. It was wonderful to meet so many members of their family—I had heard stories and seen pictures, and it was lovely to finally connect everyone.

It was a boisterous crowd, and my kids changed into their swimsuits and jumped in the pool with a dozen other people.

I was calibrated to Bean, as I always was in social situations, and I could see that he was already on the edge of unraveling. The end of the school year, the break in routine, the chaos of so many children in the pool, and the new surroundings all added up to a potential meltdown. I could feel myself start to tense up.

For the most part, he did okay. He loved water, and he had learned to swim at the YMCA over the last few months. A few times he began to honk and flap, but it wasn't terrible, and it diffused fairly quickly. One young woman was helping Abby around the pool on a floatie, and Jeffrey was having a pool-noodle fight with another boy his age. Bean floated around in his own world as I sat on the edge trying to monitor events in three different directions.

Toddlers laughed gleefully while dads tossed them in the pool, moms fussed and worried when those dads flung babies a little too high in the air, men barbecued, and children called happily to their grandparents to "look at me!" Suddenly I felt terribly alone.

Ridiculous, embarrassing tears sprang to my eyes. No reason. Nothing happened. But there I was with my three wildly different children, trying to balance their wildly different needs, and I felt utterly inadequate. Just for a second I felt like I couldn't possibly do this myself, and I felt gut-lurching sadness for my children and their lack of a father. Waves of guilt washed over me for not choosing my partner more wisely and for how that choice impacted the lives of my children. I felt an aching loss for the healthy relationship my kids were missing by not having a father present. I watched those men, and I was jealous and sad, and I wished for just a second that I could have another chance. Would life be different had I known then what I know now?

It was a brief but deep dive into the pity pool.

I pulled myself out of it and saw Jeffrey misbehaving. I called him out of the water, covertly wiping at my eyes with his towel. He was indignant and sassed me as I guided him toward the changing room. When he looked at me the anger dissolved, and he burst into tears. I closed the door behind us and hugged his wet body tightly to me.

"I want to go home, and I want to stay too, Mom. I'm sad and I don't know why." he mumbled into my shirt.

I know. I know, my sweet boy. I know.

I couldn't hide in the changing room with Jeffrey—Bean and Abby were still in the pool. I had to divide and conquer. It was my only option anymore. I had to rely on the kindness of others while I tended one child. I let Jeffrey have a cry and then helped him squirm his damp body into dry clothes and sent him to the kitchen. I fished Abby from the water and repeated the process, but without the tears. Bean was the last, lonely child floating in the pool, and he refused to come near enough the edge for anyone to grab him. In a stroke of brilliance, Mike turned on the automatic pool cover to chase him out. Bean thought that was awesome as he raced the rolling lid to the edge, where I plucked him from the pool.

By the time everyone was dry and dressed and we sat down for the barbecue, I was spent. I wear my heart on my sleeve, but I didn't want to draw any attention. I focused on the kids and getting them fed, and I avoided eye contact, lest anyone smile kindly and make me cry again. *Stupid tears. Stop. I am so lucky.*

We ended up enjoying the evening. The kids played pinball and *Q-Ball*, Jeffrey's name for billiards. When it was time to go, Mike and Nancy helped me get everyone in the car buckled up, and we thanked them for including us.

It was not pretty to admit that I was feeling sorry for myself— even for a moment. I wished those feelings didn't come unbidden and so strong. I was grateful for good friends. I was grateful that Bean held it together and that I had a moment to help Jeffrey. I was grateful for so many kindnesses.

I just wished it wasn't still so damn hard.

On Father's Day I decided to skip church and take the kids for a treat. They didn't need to know what day it was, and they didn't need to hear platitudes about how awesome it was to have a great dad.

I grabbed my keys. "Get in the car, everyone. Let's get tacos. We were all buckled in before I realized that Bean had on a pair of extra-small girl's leggings, an Under Armour swim shirt, and shearling boots. The leggings were almost indecently tight, but he liked tight things, so I let it go. The shirt was meant for the pool, but he liked the silky fabric and smooth seams, so I let that go, too. The shearling boots were lined in sheep's wool, and that solved the huge problem of seams in socks. I let those go, too, despite the fact that it was June.

There were times I thought it might be more fair to all of us if I were only Bean's mother, or only Jeffrey and Abby's mother. As hard as I tried to balance everyone, the typical kids often got shoved aside in the mad rush to manage the constant needs of Bean. While he needed familiarity and routine, the other kids needed a normal life and the occasional thing that they enjoyed, too.

There was a Mexican taqueria up the street that we frequented. It was a hole in the wall, but the staff was very nice, and they made Bean's food to his exact specifications. Jeffrey wanted to try a new place by the golf course. He was pleading, the sun was shining, and the new place had a patio overlooking the fairway. He wanted to sit outside under the umbrellas, and I agreed that might be nice. So we headed off to dinner.

I was no rookie. A new place was highly risky, but I couldn't always tell the other kids no because of what their brother might do. That just wasn't fair.

In the car, we talked about manners, about using our indoor voices in public, about not honking or biting if something was frustrating, and about keeping our *space bubble* around us. That kind of prep was really my only weapon. There was no telling how it would go. There never was.

When we arrived, the patio was empty, and the wind was picking up. The host suggested that we might not want to sit outside, but Bean was already fixated on the fluttering flags and colorful umbrellas. Abby began to cry because the wind was whipping her hair, but Bean was leaning on the railing looking out over the fairway with his arms flung wide, embracing the wind. I was thankful we were the only ones out there. I looked across at Jeffrey, Abby's head buried in my lap. He was only eight but already the peacemaker. I nodded toward the door and suggested we go inside.

I gathered our things and grabbed a window table with Jeffrey and Abby. Bean was still outside in the wind. Maybe that would look insane to a parent of only typical kids, but I had learned that this could go only one of two ways: I could force my will on him while he was still completely focused on the elements. Then he would melt down, and we would all have to leave, probably with him honking and banging his head because he hadn't had time to transition, and he might bite me in his panic. Or I could sit quietly, close enough that I could monitor him and model what I wanted him to do, and as his focus changed and the fluttering flags lost their grip on his mind, he would notice that we had moved and would happily join us.

I opted for the latter.

I knew how this dance appeared to outsiders. I know it looked like a wild kid who didn't listen to his mother, and an ineffective mother who let her kid be derelict. That couldn't have been further from the truth, but that's how it looked. I was used to it, and it only bothered me on the periphery. I had to let go of so many expectations.

Jeffrey and Abby were munching on the free chips while I watched Bean through the glass. He leaned into the wind with his eyes closed, a smile on his peaceful face. When he finally opened his eyes, he saw me watching him and scowled. I waved to let him know that he was fine.

Whatever was holding his attention finally ebbed. He bounced into the restaurant and plopped down in the seat next to me. *Exhale.*

The problems started immediately. The salsa was in the wrong type of bowl. There were red and purple chips mixed in with the yellow ones. When the waiter brought Bean's plate of french fries, they were curly instead of straight. At the other restaurant, the waiter knew his name and brought cold ketchup; this waiter's ketchup was warm, and he joked that fries were fries. *Yeah, dude, stop now. Please. Just stop.*

Bean slid down the seat, crouched in the corner under the table, and started to rock. He stayed there while the rest of us scarfed our food, just grateful that he was quiet and not honking. I quickly paid the waiter and gathered our things to leave. I managed to distract him enough to get him to the car by promising him that he could choose the route home. His sense of direction was uncanny. He guided us home along the route that his bus took to school. He couldn't eat a nonlinear french fry, but he could remember the bus route to pick up twelve other children.

I wished there were an IEP for mothers. I wished there were a thick packet I could refer to so I would know how to help him in any situation. Life with autism colored everything we did; every place we went and every decision I made, the priority was always how Bean would manage.

What would compel me to try someplace new when I knew the odds were stacked against us? And yet...I had to. I had to push now and again, and I had to find ways of stretching us, despite the chances for disaster. It was a clumsy, messy, frustrating thing, but I kept trying. It was almost instinctual. He...I...We... needed to fly. And we couldn't do it without each other.

16

School Mingled with Motherhood

JUNE 27, 2010

Thrasymachus is skeptical of the role of reason in establishing morality/ethics. His claim...

"Mom! Abby peed on the couch! MOM?! MOM, WHERE ARE YOU??? I need you quick!"

...is literally that "morality is nothing other than the advantage of the stronger party." In looking at this exchange between Socrates and Thrasymachus, I was distracted by Socrates' style of debate. While I don't...

CRASH!! "... Mom? Mom? I'm bleeeeeeding, Mom! Bean shoved a straw in my lip and now I'm going to DIE!! I need a Band-aid!"

...personally find Thrasymachus's argument persuasive, his point is an important one to consider. In recalling the introduction of the text we

are using, I found myself, oddly, thi...

Ring. Ring. Ring. "MOM! The phone is ringing and I can't find it!"

"Can I answer it, Mom?! MOM?!! JEFF!! Give me back the phone! I GOT IT FIRST, MOM!!! MOM MOM MOOOOOM!!"

...thinking of Hume.

"I'm hungry, Mom! Can I have a Go-Gurt? Abby ate the last pink one and I don't LIKE THE BLUE ONES!"

He says, "...morality is no more what is advantageous to the stronger party than it is disadvantageous to the stronger party." Thereby rendering the position impotent, as it cannot be both and have any authority...

"MOM!! THERE'S NO TOILET PAPER!! MOOOOOM-MMMM!"

It becomes amusing and looks more like baiting when Socrates proffers that Thrasymachus holds him to be a bully. Thrasymachus is—perhaps too narrowly—looking toward what he sees (fallible or not) as the ideal...

ding dong "Hi! Mom, someone from church is here! MOM? What are you doing, Mom? Where ARE you? MOOOMM?!!"

...He is rather ham-fisted in his attempts, but I don't think he's the buffoon Socrates plays him to be.

SCHOOL WITH KIDS WAS HARD.

I can do hard things. But this was another thing that looked easier with altitude and got very complicated once my feet were on the ground. It wasn't going to the lectures or taking notes or reading—that part was thrilling. I loved being back in a classroom. I loved listening to lectures where I could soak up new information, and I loved reading books with ideas that challenged me and made me stop and think and reread a page to make sure that I soaked it all in.

The hard part was leaving the nurturing protection of a classroom and heading home to manage my time while juggling three little people. It required a whole new set of skills that I hadn't accessed in years, or maybe ever. The last time I was in school I didn't really care. This time I cared. I cared a lot.

It was summer. The kids were out of school, but I had just start-ed. Instead of only having to manage daytimes with Abby, who loved to sit and read and write with me, I had three kids at home—all day, every day. Coupled with a full courseload, it was not my finest mo-ment of planning.

One of the things falling by the wayside in the crush of new pressures was taking care of myself. It was always so easy to shove my own health to the back burner. I could feel the stress curl up in my gut, and I knew that I needed to work it out. But there were always so many other things that rushed in to fill the spaces I tried to create.

The kids lost the charger for my iPod, but I was determined to get a workout in before I had to knuckle down and write a philoso-phy paper on Kant. I had until midnight to submit the paper; know-ing my deadlines down to the last minute would become a solid pattern over the next couple of years. Most of my best writing would happen between 10 p.m. and 2 a.m.

Resigned and without music, I threw everyone in the car and headed to the YMCA while giving the kids a rolling lecture on re-sponsibility, respecting boundaries, and taking care of our home. I may have raised my voice.

I got the kids checked in, threw my stuff in a locker, and went up to find an elliptical. Thirty minutes is a long time to exercise without music, but I shouldn't have worried; eleven minutes into my work-out, the play center lady came to tell me that I had to retrieve Bean. He was running away and hiding from the staff. Eleven minutes. That was a new record.

When I got to the play center, Bean was calm again and involved in a game of duck-duck-goose. Regardless, the instructor insisted that he leave. Despite the fact that he was playing politely and joyfully, I had to drag him out of the room kicking and biting because of something he had done five minutes earlier.

Once home, he stayed in the car for twenty minutes and refused to come inside. I let it ride.

I got everyone else settled and sat down to write an ethics paper on Hobbes in relation to Rousseau and Aristotle. My brain was about to burst from whiplash. I had to try and dump my temporal distractions (like a kid hiding in the car because he didn't understand why he couldn't play duck-duck-goose) so I could focus on really obscure classical ethicists who were all men and who had wives to take care of their kids while they languished in their deep thoughts.

I had just read the same paragraph three times when the phone rang. It was a sweet friend (who had a husband) asking if I could watch her four kids that afternoon. My friend was kind, and her children were well-behaved, but I felt like I was going to vomit at the idea of another child in my house, let alone four. I could not watch anyone's kids at that moment. I could barely keep my own children occupied while I wrote one paper after another and tried to keep my nose above the rolling, liquid edge of the deep blue water.

I needed to submit another paper and take a timed test for my geography class. I fed the kids dinner and got everyone cleaned up and in their pajamas. Before pressing "play" on the movie, I carefully explained that I was taking a test and that was like a time out for Mama. I needed thirty minutes to sit and think. Did they understand? They needed to let Mama have her time out. All three of them nodded. I sat down at my desk and opened the testing center website. I could see them over my shoulder, peacefully watching Marlin look for Nemo.

Six minutes. Six minutes into the timed test, the sickening sound of little fists hitting flesh and boys screaming ripped me away from my exam and back into conflict-resolution mama-mode.

Feeling the clock ticking up my back, I tore them apart, shut the movie off, and sent everyone to their rooms, grounding them for the rest of their lives. I yelled, I admit it, before racing back downstairs to try to finish my test in the few remaining minutes. I wondered if the professor had ever heard excuses like mine. *I couldn't finish the test because my sons were taking bites out of each other while my daughter hit them with her lightsaber.* I finished in time anyway, so I will never know.

I closed my computer and headed upstairs to check on everyone. Abby had peed her bed while in her time-out. I changed her sheets and fed her blankets yet again into the voracious washing machine. Bean fell asleep in my bed where I had separated him from his brother—a curled, copper-headed comma right in the center of my white comforter. Jeffrey snored softly, contraband LEGOs in his hand, in his own bed.

I wandered out to the living room, enjoying the temporary peace and quiet before I had to get back to more homework. It was a hot July night, and Little House didn't have air conditioning. A system of fans and a swamp cooler helped take the edge off the heat and contributed soothing white noise to the still night. I stared vacantly out the giant picture window, past the tree ropes and the well-watered emerald grass, as cars blurred by in the summer darkness.

The mailbox across the street caught my eye. I hadn't checked it in days, and I fished a pair of flip-flops from under the couch and stepped out into the hot night. The gravel from the drive crunched under my feet as I waited for a lone car to pass so I could cross the road.

The mailbox was full.

I tucked the pile of envelopes and junk mail under my arm and leaned against the streetlight to tear the first letter open. It looked official, but I was too tired to be afraid. There comes a point where you just don't care anymore, and I think that point was several weeks behind me.

It was a letter from the US Treasury Department informing me that they had seized my tax return for back child support. *Oh, the irony.* I had filed our taxes jointly because David and I were still married the previous year. I'd been hoping that tax return would help me, since I was not getting child support. The Department of the Treasury had confiscated my tax return to pay me child support. The taxes wouldn't even have been filed at all had I not done it. *Oh, sweet, bitter irony.* I laughed and shook my head, shoving the letter to the bottom of the pile.

The next letter was from the Federal Student Financial Aid Administration, requesting more information (and my firstborn) before they could process my loan applications for the next school year. It wasn't a big deal, just another thing I had to take care of.

The next envelope was from the State of California claiming that I owed them taxes for income I earned as a resident in 2009. That was interesting, since I had lived in Washington since 2002. But, the letter informed me, I had the burden of proof, and they needed the form back by next week.

The next envelope was a birthday party invitation for Jeffrey. Great. Another social event for Jeffrey, which would make Bean cry because he'd never been invited to a birthday party. I knew why, but my heart still hurt for him. I'd try and keep this party quiet.

I opened the next letter. It was from the welfare office informing me that all the forms I had completed the week before were accepted and we would continue to receive SNAP benefits for the next six months, until my next review. *Oh, thank heavens.* I sighed with relief. That was the letter I had wanted.

A car whipped by, and I walked back across the street toward Little House. I paused at the curb. It looked inviting in the summer night—the sprinklers had just clicked on, and yellow light shone from the kitchen window. The white fence kept the kids safe, and the giant maple tree held its climbing ropes and a hammock, while the fort waited patiently in the shadows for Bean to return. It looked like a happy home. *Maybe it is,* I thought.

I had another test to take before midnight, but at least this one wasn't timed. It was on Plato, Hume, Hobbes, and Kant for my philosophy class. I had two papers due the next day on three chapters of reading I hadn't even started yet. The truncated summer schedule meant packing fourteen weeks of work into eight. Brilliant planning on my part, yet again, for starting back to school. *Sink or swim, baby.*

The next day I had an appointment with my advisor about course selection for fall and possible academic credit for my work experience as a mature student. I'd have to take the kids with me, of course. That would be fun. Then I had until 9 p.m. to write two more papers. *No problem.*

I couldn't breathe. And I couldn't stop.

ↄ

There was no time to indulge a mind full of wind and ache, but I knew myself well enough to know it would be quicker to tap my mind and let the sticky, messy thoughts flow. I sat down and wrote a quick, emotional blog post before getting back to my books. It kept me centered and allowed me to focus. The last few days had not been kind, and I had not been kind to myself. My patience was short, and I was curt with the kids. When they fell asleep and inevitably looked like angels, I was plagued by guilt.

Mo once observed that she thought kids were like mirrors. There was no way to avoid leaving fingerprints or small scratches—the trick was not to break them. That terrified me. Every time I looked at my kids that summer, I saw my shortcomings reflected. I saw their little faces looking at me, questioning "Why, Mama?" as I pushed them off again, put in another video, and hit the books harder. I was short on patience and time, and I never got around to making fresh strawberry jam like we did every other July. I was preparing for midterms and writing yet another paper that I was starting to suspect my professors wouldn't even read. I steeled myself against the wheel, damned my fears, and pushed on.

I had taken a break from my books and was standing at the kitchen counter eating almonds from the container when Jeffrey bounded upstairs. "Mom, if you could have any wish in the world, what would it be?"

I hesitated, wary of ways I might inadvertently hurt my child with a quick, bitter answer full of adult cynicism. "I would wish I was done with school so we could have a normal life again," I offered cautiously but sincerely.

My shoulders burned from tension and my gut ached from stress, but I wanted my son to sleep well that night. He smiled. "I would wish for a billion billion dollars and some LEGOs."

I nodded solemnly. "That would be a good wish."

I was getting home from the first round of midterms when my old neighbor called about the big house—the one I left while holding my smashed heart leaking from between my shaking fingers. It was on the market as a foreclosure. It wasn't mine anymore. I had avoided that neighborhood since the day I left; it was too raw.

She was calling not to say hello, not to chat or ask how we were faring. She was calling, she tersely informed me, to let me know the yard looked like hell and I should do something about it. Stunned, I gave her David's number and told her she could call him if the yard was a concern. She unceremoniously hung up. For some reason, this crushed me. I knew it wasn't important—not really. But she had been my neighbor for three years and only cared that a house on her street wasn't looking up to snuff for the neighborhood. *Stupid neighborhood. Stupid appearances.*

I set the phone down and went to my room and sat on my bed in the dark. I was gutted, but there were just no more tears left for things that didn't matter.

Someday, I thought, *if this is ever all behind me and I have the chance to own a home again, I know two things: you get nicer neighbors in less affluent neighborhoods, and a smaller house suits me fine.*

1996

David's drug use was accelerating. He still came around, and he still spent occasional nights on my couch, but he would disappear for longer and longer stretches. I worried about him, but I couldn't make him return my calls. I was starting to understand that I had drawn from him more than I had given, and that being a grown-up meant respecting boundaries, even when they didn't suit my desires. I couldn't continue to rely upon him but deny him the closeness to me that he wanted. I also couldn't build a life with an active addict.

I hadn't seen him in weeks when the phone rang one afternoon. It was Danny, and he was worried. He wanted to know if I could come over and talk to David.

When I got there, David was in the backyard. Danny told me that David had been awake for a couple of days, and had spent the last night in the backyard walking in circles around a fire pit. In the now-afternoon sun, David was still circling the fire pit.

The backyard was dirt and weeds with a tall redwood fence. In the center was the fire pit, coals and embers of what was once a roaring fire now giving off a dull glow in the daylight. I stood by the back gate, the paint rough under my hands as I watched.

David was alone, wearing rolled-up jeans, his feet bare, his long hair grazing his sunburnt shoulders, while he walked in a wide circle around the coals. He was dragging two heavy chains behind him in the soft, dry dirt. He talked to himself as he stepped carefully in a pattern only he could see.

I stood silently. I knew he knew I was there.

He circled the fire several times more, ignoring me and softly talking to himself, before he stopped and looked toward me, his eyes wide black pools of chemical dilation.

"Boo!" he yelled, then laughed. I didn't move. "Aren't you scared? Run away! The Big Man is scary!" He waved the chains he was clutching, mocking himself.

I continued to stand quietly. I knew how he looked, and I knew any outsider would easily and cheaply label him "crazy"—even some of his friends might. But just like the first night I met him, and every night afterwards, I wasn't afraid. It was clear he was angry and felt abandoned and judged and alone. *Anger masks other feelings.* He was fighting his demons, and demons are not pretty.

My Al-Anon and codependency meetings had given me tools to better engage with people without being subsumed. I knew I couldn't fix any of this for David, but I could be there to bear witness, as long as I felt safe and it was my choice. What I saw was my dearest, oldest friend, and he was hurting. All the other kids on the playground had run away from him when he'd gotten too serious and let them see his heart, and he was covering his pain with substances and rusty iron links.

There were stacks of firewood near the gate; I picked a round log and sat down.

"Hey," I said softly.

He stood near the fire, his feet planted widely in the dry dirt, rusted chains still in his hands. "They called you." It was a statement, not a question.

"Yeah." I paused, looking at him across the distance.

"People suck." He started walking the other direction around the fire. It may have been unconscious, but he'd been moving clockwise when I arrived. I watched him now walk the other direction around the cooling embers until he visibly relaxed.

"People suck," he repeated. "People just want things from you, and then when you are real with them, they run away and get their pitchforks because they can't see you through their own projected bullshit."

I nodded, but didn't say anything. He didn't need me to fill in the blanks.

"Why are you here? Why did you drive all the way over here? You don't belong here anymore." A flash of anger crossed his face, and dissipated just as quickly.

"How is it..." he began loudly, rattling the chains, "that you are the one damn person who always shows up? How is it that you're that person? How is it you can come back here in this spiritual, metaphysical mess, and you can see me? *Why?* Why the hell is that? It's like it's some damn grand joke on me. You. *Why is it you?*" He laughed bitterly, and started walking again, the chains dragging a serpentine path in the dust after his bare footprints. "God is laughing at me..."

He continued walking while his stream of consciousness trailed behind him. I listened. I didn't know what else to do, and that was okay. I was there to witness his pain and sorrow, and to be his friend.

He slowly unwound, the tension leaving his arms and body, until he finally dropped the chains near the dying coals and sat next to me on the log pile.

"I'm tired of hurting," he said softly. "I can't even numb myself anymore."

"I know." I looked at his dilated eyes. He'd clearly been trying.

He breathed deeply and pulled his red-tasseled mala beads from his pocket. "I have to do something. I have to make a change. I want a life I can see through the glass, but I cannot figure out how to reach it. And it's killing me. I have to get out of here."

Heartache rolled over me.

"It's hard to think clearly when you haven't slept in days. Let's get you some rest, and I'll feed you...." I offered tentatively.

"Yeah, okay." He nodded. "I'll get my stuff. Can I crash on your couch?"

"Always."

He stood and looked down at me. "Thank you."

"Yeah." I watched from my log as he pushed the gate aside. Danny's eager dogs squeezed around his legs and ran toward me, all perfect dog happiness and love.

A friend generously offered to watch the kids while I took my last midterm. She lived on several acres out in the country with dogs, dirt, hills, tall grass, chickens, tractors, and things the kids love.

After my exam I ran by Little House to pick up a thank-you plate of lemon bars for her and then headed to pick up the kids. The sun was sinking low, and the light was golden as I rolled down the windows. The surprisingly balmy July breeze sent my hair whipping around my head.

As I pulled in the drive, all the kids and my friend were to the side of the barn. The boys were dusty and happy, and they smiled and waved at me. Abby was wearing her Snow White dress as she marched across the dirt road, hand on her hip. She had a pair of clear plastic safety goggles pushed back onto her hairline and a Red Rider BB gun slung over her shoulder.

"MOM! They won't get out of the way and let me have my turn!" She spun on her heel and stomped back toward the barn.

They had set up a row of root-beer cans on a large log. Each kid had a BB gun, and they were taking turns shooting at the cans. Abby marched up to the firing line, planted her feet, cocked the BB gun, and leveled it at the makeshift targets. The back seam of her dress was split open from such hard play, there were beads of sweat on her nose, and her eyes were fierce with determination. *Ping! Ping! Ping!* The cans scattered.

The rest of the summer continued in that pattern until I submitted my last final and relaxed with an overwhelming sense of relief. I thought that I had been dealing with the pressure well enough, but it was another situation of the frog in hot water. Until the valve tipped and the steam released, I didn't realize how heavy it was.

I thought my dreams of a perfect quarter were in shreds, but I still hoped to pull high enough grades to earn some grants and scholarships. I knew I had perfect numbers in one class, but the other two had weighted totals, so I had to wait to find out. At that point I hardly cared. I had done my best.

My first day of summer vacation was deep into August. My poor kids had lived with a tense mama who hadn't been much fun. Jeffrey estimated the amount of homework I did in eight weeks to be more than he did in four years. But it was finally summer vacation for me, and almost a month of languid days lay ahead of us. I planned on saying yes to as many things as I could possibly manage.

The guilt, fear, and frustration melted away.

And then, surprisingly, came buoyancy. Like a saucer floating over the tides. Somehow, what seemed impossible had come to pass, and I was standing on my lawn with my painted toes in the damp grass, watching the sun set while my children played in the sprinklers in the tiny yard of my Little House. I was happy.

It was like a light I couldn't look directly at—but I knew it was there, and I could feel its warmth.

17

Harvest Moon

SEPTEMBER 18, 2010

The kids were up early, and I lay in bed longer than normal listening to them chatter, peppered by bits of bickering. The seasons are changing, and it's probably time to close the windows,' I thought, as the almost-chilly air slid over the sill and down onto my head. I love when the seasons change; the air turns before the leaves even begin. I've been watching my big maple in the front yard, waiting for the first edgy haze of orange and yellow—but not yet.

Jeffrey asked me where my wedding ring was. It's the small pebbles in your shoe that trip you up, like a child thinking his parents' marriage imploded because he lost the cuff links on the dresser. No, my sweet, it's not, no never, not ever, your fault. My wedding ring is shut away, with my popped heartstrings, in a tiny white leather box lined in red velvet-crimson on the inside, and when you crack the box, it's like cracking my heart. "Can I have it Mom?" Innocence. You already do, son.

The others chime in, nervous the lion's share is being commandeered

by the firstborn yet again—"I want it Mom! I want it! Where is it?!"
"Mama, can I have your pretty diamond ring, the silver one?" It's not
silver, I hold the words in my mouth, unhatched like a robin's egg. It's my
remnant, my fossil, child. We shall wait and see. You do not know what
you ask....

UNDER THE FRONT WINDOW WHERE I sat, the
pumpkin vines were taking over my flower bed and creeping amid
the rusting rose bushes and the last, brave geraniums. If we were
lucky, the egg-sized pumpkins might actually be softball sized and
maybe even orange by October. The lawn was still lush green and
in desperate need of mowing, but since school had started again, I
hadn't been able to light enough of a fire under Jeffrey to get him
out there. The American flag on the porch had blown and caught in
the tall sunflowers by the front door, and they swayed and tangled
together in the breeze. Is that disrespectful, letting my flag dance
with my sunflowers? I decided it was fine and left them to their jig.

The washing machine was churning away in the basement, stoi-
cally chewing through the ongoing casualties of teaching a little girl
to sleep in big-girl pants, and piles of fresh-smelling laundry spilled
from plastic baskets near my feet. I was ignoring the T-shirts and
grass-kneed jeans for the moment, but I knew they were patient and
would always be waiting.

But that wasn't true. A friend once told me that the days take
forever, but the years fly by. She was right. There wouldn't always be
grass-stained jeans and a small girl trying to master her bladder. As
impossible as it felt in that moment, my children would grow up;
someday they would need me less—if I did my job well.

My nose was cold. I tucked my hands under my laptop now and
then to warm them on its little whirring fruit-heart. It was the time
of year where the mornings were still chilly, but by afternoon everyone was pink cheeked and covered in a sheen of sweat from playing hard. Too cool for the fans, too warm for the heater. Instead, I
grabbed a zippered sweatshirt from the back of my closet and began

the annual rotation of the clothing. Soon enough it would be parkas, boots, and searching for missing stocking caps and mittens.

It was going to be a big, swollen fat moon that night. A harvest moon. I loved the Equinox. I loved the perfect balance between light and dark found twice a year for a fleeting moment. The dance between dark and light, the journey back and forth, the sun surrendering to the night and being reborn at the nadir of the year. It was a beautiful and timeless rhythm that made me feel safe and grounded.

It was the first day of fall classes at the university. My syllabi and calendars were printed, my folders labeled, and my books stacked on the Craigslist table. On the counter near where I studied was a cup with an entire box of new No. 2 pencils, all sharpened to wicked points and waiting—prettier than a bouquet of flowers. I loved school. As hard as my first quarter was, I loved being challenged and having my mind stretched. I loved contemplating new ideas and information, storing it away to be drawn upon at some future date.

The boys were back in school and Abby was starting preschool two days a week. I had managed to stack my classes around the kids' schedules and thankfully would need less help than I had needed during the summer. Summer had been brutal, and while I was carrying a heavy course load, I felt confident in anticipation of a regular, uncompressed fall quarter.

I looked back out the window, contemplating Bean turning seven that week. All he wanted for his birthday was a turkey baster. He'd seen one somewhere and found them magical. No matter who asked, or where we were, he was steadfast in his desire for a turkey baster. *Add turkey baster to grocery list.* I could see the mailbox across the street, and I was dreading both the bills that it would surely contain and the emptiness that I feared in the coming days.

It had been almost ten months since the children had seen David. I didn't know when—or even if—that would change. I had been holding the thinnest threads of hope that he might be able to function as a father at some point, but the more time passed the more that fragile hope dimmed. The kids had stopped asking about him, and that made my heart ache—for them and for him. There was nothing I could do but keep moving forward.

My pattern business was keeping us afloat, supplemented by my rental arrangement and SNAP benefits. In a normal situation I would have been working up new designs for my stores, but for the life of me I could not figure out how to squeeze more hours out of the day. There was also the elusive issue of inspiration and creativity—I could not simply sit down and command myself to draw up new ideas. I needed time to play with fabric, sketch, piece things together, and find the theme for a new line.

Inspiration just wasn't there. I had made a choice when I started school. Was I going to be an entrepreneur? The answer was yes, but it was also qualified—I was investing in what I hoped was a more certain future with a college education. The book was due out after the first of the year, and that would be an important source of financial support.

In the meantime, I felt the pinch and grind of living on the edge of my resources. It was like looking down from a tightrope over a canyon and having the world swim before my eyes. Just hang on. Don't look down. Keep going.

I was sitting at my fabric table in the windowless basement thinking about fabric and money when Bean bounded downstairs, his two front teeth in his hand. "Can I show them to Ava?" he asked. He had lost them the week before, immediately after his birthday (he got his turkey baster and took it for show and tell). He couldn't leave the hole in the front of his mouth alone, and he looked so precious with his gappy smile.

"Sure. We're picking her up for carpool today." I set my fabric worries aside, checking the clock on the wall by the stairs.

Bean had met Ava in the childcare center at the YMCA earlier in the year. He didn't make friends easily, and it warmed my heart that she seemed to enjoy his company. Ava's mom and I shared smiles in passing, but that was the extent of our interaction.

Toward the end of the school year, the woman I carpooled with phoned to tell me that she had a new neighbor doing the same route. Three ways was better than two, and we worked out a new schedule. The first morning the new mom pulled into my driveway, Bean bounded out the door—it was Ava's mom.

I was holding my breath hoping that he might finally have a friend. The first thing out of Ava's mouth was, "I want to sit next to Bean!"

She wedged her booster seat into the center spot between Bean and Abby. When she couldn't get her buckle fastened, Bean unhooked himself and carefully fastened her belt. They giggled and laughed all the way home.

In her driveway, Bean offered to carry her booster to her front door as I helped the other kids from the car. I turned to see Ava enthusiastically throw her arms around Bean and give him a big hug. And he let her. I suddenly had something in my eye.

As Bean ran back toward the car, Jeffrey began teasing. Whirling around and shooting mom-daggers at him, I threatened his existence if he uttered a word. *No, son. Do not take this innocent friendship from your brother. Shut it. Now.*

Bean climbed in his seat, buckled up, and looked out of his rolled-down window with a half-smile on his rosy cheeks the whole way home. *I loved Ava, too.*

In the same week, with no fanfare and surprisingly few tears, I passed the one-year milestone of filing for divorce and the one-year anniversary of signing a book deal in Houston. At my publisher's urging, I celebrated by having a head shot taken for the forthcoming book cover—I put some makeup on and Jeffrey took pictures with our digital camera. It worked.

I also had a birthday. I cannot stress how little I cared or how old I felt. The weight of the world was on my shoulders, and I felt like a tired old turtle. Carpool, school, kids, study, homework, kids, bedtime stories, homework. Day after day. There were glimmering moments of joy sprinkled in, like bits of glitter left over from a craft project, but it was still a foundation of mostly hard things.

But the glitter was a nice reminder that joy was real, too.

Visitation rights are not tied to child support.

I understand the complicated wisdom in this rule looking back with the hindsight of years, but at the time it rubbed salt in some deep and fine wounds. You could be a total deadbeat parent, not contribute a dime to the support of your children, abandon the other parent to protect and juggle three children with full-time school and bill collectors, and still regain visitation rights.

My lawyer had the joy of explaining this to me the night before I had a giant comparative literature paper due and I was already short on sleep, already stretched thin. Instead of writing my paper that day as I had planned and prepped, I scraped the bottom of the barrel and drove to the electric company with my pink bill in hand, a gift from the nice man who had come to turn off my service. I used my birthday money from my mom to keep the water on. Nothing like living on the edge, babies.

And then I had to go back home and prepare the kids to see their father, whom they had last seen convulsing on their grandmother's floor while paramedics and fire fighters worked furiously to keep him alive. I had to prepare myself and them.

There was no glitter anywhere that day.

Interlude
Return

HER BLOG WAS PEPPERED WITH one recipe after another that month. It was something she did when things were too hard, when she couldn't look right at what was happening. If she was only telling people how to make things, it meant she was not okay. October overflowed with one recipe after another, and when she ran out of food to write about she moved on to craft projects. All instructions. All the time.

The call from her lawyer informing her that her ex-husband had finally made the sobriety benchmark sent her reeling. She didn't think it was possible to feel so many things at once—relief that he was sober, happiness for her children, deep concern for how her children would process things, stress at managing the logistics of the visits amid her already hectic schedule, and anger. Deep, roiling anger at him for putting her in this position. Not just the divorce, but the abandonment—what it had done to her, what it was still doing to the children, the ongoing repercussions of his actions she kept having to field while he focused on himself in rehab. *Must be nice to just think about yourself.* Resentment and fury coated her like hot tar.

She didn't have time for this. It didn't matter. She was forced, bound by the same court order he was, to allow him to see the kids for three hours a week. It took ten months, but he'd proven himself sober for six continuous months and had completed his drug rehab program. His visits were still supervised. She could allow the courts to take care of those details, or she could make her own arrangements.

The kids' grandmother could still be a supervisor, but that meant taking them back to the rooms where they witnessed the confusing and frightening violence of heroic firemen pounding on their father's seizing body. Their counselor agreed that she needed to protect them from those memories if possible. That was a bridge she could help them across later.

However, if she shoved it off to the courts, they would assign a county facility with a stranger sitting in. The idea of subjecting her kids to a correctional environment was more than she could bear. She couldn't do that to them. She hated her ex-husband at that moment, but she loved her kids more, and she was furious at what she knew she had to do.

If she were truly going to put the needs of the kids first, the safest place for them to see their father was right in their own home. *Dammit! Dammit, dammit, dammit!* The thought of inviting him into the place she had pieced together with the ashes he had left her made her feel physically ill. She held onto the kitchen counter, her head swimming, and forced herself to breathe deeply.

It didn't matter. It didn't matter that she wanted to chew her arm off before opening her door to him. She knew it would be the best thing for her children to be in their own home where there were no bad memories and where they knew they were safe. She balled her fists in frustration and fury and fought back tears. It wasn't fair. It wasn't fair! *It didn't matter if it was fair or not*—rock. She picked up her phone with shaking hands and dialed her lawyer.

Her lawyer was surprised. He informed her that she didn't have to set things up that way. *Yes, I do. If I love my children more than I love my own anger, I do. I have to do it because it is the right thing to do.* It was a defining moment—she stood on the edge of the known world and could see the path visibly fork.

In one direction was resistance and punishment. She could justifiably allow this story to define her life—it would be easy, and it would be understandable. It would also freeze her in that narrative, crippling her and the children from ever moving forward with whole hearts. They would be trapped in amber, broken.

In the other direction was healing and forgiveness. She could set down her pain and disappointment. It would not be easy in the beginning, but she knew it was the only path out of sorrow and heartache. It was the way she could write her own story and not allow herself or her children to be defined by bitterness. For that to happen, she had to let go. And she had to forgive. She didn't know how to do it, but she knew it was the only way.

If she was who she believed she was, this was where she would have to prove it. She could not say she loved her children but then allow her choices to give lie to her words. It must be love made visible.

I have made so many mistakes in my life. Please God, let me do this right. If I do nothing else right, let it be this.

She opened the kitchen door, and her heart lurched.

He stood on her step, head freshly shaved and wearing a blue woolen shirt. She hadn't seen him since the ER ten months earlier. The planes of his face were as familiar as her own, but they were etched deeply with new lines carved by the sorrows of the last few years. His clear eyes were naked, raw, no longer clouded as they had been the last hundred times she had seen him. The insulation of chemicals protecting him from the reality of what he had done was gone, and he stood openly before her.

She couldn't look in his eyes, it hurt too much. So she looked toward his mother standing behind him, holding a paper bag of groceries and her purse, and dabbing at her eyes with a tissue.

"Please, come in..." she whispered through tears, pushing the storm door open for him. He stepped gingerly into her Little House.

18

A Day in the Life

OCTOBER 23, 2010

Like a dog who's been kicked, I am kind of cowering in the corner—I don't want to tempt the fates and speak up too loudly—it's better to be invisible. I might not exist then, but no one can hurt me, either. My breath catches in my throat, and the part of my brain that is not primeval medulla recoils from this base reaction and begins to try and reason. You don't reason with the primordial ooze.

The needs of others cut me like slivers of glass. Like a plate spinner in the circus I keep running between delicate balancing acts. Three essays due for school today, two discussion commitments, a large paper and a test due Friday. Between now and then I have preschool, carpool, a field trip for one child, enrichment craft day at church, visitation with David, and an appointment with financial aid.

Yet oddly, one just keeps going. There is great joy in small things, and I am getting better at recognizing that often pain is as transitory and fleeting as happiness. There is comfort in remembering that. "This too shall pass" really applies to everything.

6:46 A.M.: IT'S UNCLEAR IF it was the sound of rain gurgling down the gutters that woke me or if it was my daughter's cold little feet pressed against me as she flopped sleepily, arms akimbo, in the pre-dawn light. When I fell asleep to the muted late-night monologue, I was alone in my bed, but as happened so often, I woke with one or more smaller people pushing on my warmth and needing their mama.

7:20: All three of them were in bed with me watching cartoons, as I was slowly shoved toward the edge of the bed, as sleepy snuggling gave way gradually to the gray pallor of the drizzly day. Bean's ability to tolerate jostling and touch diminished as hunger kicked in; the clock was ticking to get him fed before he came unglued.

7:30: In the kitchen, the gray weather made me feel like making a nice breakfast, so I whipped up a batch of cinnamon crumble muffins and threw them in the oven. I enjoyed the sound of rain and the cozy feeling of a warm kitchen. Abby wandered in, rubbing her eyes, and wanted to help, but I was distracted as I tried to look over my homework while the muffins baked. "They're already in the oven, toots. Can you get the milk out?" I had an assignment due the night before, but I had some leeway and could turn it in a few hours late and be fine. I shooed Abby from the kitchen and started cooking some bacon in the cast iron skillet while I thought about reworking my paper on post-colonial Africa.

7:54: I put breakfast on the table, and in a rare moment of inspiration, I even lit a small candle to make it feel cozy and warm. I called the kids. I could hear cartoons and giggle-bickering. "Breakfast is ready!" *No response.* For some reason, this ticked me off. *I have so many other things I could be doing besides fixing a hot, homemade breakfast, and they can't even come eat?* My mood soured, and when they came to the table, Bean immediately yelped and ran to hide, apparently because his muffin was in the shape of a heart and not a proper circle. *Dammit, why did I even try?*

8:00: Bean came back to the table after I wrangled him out of his squeeze-spot—with much honking on his part. He wasn't happy, but I cut his muffin into a circle. They ate their homemade breakfast in the kitchen without me. I wasn't hungry, and I went to my room to cry—quietly, because I don't want them to hear me. *I am so tired of crying.* I am annoyed with myself, with my eyes, with my heart. *Come on.* I turned on PBS and watched through angry tears as some guy made dovetail cuts in a beautiful piece of wood with a hand chisel.

8:22: The kids were off playing, and I dragged myself to the kitchen to clean up breakfast and start a load of dishes. *So much work for only a few fleeting minutes of happiness.* Did it matter that I still did these little things? Was the effort worth it? Did it make a difference? It's another series of questions that lead to nowhere and to which I would not have the answer for years. *The answer is yes, it mattered, and yes, they do remember it, and yes, it helped them feel like they were loved when things were hard.*

9:00: Bean requested that I move his therapy hammock from my room into the TV room so he could watch movies in it. Any time he could tell me what he needed with actual words I was grateful and would try to do it. I had already unfastened the hammock from the bracket in my ceiling joist when I realized I didn't have the proper tools to install a new bracket. Digging in the kitchen junk drawer, I found a hammer with part of the claw missing, some screwdrivers, and one mangy crescent wrench. I could make that work.

9:40: After hammering small holes in the ceiling to determine the direction of the joists, I found a good spot and attached the anchors. It was hard with no drill to make pilot holes, but I used a screwdriver as a lever to get some torque on the eyebolts and got them seated well with some elbow grease. Standing on one of the kid's chairs, I was attempting to clamp the carabiner into the eye bolt on the ceiling when the wrench slipped and smacked me in the mouth. My lip was bleeding, but my teeth seemed to still be intact.

10:00: With some ice in a plastic bag pressed to my swelling face, I sat down to crack my textbooks and work on my post-colonial Africa paper. The kids were happily playing in the basement, the dishwasher was finishing the dishes, and I was comfortable at the Craigslist kitchen table. I got about a page and a half written—a decent start—and was only interrupted three times. Bean was very happy and content with his new swing location, and I reaped a small reward in uninterrupted time. The Wii was babysitting so I could get those pages written.

11:00: Everyone was still happy and occupied downstairs, and I was hungry. Cooking myself something sounded therapeutic and nice. On my counter were some plump late-summer onions brought over by some friends from church. I sliced them up and got them caramelizing—not sure what I was going to make, but caramelized onions were always a good start. I learned a long time before not to toss apple or potato peels down the disposal, and I was about to discover that the same thing applies to onion skins. Just as the pan was beginning to sizzle, I turned on the disposal and it erupted all over the kitchen. I flipped the stove off with a sigh.

11:25: Everything under the kitchen sink was on the floor, and I had unscrewed all the pipes and cleaned them out. There was a pile of towels and a bucket full of nasty water, and I decided that pouring the water down the toilet was the best plan. It was a good choice. Briefly I had contemplated calling Mike when I thought I had fixed it the first time and water shot up all over my clothes. I screwed up my resolve—I didn't want to ask for help. Again. *I can do this.* Carefully I fit the pieces of pipe back together and tightened everything down. *No leaks.* Exhale. I did it. Time to start a load of towels.

12:00: I washed up and finished cooking my onions and spread them on toast with some cheese. It was astoundingly delicious. I heard Bean in the basement and smiled—he'd found his trumpet. He loved his trumpet and thought we had lost it in the move. I made myself a cup of peppermint tea and realized no one had had a bath or shower yet, and I needed to go to the grocery store. I shoved aside the paper I was working on and noted on my calendar that I had a test to prepare for, too. If I played my cards right, I could get to it all.

I lagged a little, enjoying the warm cup of tea in my hands. It was still raining, and heading to the grocery store on a Saturday with all three kids was…not my favorite.

1:27: Two showers, two baths, everyone dressed, towels hung to dry. Trying to get everyone out the door was like herding cats. Abby was weeping because she left her favorite fluffy coat at preschool and the world would surely end. Bean would not stop trumpeting, and Jeff was ready to kill him. I really hoped my cloth grocery bags were in the car. No progress on my homework.

2:31: That was fun. The grocery store with Bean is always a challenge. All those colors and smells often push him over the edge, so we ran through with our list and got the heck out as fast as possible. He only ran away and hid twice, which wasn't bad. My neck prickled with self-consciousness as I scanned the aisles calling for him. I don't know how much was real and how much was imagined, but I was sensitive to people looking over the tops of their glasses at the *terrible mother who clearly cannot control her child*. I'm used to it, but it still hurts. When I found him the second time, I shoved the food aside and put him in the cart, where he kicked and honked until we were through the check-out line, where I paid with my SNAP card and was grateful the checker was kind. I saw a friend's husband in the store with one of their kids and I had a moment of envy at their ability to divide and conquer. It was afternoon and I was no further on my paper, the laundry hadn't been changed over, and the beds needed stripping. There was a single-adult dance that night at our church, and I had tossed around the idea of going, but from where I was at the grocery store, I just didn't see it happening.

2:55: The groceries were all put away and the kids took their laundry to the wash room, so that helped. On the couch, the boys snuggled in brief brotherly harmony as they peered intently at the screen of Jeffrey's Gameboy. I could hear Abby singing to herself as she spun on the computer chair in the basement. *Whirrrrrr… whirrrrr…*I had to go coax her to move so I could actually get started on my homework.

5:02: I got a solid hour and a half of studying in while Abby spun herself on the desk chair next to me, occasionally asking me to loosen a LEGO for some big, delicate thing she was building. Bean hung out in his hammock, swinging contentedly, and played Wii with Jeffrey. I was able to log into the university website and watch a lecture I had missed earlier that week and then scored 96% on the fifty question quiz that followed. My tea was tepid on the desk next to me, but it was time to cook dinner. I had no idea what I was making, and the laundry was still forlorn and undone.

5:35: Dinner was on the table, and all children came when called. Soup and grilled cheese sandwiches left most happy, with an English muffin with peanut butter for Bean, of course.

6:15: The kitchen was cleaned up and the dishwasher was running while the kids got their pajamas on. I believed in early bedtimes. Early bedtimes saved my sanity as a single mother. I bribed them and promised I would read two chapters of Harry Potter that night if everyone was compliant. They looked at me oddly. I loved reading to them every night though—even when I was stressed and too busy. *All the time?* It calmed them and let us end the day on a good note, no matter how off things might have been earlier. I ran to the basement to start the long neglected laundry.

7:24: Abby was in her room alone because she couldn't keep her feet off her brothers, but she was happily singing to herself. The boys went to bed with their flashlights and were given permission to read Calvin & Hobbes until 8:00, when it was lights out. I still had my paper to finish on post-colonial Africa, as well as two other assignments due the next night. What I really wanted was to curl up with a novel. So much for the church dance. *Like that was ever going to happen.* I laughed to myself and sat down to write.

8:16: The doorbell rang. It was Jeffrey's Sunday school teacher, who also happened to be the nicest man on earth. He brought us a pizza, as he did many weekends, from his restaurant. The kids would be bummed they missed him, but they were already asleep. He and

I visited for a few minutes at my kitchen door before he left on his motorcycle. Bean loved that motorcycle.

8:32: I put the pizza in the fridge—the kids could have it for lunch the next day. It was time for real homework. Forget social life, forget dating, forget church dances for singles. *Where on earth could I fit anything else in?* I knew most of what filled my days was part of every other mother's day, too. Not the full time school, but the other things. The part that stuck out for me was not having anyone to share the joys or the tiny triumphs with—I was alone with three kids most of the time. If I did well on an argument paper, they didn't understand. If I got a really good grade on a lab I worked hard on, there wasn't anyone to celebrate with me. I valued solitude, and I liked being alone. I didn't like being lonely.

I knew if I did my job right, I would be sending my children off, like arrows, into their own futures. That meant I was standing alone. Had I planned better, maybe I could have gone to that dance? *Oh hell no.*

I sat down to finish my paper and start the next day's assignments.

19

Empty Bookshelves

NOVEMBER 18, 2010

Most of the time lately, I cruise along just fine. It feels like so much hard stuff is behind me now—and while I still have hard stuff in front, it's hard stuff of my choosing, and not someone else's mess anymore. I'm not foolish enough to think it's all smooth sailing from here, but I know seasons change—it can't stay this way forever.

I'm killing it at school—I have a graduate program picked out and a better than fair shot of getting admitted. There is even a potential plan post grad school, about which I am reservedly excited. My kids are doing pretty well—I mean, they act like regular kids, which is a good thing, right? We have Little House, and a paid-for, working, decent car. My kids have great teachers and wonderful friends, and I do too. I have some happiness and satisfaction.

So why do I still feel like I have failed? Tonight, I was talking with a friend, and she gently pointed out that I needed to stop beating myself up for marrying David. It stopped me short—she was right. There is a tiny part of me that secretly feels if only I had done more, tried harder, been better...I would not have lost everything. Intellectually, I understand the folly of that thinking—and yet it's still there, like a rusty, forgotten bucket that I trip on in the dark.

I don't know how to fix this. If I know what needs doing, I am unflinching. But this? I have no idea how to heal that part of my heart. Bitterness has mercifully been absent from me for most of this process, a fact for which I am profoundly grateful. I don't want bitterness within a country mile of my heart...but how do I cull the seeds of rust from that old bucket and keep my heart supple and open? How do I keep my heart from turning to stone? How do I forgive myself?

I SPENT DAYS CLEANING UP the emotional wreckage after David's first visit with the kids. The powerful emotions of being able to see him again were hard for little bodies and minds to process, and it was my job to help pick up the pieces. They were so happy to be able to see him. He was tender and gentle, and he talked with them quietly about love, mistakes, and forgiveness. He was trying hard to do what was right in the face of some really awful truths.

Looking back, I cannot fathom the courage it took for him to knock on my door and stand before me that chilly autumn day. He knew he had harmed me, harmed his children, broken the things most perfect and precious that a person can hold. He also knew his children needed to see him and that hiding from what he had done would not facilitate their healing and recovery.

He made no excuses and did not try to shift the blame for what he had done to anybody else. He was willing to stand before me and accept and absorb whatever rejection, pain, or fury I chose to hurl at him. It was a hallmark of progress in twelve-step work—looking honestly at oneself and taking a fearless moral inventory.

At first I couldn't talk to him; my words clotted in my chest into an immovable, chaotic dam. Where does one even start after what we'd been through? That first *Please come in* was everything I could muster through the tangle of sorrow and anger. It was as much a prayer for him as it was for myself.

It stayed that way for a long time.

His mother and I worked out a schedule, and she accompanied him to Little House each week for his visit. The kids loved their Nana, and she was not only a help for David, but also for me. It was still hard for him to manage jumping back in with three rambunctious kids, and she acted as a buffer to support everyone. Her presence helped me relax and enabled me to step gradually back safely.

As expected, Bean had the hardest time with the transition. He didn't understand why his dad had been gone for so long, and he didn't understand why he had to leave each time he visited. In Bean's mind, I imagine, it was a confusing swirl of uncertainty—*Is Dad back? Why is he gone again? What's happening next?* Abby had very little functional memory of David, and I think she had the easiest time with his visits. Jeffrey...Jeffrey remembered things. He remembered hard things I wished I could shield him from, and that manifested in him being very protective of his father and his visits. Our counselor told me to expect this, and I did my best to guide him through the thicket of big emotions. Some days we did better than others.

One night after David and Nana had left and I was juggling homework and baths and my own emotions, Jeffrey told me he hated me.

I stopped, stunned, trying to breathe amid the chaos of holding this little ship together. This child who had split my soul wide open and cut a chasm into the wilderness of motherhood with me, this child who had introduced me to God and allowed my bright tears to fall on his fiery copper hair while he was still wet and trailing clouds of glory, said he hated me.

This is what the counselor was talking about. . .be still.

It didn't matter why he said it. It was trivial and meaningless in and of itself—it was selfish in the way only a child secure in the love of his parent could be. Even as part of me recoiled at his words, I recognized what was happening. I leaned carefully on the doorjamb as he glowered over his scowled brow at me, arms crossed and using his stocking feet to shove away the messy piles of LEGOs and dog-eared comic paperbacks littering the floor around his bed.

Parenthood teaches us enormous lessons at inopportune times. Somewhere, deep down, I had the presence of mind to realize that this lesson was about the removal of yourself—the you who is unique and hurts and hopes and wants—when your child needs something precious and specific from you.

In that moment, watching him kick tiny plastic toys and throw his anger and rage about things he couldn't control at me, it was my job to understand, to actually see him and help him have what he needed. My own feelings were inconsequential. That was why I was the parent.

He trusted me. The stresses of his life, though they might have seemed simple and childlike from an adult perspective, were all new to him—and they were not small. In the course of one year, he lost the only home he remembered, the freedom and security of having a stay-at-home mom, and most devastatingly, he lost his father. The shadow of David, who occasionally showed up and looked like the guy who used to function as his father, was fragile, untrustworthy, and had to be handled with great care.

All three of my children clung to what they could eke out from the three hours a week with their dad. He was still not entirely dependable, canceling at the last minute if he was having a rough day. Jeffrey was watching himself and exercising protective care over the repository of his ideas about what "dad" meant. He could not, at this parting of paths in the road, tell his father that he hated him—it would blow apart the fragile relationship that they had cobbled together.

It was for me they reserved their expressions of pain, anger, and sorrow. It was with me that they were safe enough to throw themselves on the bed and wail about the breaking of their hearts—and this was what I thought of as I sat down next to my angry son and laid my hand gently on his back. He folded his arms and harrumphed, scowling at me deeper. Taking his face in my hands, I told him how much I loved him, and how proud I was of the vastness of his heart, the courage of his convictions, and the soul contained within his growing body. I reassured him life would not always be this way, but that, when it was, we could do hard things.

His face softened, and he leaned over into me, flushed and a little embarrassed, trying to hide a chagrined smile. "I'm still mad at you," he mumbled into his folded arms, brows still drawn down, but eyes a little brighter.

I leaned gently into him. "Yes, I know. It's okay. You can be mad at me. I'll still love you forever. I may not always *like* you—but I will *always* love you."

His head popped up, surprised and indignant that I would say such a thing. I met his eyes. "Well, you do have the power to hurt my feelings. I'm a person, doing the best I can, just like you."

Contemplation rolled across his stormy eyes, and I could see him processing the idea of *mom* as someone, not just the filler of bellies, of laundry baskets, of backpacks, and of bathtubs.

He was nine years old. Too young for the load placed upon his shoulders—oldest child, addict father, full-time-student mother, courageous boy with a heart of gold—but I saw those shoulders broadening already, and I suspected he would someday be quite a man. *I wasn't wrong.*

2008

The summer before Harold and Maude kept me company in the backyard while my world crumbled, I took Jeffrey, then six, on his first road trip. I was headed to Salt Lake City for a conference, and I thought it would be the perfect time to bond with him before school started.

It might have been quicker to fly, but road trips are a rite of passage I wanted to share with him. I loved the idea of having time with just him, away from the distractions of everyday life, siblings, and a dad who was growing more and more invisible. There would be other kids at the conference, and I would have plenty of free time. He was excited to go, and piled his pillows and toys in the backseat with puppy-like exuberance.

Ten hours and a ghastly amount of "Are we there yet?" later, we pulled into our Salt Lake City hotel. Our room was right off the pool, and I promised my tired boy we would hit the water as soon as we got dinner. We unpacked and decided to walk to a restaurant up the street.

It turned out that Salt Lake City addresses are encrypted so strangers can't find anything, and the restaurant was much farther than I had imagined. It was also July, and the outside air was like the inside of a furnace. I felt the moisture being sucked from my body as I dragged my hot child through the arid desert, looking for something called the Blue Iguana.

We found it. *Underground. Of course.* After a short wait, we got our food, but the look on Jeffrey's tired face told me he was going to crash into the guacamole if he didn't get some sleep. Chugging a pitcher of water while the waiter boxed our food, I temporarily rehydrated and made ready to enter the furnace heat.

The shortest way back to our hotel was walking down West Temple, where we unexpectedly found ourselves at our church's large Conference Center. We had seen the building on TV before, but we weren't prepared for the enormity of the actual edifice.

Jeffrey immediately recognized things he had seen in pictures "Can we go in, Mom?"

I paused. "I don't know."

I tried the doors nearest us, but they were locked, and we couldn't see anyone inside. A guy on a Segway whizzed by, shouting over his shoulder, "The doors on the other side are open!"

Looking down at Jeffrey, I shrugged. "We can go in, but it might take up our swimming time. What do you want to do?"

His copper head shone in the sun, and the freckles were popping out on his alabaster nose. "I want to go inside."

I think it might have been the promise of air-conditioning more than anything, but either way, he made his decision and we moved toward the doors that Segway Guy told us were open.

When you are hot, tired, and unsure where you are, that building is really, freaking big. We finally found an open door, and the blast of cold air was disorienting for a few seconds. There were scattered people, but no crowds.

A kind-faced older gentleman approached us holding out a paper. "Are you here to see the choir, or for a tour?"

I was confused. "Choir? What choir? We were hot and came in to see the building." *The cool air was a bonus.* I looked at the paper the man placed in my hand, and then back at him.

"Sister, the Choir is practicing here tonight, and you and your son are welcome to watch if you'd like. The orchestra is warming up right now, and you can go through those doors to your right." I still wasn't accustomed to the way Mormons addressed each other as *brother* and *sister.*

Jeffrey was jumping up and down. "Let's go, Mom! Let's GO!" He was yanking my hand and flapping his own arms in excitement; I mumbled my thanks to the man and we headed toward the doors.

Who knew the Choir was practicing, and that we would stumble in at the exact right time, on the exact right day?

Honestly, I wasn't paying a whole lot of attention. I had been driving since before dawn, our still uneaten dinner was boxed and bagged in my hands, and I was dizzy, parched, and a little grumpy from our unexpected walk. I wasn't thinking of anything spiritual. I wasn't thinking much of anything at all.

So when I walked through the doors and smashed completely unprepared into a wall of my own emotions, I was blindsided. Standing there, looking out at the arc of seats and the smattering of people, I felt connected to my faith in a way I never had before. There was nothing special happening—someone was folding some chairs near the dais, a musician in the orchestra was tuning a violin, the choir was milling on the stand in small groups, and there was no music yet. So what were all the feelings? Why were my feet refusing to move as electricity arced up and down my back?

"Mom! Come on!" Jeffrey was yanking on me again, and I wiped my eyes with the back of my hand.

"Why are you crying Mom?" Jeffrey looked up at me.

"I don't know," I answered truthfully. Why was I crying? What was wrong with me? An empty building, a few people idly chatting, my son excited to hear some music. It was all perfectly ordinary. Why was I crying?

Jeffrey skipped toward the front of the cavernous hall, and I followed, searching my purse for a tissue. I just wanted to sit in the cool air and feel what was happening. There were thousands of empty chairs, and I slumped into an aisle seat as Jeffrey bounced from chair to chair, seeing how close he could get to the organ and counting the tall brass pipes.

My body looked warm and solid, but things were stretching, moving, slowly leaning on the shelves inside my mind. How odd to be a spectator in my own life—gently at first, like an oiled toggle on an old lock falling into place, then quicker and hotter, the ideas beginning to tip and slide. My breath caught in my chest as a channel opened and suddenly missing pieces shot home and everything fell off the shelf inside me.

Stunned, I sat still, my thoughts cascading over me like a roaring waterfall.

Holy crap. This is my faith, my home. This isn't just an experiment. This isn't something I'm just trying out, until the next interesting thing comes along. This isn't something I can ever walk away from—not ever. This Is Who I Am. This is eternal progression. This is lead into gold. This is man into God.

Holy. Crap.

The music had started, but I hardly noticed. Jeffrey snuggled into the crook of my arm, and I turned my focus back outward. Everything looked the same—but I was not the same.

An hour later, we left the cool of the building and walked into the late blue twilight. The heat was abating, and the sky showed only the last strands of color on the horizon. We were both quiet as we walked across the courtyard, lost in our own thoughts.

Jeffrey reached out and took my hand. "Mom?" There was a hitch in his small voice.

"What, sweetie?" We stopped on the sidewalk.

His voice was surprisingly thick, emotional, and I could see his face full of concentration as he worked to find words for his feelings. "I'm so full of something right now, and I don't know what it is."

I nodded. "Yes. I feel that too." The breeze whispered across the empty shelf inside me. I squeezed my son's hand, letting him know he was not alone.

❧

Within our church community, we had an abundance of kind, thoughtful, helpful and consistently present friends. My children were never forgotten in activities. There were people who would simply stop by to chat or to offer some love or help. I don't know if it was because we lived on a main road near the church and we were easy to find, but it was a huge blessing that left me a little awed.

I had friends who were willing to help on short notice if my child care fell through and who were willing to help get a kid to Scouts, or watch Abby while I took a test, or just come by and hang out around my kitchen table. It seemed like every time I turned around there was someone happy at my kitchen door with a note, or a small gift, or just a smile and a hug. I was grateful.

One Sunday at church, the women's leader—the same one who helped find and prepare Little House—stopped me in the hallway. She leaned in and whispered,

"Tracy. You... look...smokin'!" then winked and walked away. I guess she was used to seeing me in my mom-student sweats. *Maybe I need to put in a little more effort—there was that boulder again. Why is it so hard to remember myself?* I was both slightly embarrassed and flattered—I mean really, what struggling mom doesn't want to feel pretty at some point?

I got pulled out of Sunday School because Bean was melting down in his class, but even when they came to get me, it was done with such love. He had kind teachers who tried to understand him and help him with love and compassion.

When we got home from church, there was a message from David canceling his visitation that afternoon. I sighed in resignation. It happened more than I wished, but there was nothing I could do. There was also a message from Mike and Nancy saying they would drop by to fix a draft in the back door, but they also wanted me to know there was a singles mixer that evening at church and that I should definitely go. They volunteered to watch the kids, so I had no excuse.

There was nothing on earth we could have done to deserve the community that circled their wagons around me and my little family. To this day I am grateful for the vastness of those human hearts and their ability and willingness to choose to love us.

That evening, armed with the compliments of the day, and with Mike and Nancy literally pushing me out the door, I took my first reluctant steps toward a personal future where my heart might once again not be stone.

20

A Low, Quiet Calm

FALL, 2010

The pillars of my faith are planted in soil that is still soft and freshly turned. The ground where they rest is still marred by the plow, loamy and verdant from only relatively recently having been broken and turned. This loose fresh soil makes my pillars more like stakes, sprouts… wisps of what they may someday be, but the seeds are planted nonetheless, and I have seen the seeds sprout that may someday have the breadth of oak, the strength of cedars. Not yet, but the promise makes me willing to gamble on faith.

MY SEARCH FOR GOD STARTED early, much to the bemusement of my multi-generational atheist family. My childhood was idyllic, just south of San Francisco on old orchard land. My hippie parents and I had happy, carefree days tending our chickens, picking fruit from our trees, and making jam. We even had a goat before having a goat was fashionable. My memories are tinged with happiness and the scent of freshly tilled soil, the tang of salt spray on my lips, and the tingling feeling of sunlight breaking through thick banks of fog.

Family and friends were always close. My mother's sister and her family lived down the road, and my grandmother was only a few minutes beyond. Doors were always unlocked, and I spent as much time with friends and extended family as I did in my own home. It was a good and happy upbringing in a good and happy home.

And yet, even at a young age, I felt something missing. No one else seemed to notice, but it was like a tiny pebble in my shoe that only I could feel. Keenly, I didn't have the words or frames of reference to give it voice—I only knew there was a space inside of me where something important belonged.

I recall being in first grade and studying the nativity that my mother would put out at Christmas. It was a family heirloom, and my mother would set it out as a nod to tradition. She loved Christmas, and that was good enough. I was mesmerized by the little statues. That little ceramic Jesus was the recipient of the first prayers of my life. Without understanding why, I pulled my child-sized rocking chair up to the shelf where the crèche was placed, and I started to cry. Quietly, I poured out my heart to the tiny glass figure. I was fearful of being discovered doing something so oddly unfamiliar, but so compelling. I could not stop myself. It felt like someone was listening.

As a young teen, I tagged along with a friend and her mother to a bookstore, and I purchased my first Bible with my babysitting money. I picked a green leather volume with the words of Jesus in red, and my friend would go over passages from the New Testament with me, showing me how to highlight words I liked with a yellow pencil. At home, I kept my Bible shoved behind other books on the crammed bookshelves in my room and hoped my mom wouldn't notice. Most kids hid Judy Blume novels—I hid the Bible.

As I grew, so did my yearning for answers. My parents allowed me room to explore religion, even though they didn't share my need.

I would go to any church with anyone who would take me. I attended synagogue, the Kingdom Hall, Catholic Mass in Latin, Hebrew school, a Charismatic Christian church, the old Lutheran A-frame down the street, the small chapel across from my elementary school, a Sikh service with a classmate, and Mormon services with another friend. I was searching.

As my idyllic family life began to unravel, my parents divorced, leaving me floating and on my own before I was quite ready. I continued to search for faith, for God. I searched in secret places and places regular and simple. There was not a church or school of thought I wasn't willing to consider, but still I wandered, unsatisfied, searching. What I was looking for was that feeling I had from that little Christmas Jesus. I was looking for someone who was listening for me.

I made some mistakes. It took fifteen years of being mad at a silent God I wasn't sure was even real before the answers came pouring down on my parched spirit.

The birth of Jeffrey finally caused my vague, sputtering faith to burst into vivid flame. When he slid from my exhausted body with that final great push and they set his slippery newborn body on my beating heart, I knew God was real. Years of searching fell away as I looked in awe and wonder at my first child, and I knew, *I knew with all my heart*, that there was a God and that he was right there with me. I sobbed—in exhaustion, and for my son—but also for answers to lifelong questions. In every picture of Jeffrey's birth, my face is bathed in tears. Only I knew how long those complicated tears had been waiting to fall.

After that awakening—a birth for both Jeffrey and for me—I found myself seeking a church in earnest again. I wanted my child, and my future children, to have a foundation of faith. I wanted them to know God as part of the weft and weave of their daily life, to know Him as a cornerstone and not feel the void I had longed to fill. I understood I could not really provide that for my children, and that their paths were their own to walk, yet I wanted to at least give them some literacy, some familiarity with liturgy and holiness in different forms. I went church shopping each week. One Sunday, purely because I liked the building—which is really peculiar in retrospect—I went to a local LDS church in our neighborhood. I knew very little about it except that Mormons had a reputation for being nice, and I had a vague recollection from my childhood co-op days that they stored bulk food. I sat alone in the back with squirmy Jeffrey on my lap and left immediately after the service. But something stuck with me. It was an odd service, where people from the congregation gave little sermons themselves, speaking of their beliefs, and everyone was invited to come to the podium if they wanted to speak. I was intrigued by the parade of young people talking about God with knowledge and confidence and obvious love. At that service, the vocabulary and vernacular were unfamiliar, but I left with a feeling of perplexed curiosity.

The next Sunday, with the slight, shy defensiveness of someone on new ground, I announced to David that I was going to church again. He glanced up from the couch, nodded, and smiled his encouragement, before going back to watching the baseball game. He was happy with his faith but was supportive of my searching. I gathered Jeffrey and headed back to the curious building. Two months later, still incognito in the back, I approached the missionaries after the services, and asked what I needed to do to be baptized.

One of the things that frightened me most about getting divorced was not having a close father figure for the kids. I didn't doubt my competence as a mother, but I also knew children needed healthy models of loving male relationships. We lived far from my family—my dad and brothers were all in California, and I had no idea what would happen with David. No matter how good a mother I might be, I couldn't model loving men by myself.

There were parts of church life that I sometimes avoided, just to protect the little hearts in my care. We skipped services on Father's Day. *We still do.* If families were being talked about in idealized form, I would quietly gather up my children and go home to play instead. There were small, bumpy reminders sometimes that we were a different-shaped family. My kids were tender, a little raw from what they had experienced. David's absence was never far from their awareness, and we didn't need reminders.

That spring, my church was planning a father/son campout. Mike came to visit, concerned about the feelings and hearts of my two boys. He had spoken to the bishop, and they wanted me to know that they understood how hard this might be, but they wanted to include Jeffrey and Bean and make them comfortable.

The boys had never been camping before. They were eager and excited, and that afternoon they waited by the fence in front of Little House watching the cars pass and waiting for Mike. Their carefully packed bags, pillows, and food were stacked by the front door, and when the car pulled into the driveway they jumped in and waved happily at me standing on the porch.

Around midnight the phone rang. It was my bishop. He had Jeffrey and Bean in his tent, and they were sobbing. He told me that everything had gone well, but when it came time for bed and they settled into their small tent, they both were overcome with tears and wanted to go home. He had tried to soothe them, but they were distraught. He passed his phone to them, but hearing my voice only made it worse. I prepared to wake Abby and drive to the campground. I was unsure exactly where they were—they had hiked in, and I didn't know if I could actually find them, but I was going to try.

A few minutes later, my phone rang again. It was Mike telling me to sit tight and not wake Abby. They would get the boys home. The bishop carefully packed my tired, weeping children onto the four-wheeled ATVs with which they had trekked in supplies, and they slowly made their way down the mountainside in the dark night. Then the bishop, leaving his own son asleep in his tent, drove my boys home. He even carried Bean, who had fallen asleep on the drive, into the house and put him in his bed. Jeffrey curled up in my lap and cried.

That camping trip could be seen as a disaster. But it wasn't. Bean and Jeffrey were young, and the next morning they talked about how great the bonfire was, how much they loved making s'mores, and how awesome it was to pee on a tree. When it got late and dark they were frightened to be away from the familiar, but there were good men watching out for them, protecting them, who took the time and care to usher them to safety. That camping trip would have long, gentle repercussions for my sons. The take-away was far greater than the surface-story of small boys who wanted their mama and their own beds.

It was 5:03 a.m., and the kicking, flopping, gently snoring boy who had crawled in bed with me shortly after midnight finally drove me out and up. My eyes stung in the pre-dawn dark while I felt around for some socks, and I padded down the hallway to steal a fluffy blanket from Jeffrey's bed. The boys had haphazardly draped a string of colored Christmas lights around their window and over their desk, and their room was bathed in a soft, low rainbow. I smiled to myself.

Warm air poured from the floor vents as the heater kicked on quietly somewhere under my stocking feet. In the kitchen, dragging Jeffrey's blanket and holding my laptop, I clicked on the star-shaped light over the kitchen window. It was a souvenir from my visit the week before to see Mo in Seattle, and it made me happy. My mind was slow and groggy, but the tiny golden stars the lamp threw over the walls and ceiling decorated everything in the room with a low, quiet calm. I twisted the knob on the stove and watched as the blue flames danced under my teakettle. I was grateful that firewood and stoking a cast-iron stove were not part of my morning.

If I let it, the weight of the day would settle on my shoulders. There were always things that needed my attention—too many things. Yet I had found an odd and surprising balance in faith. If I tabulated and correlated and focused on all the things that I could not get to, the entire focus of my life was on where I was falling short. Over the dismantling years, I found that the things that were actually important were far fewer than I imagined. Shelter, love, food, direction, and faith. I had that covered. Most months I had no idea how we were going to make it, but the last year especially had taught me that somehow, every month, we did. And so I had stopped worrying so fiercely. It always worked out. It was like standing on a ball: if I thought about it too much, I would fall. Faith colored my gratitude daily.

My teakettle rumbled importantly to itself, bringing me back to my kitchen. A cloud of steam billowed up as the peppermint and chamomile mixed with the drizzle of honey in the bottom of my favorite Japanese teacup. Cradling the cup in my hands, I sat down at the Craigslist table and opened my laptop. Time to begin writing yet another paper.

I was mulling over heading into another round of finals and the impending holidays when the phone rang. It was Nancy, inviting me and the kids to join them that evening for a family dinner and a walk around the lake to look at holiday lights. It sounded lovely. My spirit was buoyant all day. School was going well, and that might have been part of the bubbles of happiness—there was no pressing homework at hand, so I could relax. I found myself stepping outside of myself for moments just to observe the many miracles in my life.

One of the miracles of modernity was the connection I was able to achieve to the outside world despite my humble circumstances. Writing and blogging openly about what life was like allowed me to make incredible connections. Friends around my kitchen table helped me be a better person. At school I took part in heated and passionate discussions with intellectual classmates, and I was grateful that I got to keep company and learn from so many inspiring, smart people. These interactions helped me look beyond where I was and imagine where I could be.

My children were happy, and that amazed me, too. They rolled into the house after school, each one a boisterous ball of noisy, giggling energy. Abby inhabited both her brothers' world and her own. She still got one-on-one time with me while her brothers were at school; this was when Darth Vader retreated and the crayons and tea-pots came out. I was delighted with the way that she straddled the worlds and owned them both.

It was a long-standing policy of mine to have an open door. I loved when people stopped by. I loved seeing happy faces at my kitchen door—no one used the front door at Little House. My kitchen would never be spotless, but anyone who wanted to sit around my Craigslist oak table and chat was welcome. Only the day before, a friend I hadn't seen in ages had stopped by for help with a project. We fixed it up, and her baby fell asleep in Abby's lap while we talked. It was precious, unplanned, and beautiful.

David was doing better about showing up for his visitations, and he was staying sober and working through the twelve steps. It was still very hard to be in the same room together—the air was heavy with things we just couldn't bear to brush against, but we had settled into a simple routine. I realized that the loose ends between us would never be fully cut. There would always be raveling strings blowing in the wind, and as they unwound, they knotted together in new ways, becoming nests of their own. Despite the divorce being legal and final, there was no such thing as "final" when you have three children you both love. It was more a matter of what new relationship would be knitted from the old strings.

I was content for the first time since my life had fallen to pieces. I wondered if maybe those tiny moments of pause—when you notice your place, notice your heartbeat—were what make up the body of who you actually are. *I don't know. I only know this moment.*

It was time to gather the coats and boots and get ready for our walk around the lake. One last hurrah before I had to disappear down the rabbit hole of studying for finals. Once finals were over I would think about Christmas.

A few weeks earlier I had searched eBay for nativity sets. In a few simple searches, I had found an exact replica of the crèche my mother had when I was a child. There was the tiny little ceramic Jesus wrapped in swaddling clothes, and the straw-covered stable with the cow and donkey, while Joseph and Mary knelt. My heart pounded in my chest. *There it was. The same one.* With the last of my birthday money I had squirreled away, I bought myself a Christmas present.

21

Perfectly Bent Petals

MARCH 25, 2011

As my mind wandered, I found myself looking at a giant spray of spring roses filling a vase on a table. Each flower was so beautiful, and yet when I looked closely, each petal was unique, different—bent here or there, a curl in the edge, a tiny ripple in the textured leaf, a frill here, smooth simplicity there. Yet the imperfect petals, when placed in the context of being a flower, became perfect. And each rose, a collection of imperfectness, then was part of a greater bouquet which in turn became a masterpiece.

I think this is what we all are—Imperfect Petals. We are made perfect in how we put ourselves in God's hands and allow Him to do with us what He wants. When we beat ourselves up for having bent our petal, or for our edges not being as smooth as the petal next to us, we are devaluing the beauty and perfection that lies beyond ourselves. I don't think God cares so much about the marks on us nearly as much as we do—because he sees the whole, and knows if the petals were all the same, the rose would not be so beautiful. It's the differences and so-called flaws that create the beauty.

Life is going to mark us. We are going to be bruised, torn, and scarred by what happens here. But it doesn't matter. The bend of my petals is what makes me useful to God, what makes me unique, and precious. God does not need—nor want—me to be like anyone else, or for us to be perfect copies of each other; indeed, such an idea is an affront. We only have to trust, and know that we are loved, and hand ourselves, flaws and all, over to God in order to be made perfect.

EARLY THAT SPRING, SOMEONE DROVE their car through the fence around Little House. Thankfully no kids were outside, and everyone was okay. It was an unseasonably warm day when my hero Mike came by to assess the damage so we could get Bean back his yard. We stood out in the warm, thin sunshine talking over my battered fence.

Mike told me a story about his own family, about a time of need and how help was granted with love—only for me it wasn't a distant story padded by the patina of years. Per court order, my children were supposed to receive support from David. It was a modest amount, and I had not asked for more, but it was still a bar that he could not meet. Any support at all would have made a difference, but the way things stood, I was running on fumes. Each month I had been robbing Peter to pay Paul, and it had finally caught up with me. Mike gently reminded me that my pride was hurting me and that I was not allowing others to bless us.

On Sunday the bishop greeted me with a smile and told me he'd been expecting me. Mike had called to warn him that my pride might prevent me from coming to him, and he wanted to make sure that the kids and I were okay. Safety net in place: check. He gave me a short list of things he wanted me to do, one of which was to call David and explain the importance of him taking some financial responsibility. Even if he didn't have much, helping me and the kids needed to be a priority.

The boys had been acting out terribly, and Abby was compensating by being as sweet as she could be, sneaking in to kiss me and tell me she loved me at all hours. I'm not sure which concerned me more. I didn't want them to feel responsible for me or my feelings. I wanted them to be safe and happy, and most of the time I thought I was doing a good job. Then something would happen that made me feel like I just got off a carousel and was dizzy with confusion.

The next night, heading home after a huge craft-project meltdown at the YMCA, Bean sat in the back of the car honking and wailing. Jeffrey was up front next to me with his hood pulled over his face and his arms crossed, furious at me for making him leave, and Abby was kicking the back of my seat because her water bottle was empty. I burst into tears.

Bean began to howl plaintively, and then we were all crying. One big happy family rolling down the road toward home, which is not really home at all, but a borrowed Little House lent to us in charity. As I pulled into the driveway, Bean wailed, "I don't like this life, Mama, I want a different one! I don't want to live in this stupid house and have you in school and I don't wanna be sad!" *Me too, Bean, me too.* I sat in the driveway, clutching the steering wheel, my shoulders shaking under the weight of too much. Too much, and not enough, and it just didn't matter.

I got out of the car and looked up. The sky was clear and warm with stars just beginning to rise.

Keep going. Don't confuse what's happening for who you are.

Abby was still kicking the seat and waiting for me to open her door, but the weight shifted inside me, and I smiled from somewhere deep and real.

I woke from a dream that made my heart ache and my limbs twitch with the need to escape. Years before moving to the Northwest, I had lived in a tiny post-war California flat-top. It was a crappy little house, but I loved it. It still sat empty, a forlorn tissue box on the window sill where I had left it a decade before.

In my dream I was back in that house, only with all three kids. The neighbor knocked on my door to inform me that my landlord was evicting us, and she told me that I needed to pack my kids and get out. Panicked, I raced around in distended dream-time, looking for my landlord. I couldn't find her number, the phone didn't work, cell reception cut out, Wi-Fi dropped—every path to an answer of my fear of being cast out was broken. It was hellish in the way that only panic-and-loss dreams can be.

Still wrapped in the cobwebs of that dream, I lay in my bed a thousand miles from where I had started, in yet another rental house, with three kids, and with all the dreams that I moved from California trailing ashes behind me. I felt vulnerable and powerless.

In that other little house in California, I had kept a Norwegian proverb that David had given me tacked to the wall in the kitchen:

"In every woman there is a queen. Speak to the queen, and the queen will answer."

Like so many women, I struggled with doubting my worth in a million tiny ways. The little proverb would catch my eye and remind me that, when I held myself as someone of value, others would respond accordingly. That was before I found my faith, but I still found those words meaningful and helpful.

A queen does not need validation from the world. A queen knows, even if her circumstances change or she loses her crown or her head—*Henry VIII was such an ass*—she is still a queen. There is a calm certainty about a woman who knows her worth. People inherently respond to her dignity. When I would get lost in powerlessness, I needed these gentle reminders that, no matter what outward chaos prevailed, I was okay. The feeling of powerlessness was a reflection of the world, not necessarily of what was real. I could lose my home, my marriage, even my extended family—and it did not change the bedrock of my identity.

These subtle, tiny shifts in belief reflected in how I interacted with the world. When I saw myself as valuable, it showed in my countenance, my posture, the set of my shoulders, and the look in my eyes. It showed in how I spoke and how I listened.

I still found the proverb of the queen both appropriate and beautiful. I needed reminders. When the world threw me down, or when loss swallowed me whole, or when seeing through the glass darkly was just too damn hard, remembering the queen made all the difference.

When I value myself, everything has more value.

1998

David left California. In a move that took Herculean courage and resolve, he packed up his belongings and moved in with his mother in Washington State, more than a thousand miles from his existing life. He said he knew he couldn't get himself in order, get himself clean and sober, by staying in the same place and doing the same things he'd always known. He needed a clean start, in a new place, and it had to be far enough away that he was safe.

I missed him.

But at the same time, I was so glad he was gone.

For the first time in years, he was actively taking care of himself. He was attending twelve-step meetings voluntarily, and he'd gotten a job working in a construction supply company—it was exhausting, physical work, and he said the distraction of being so tired at the end of every day kept him sane. He preferred it to the cerebral electronics and engineering work he'd done for so long. He started biking to work and lifting weights in his spare time.

Part of what he was practicing was boundary maintenance. He felt that if he talked to me too often on the phone, it would distract him from his recovery focus and from the work he was trying to do

I started writing him letters. I wrote him letters about what he meant to me, and how I could see, with the hindsight of years, how he had nurtured me and helped me to become who I was. He had guided me through growing up and shown me how to choose the paths of mercy over the thorny brambles of severity. He had shown me how important it was to decouple emotional reactions from moral valuations. He had helped me navigate leaving bitterness behind and taught me to choose forgiveness—even toward people who had hurt me. Just about everyone was battling their own demons, and they were also doing the best they could with what they had. He taught me all of this.

He'd been gone more than a year. I was coming home from a particularly disastrous date when a Bob Dylan song came on the radio as I flew down the freeway:

When the evening shadows and the stars appear
And there is no one there to dry your tears
I could hold you for a million years
To make you feel my love
I know you haven't made your mind up yet
But I would never do you wrong
I've known it from the moment that we met
There's no doubt in my mind where you belong.

It was David. It was David who was waiting for me. It was David who would never do me wrong. It was David who had done everything he could to give me the space I needed, while he did what he could to live with what I offered. *It sounds so stupid now, to look back and acknowledge what a revelation this was to me—it was clear to everyone else.*

Waves of realization rolled over me, and the internal arguments began. *He was a drug addict. He was a thousand miles away. He was doing so well. I was selfish—oh, how selfish was I? Could he be a husband and a father? Would he want to be? Did he want the same things I*

234

wanted—stability, parenthood, the white picket fence? It was insane to consider this at all. And it was terrifying.

When I got home, I sat on my bed staring at the phone on my nightstand. It was late, and I argued with myself over the wisdom of calling him.

I picked up the phone, hands shaking, aware I was risking something very great.

He answered on the first ring. "Hey." His familiar baritone crossed the long-distance line.

"Hey. Did I wake you? Sorry for calling so late." My breath was shaky as I tried to calm myself. I asked him if he knew the Bob Dylan song I had heard.

He chuckled, and started singing, *"When the rain is blowing in your face, and the whole world is on your case, I could offer you a warm embrace…* That one?"

Of course he knew it. I had never found a song he didn't know. I took another deep breath and dove in. "So I think I realized something important tonight. Can you listen to me for a minute?"

"Of course," he replied.

"It dawned on me. Maybe…maybe…it's you."

He was silent a thousand miles away on the other end of the phone.

"I have never understood why, but maybe it's because…" my heart was thudding out of my chest, but I pressed on, "…maybe it's because we're supposed to be together."

Silence.

I could hear his breath, and suddenly all of the pain I must have caused him over all of the years came rushing in, and I felt like a monstrously selfish child. At the *very least*, I owed him the space now to consider his own thoughts without my needs pressing on him.

How could I expect him to be waiting for me nine years after we met? I waited—in what might have been my first truly adult moment in life—preparing myself to accept whatever he said, whatever boundary he needed, or even outright rejection. I owed him that.

He broke the silence, saying with quiet gravity, "You better mean what you are saying."

His words hung in the air, heavy. This was his heart, his bones cracked wide, naked, and raw, vulnerable in a way he chose to be only with me.

"I do," I whispered into the phone.

"I'm proud of you." David sat at my Craigslist kitchen table, running his mala prayer beads through his hands. Years before he had joined our church, but in his slow climb toward recovery he'd found solace and comfort in the traditions of his previous faith. Whatever helped him stay sober was good. On the table between us was the advance copy of my quilting book, which was being released the next week. It had been a long year.

Over the months we had settled into a careful emotional space where we were learning to talk to each other again. The glassy brittle tension of that first day when I could only whisper was gone, and his willingness to take responsibility helped both of us heal. The kids had grown used to having him in Little House several times a week, and he even successfully stayed overnight while I visited Mo in Seattle. Baby steps in the right direction.

There were places that hurt too much to go near, but he continued to be willing to absorb whatever arose—whether from me or from the kids. There were no emotions off limits, and while I am certain it was personally taxing and costly for him, he accepted and allowed our children—and me—to process our feelings openly and without defense. He wept openly when I shared some of the details of his overdoses—the opiates had destroyed many of his memories.

He didn't make excuses, and he didn't flinch, though I know it hurt him. That was how I knew he was getting better.

We decided that we were still a family even if we weren't married. That meant putting the kids first. That meant being kind to each other and presenting a united front as parents. That meant celebrating holidays and birthdays by including each other—even though it was hard at first. His mother had celebrated his birthday at our local taqueria, and packing the kids up to go sit with him had taken all my courage. But I did it. And the next time, when he joined us at Little House for Abby's birthday party, it was easier. Baby steps in the right direction.

I talked with him about school, about how I was doing, about how everything was affecting the kids. I talked to him about my first thoughts about graduate school and what that might mean. He smiled, his eyes sparkling as he looked across at me. "Duh. You were always the smart one." And he laughed.

He told me about his rehab meetings and the characters he met. He talked about his frustration at not being able to find work and his grief at his own fragility and his sorrow for how he'd failed his family. His mom would make dinner in the kitchen while the kids pestered him to play another game, and I would then excuse myself to study or go to run errands. I wanted him to have time with the kids without me in the background. Those relationships were theirs to cultivate, not mine to control. David and his mother became a regular part of family life at Little House, and it was exactly the balm each of us needed.

I had found my oldest and dearest friend again, and while we were both scratched and scarred, and nothing would ever be the same, the shine was still real.

My quilting book dropped, and suddenly I had a paycheck again. I received the remainder of my advance, and I could look forward to and budget for a royalty check every three months. It was also fun to walk into the fabric store and see my work displayed right on the shelf. The book, and the royalties it produced, were my life-preserver as I wrapped up one quarter of school and headed immediately into the next.

In order to finish early—which had always been my goal—I had talked my advisor into allowing me to carry an overload. At first he was reluctant, but as long as I kept my GPA up, he was willing to sign off. It felt like running the last leg of a marathon or eating the back half of a whale. If I carried an overload for the next year, without taking summer off, I could graduate the following spring.

I had a plan and an end date.

22

Dragging the Parachute

AUGUST 29, 2011

She bends down to kiss the rosy cheeks of her giant sleeping boy. How did a decade pass and her cherubic copper-headed baby turn into this giant man-child who shares clothing sizes with her? She brushes the haystack of red curls from his face and presses her lips to his freckled forehead. He doesn't stir, deep in the arms of sleep.

Stepping back, she lands on a Lego and smacks her head on the top bunk. She stifles a cry, but the boy stretches and rolls and cracks one eye at her. She smiles and rubs her head, and he mumbles, "Love you too, Mom," as he rolls over and sprawls on his stomach in front of his whirring fan.

She stands in the darkness looking at her boy. Lightning flashes outside, and the hum of fans floats in from all rooms. She had never said a word... but he had seen her and assumed her love. Maybe she's doing something right after all.

I SAT ON MY FRONT stoop in the late summer sunlight. The pink sky and warm air draped over my shoulders as I watched the beams of light that were my children as they ran around the lush emerald lawn. The grass was freshly mowed into wildly uneven stripes by a boy giddy at finally being given the responsibility of a power tool. He was followed closely by his copper-haired and equally shaggy brother, slurping a purple popsicle and kicking the fallen piles of grass with glee. Abby was sprawled on her belly next to me on the warm concrete walkway, inspecting ants and dripping popsicle puddles for them to feast on.

The day before, on a brief break from school, I had decided to riffle through the garage and bring organization to the chaos. It didn't work, but Abby had found a treasure—my wedding dress. Even little girls who dress as Darth Vader most of the time fall in love with wedding dresses, and her eyes lit up as I slid the zipper down on the thick garment bag and pulled out the confection of tulle, satin, and pearls. In the bottom of the bag were my shoes and veil from that happy day so long ago, and we spread them out across the living room.

"Mama! It's so beautiful! Can I put it on?!"

I had zipped the dress away twelve years earlier and had not taken it out since. My world had changed several times over since then—three babies, several moves, two houses bought and one lost, my marriage destroyed; I wasn't sure how I would feel pulling out that giant pile of fluff and tulle. Oddly, I hadn't felt anything—no gut-lurch, no hot tears I had to blink back—just kind of quiet detachment, looking at a pretty relic that didn't have much to do with me.

"Sure, sweetie, you can try it on." I gathered up the yards of white fabric and let them fall over her small form. She'd stripped down to her undies and wiggled with joy.

She was right—it was a beautiful dress. I had fallen in love with it when I saw it in the window of the bridal shop; it was the only dress I had tried on. I knew it was perfect before I even put it on.

Of course it was huge on her, the tulle ball-gown skirt swamped her and puddled in a cloudlike poof—but she felt beautiful. "Like a princess..." she whispered.

And that's just how she should feel in a wedding dress. It was hers now. A beautiful reminder of something that was, but wasn't anymore. My scars were healing, smoothing over with time. *What I really want, though, is to see her try and put the veil on with the Darth Vader outfit.* I giggled to myself. Turns out time does heal all wounds.

"MOM!" Bean yelled from the backseat of the car. He always yelled. "There's something I was afraid to tell you, but I think now is a good time." *Oh, dear Lord....* I steeled myself. "Yes, Bean? What happened?"

"Well, you know the TV downstairs?" He grabbed his water bottle as he unbuckled his seatbelt.

"What happened, Bean?" *I am calm I am calm I am calm.*

He got out of the car and hitched his pajamas up. "Well, it's kind of on the floor now. It kind of fell. But don't worry! It still works!" Jeffrey looked at me and shrugged.

"Bean, what happened, and why didn't you tell me? It still works?" I opened the kitchen door and the three of us headed downstairs. Face down on the floor, talking importantly to itself, was our very large TV. With Jeffrey's help, we flipped it back up, and all I could think was *what if it had fallen on him.*

I sat Bean in my lap and explained that he was more important than any TV and that he should always tell me if something like that happened. *How did I not hear it?* I wondered.

As I was wrangling it back into the armoire, I noticed all the wires and cables leading from the cable box and the DVD player were neatly snipped, right at the connectors. "Bean? Tell Mama what happened. What were you doing? Is this why the TV was on the floor? Why are these cables all cut?" *Calm. Calm. Calm.*

"I didn't do it Mom!" He wouldn't look at me. "Bean, tell Mama the truth. It's way better to tell the truth—I will always forgive you. I love you even when you do bad things."

He looked at me, all missing teeth and copper hair. "Mom, if I were going to do that, it would have been because I was looking for a place to plug in my headphones, and I would have put the scissors right over there." He pointed to my easel, where the orange handled scissors were sitting. *Exhale.*

That night, as I was sweeping the kitchen and waiting for Jeffrey to arrive home from Scouts, Bean came in and offered a highly unusual unsolicited hug.

"Mom. I've decided to forgive myself for my fibs and to ask you to do the same. At church I learned that when I lie, I need to forgive and not do it anymore. That's what I've decided to do."

And with that he went in his room and crawled in bed, while I stood in the kitchen holding the broom, staring after him, wondering what else life had in store for me that I could never, in my wildest dreams, have imagined.

For weeks I had been battling with the Financial Aid Office at my school. That morning, with all three children in tow, I met with a new financial planner and finally emerged victorious.

We ran over to Senior Hall, where I met with a new advisor who provided me with more concrete information in thirty minutes with three kids dancing around the desk than the previous nincompoop did in five full quarters of college. We went over everything, and I left with a written plan of exactly what I needed to do to qualify to graduate. When I left the new office, I had all my classes secured, the next two quarters laid out, my senior capstone reserved, and graduation slated.

My course load was going to be really heavy for the next three quarters, but as a college Senior that was expected. If I kept up my grades, I could plan on walking in robes, a mortarboard, and maybe some honors cords too. I felt like Will Smith in *Independence Day* when he was dragging the parachute behind him in the desert, only I was trailing children as I walked across campus toward my car.

The next week, Abby started kindergarten the same day I started my senior year of college.

Interlude
Driving Home

SHE ROLLED THE WINDOW DOWN and dangled her arm into the still shimmering late-summer heat. Her eyes drifted out of focus, the red light allowing her a moment of stillness in the sweltering night. The air-conditioned quiet of her car without the children had only amplified her loneliness, so she switched it off and rolled down the windows. She welcomed the street noise, the diesel fumes, and the un-muffled exhaust pipes of the teenagers cruising in their muscle cars. Somehow the chaos banked the echoing emptiness inside.

She had been parenting and managing to get by for so long alone that she barely noticed it anymore. Or at least that's what she thought. Isolation had been a part of her life for what felt like decades—isolation from her family, distance from her friends, geographical isolation when her marriage crumbled, emotional isolation as she picked up the shattered pieces and cobbled back together something of a life. *"I am a rock, I am an island...."* Paul Simon's words meandered through her brain as the light changed to bright green and she pushed the car into gear.

She moved off the main drag and turned down a back road. Her path was inky black, and the humid night air whipped her hair into an untamed halo, catching on her earrings and spilling out the window into the night. She was living on borrowed everything—borrowed loans for college, borrowed house until graduation, borrowed light for her soul.

The loneliness inside permeated the layers of her spirit and reached toward heaven to her God. Living on memories. *Is that borrowed light?* She didn't know. She only knew she didn't really know anything, and she missed feeling closer to God, missed feeling like she was heard and loved. The silence echoed through the canyon of her heart. *Is it borrowed light if you are using your own stockpile?* she wondered idly, downshifting at a deserted crossroads.

How much can one person handle? Her thoughts wandered. Platitudes rolled through her mind—*put your shoulder to the wheel, you must be so strong, God doesn't give us more than we can handle, I don't know how you do it, count your blessings name them one by one.* On and on the useless words rolled. People meant well, she knew, and they didn't realize what they were saying. And the loneliness grew.

A man at church had told her a few days before that she was a hero. She had smiled kindly but was internally baffled. *For what?* she wondered. For taking care of her family? For getting up every day? She didn't know how to explain to people that their compliments made her feel more alone. The worst was when people said, "I don't know how you do it!" She would look perplexed. *What else am I supposed to do?*

How much could she absorb, take in, buffer for those she loved before she broke? She was honestly afraid to really ask that question, afraid that the answer would terrify her or that God would take it as a dare. Rationally she knew that was crazy—but emotionally her shoulders shook and she worried that her knees were going to buckle. How many times can you get knocked down? How deeply can your heart be cut and have it still go on beating? Why does loving someone, anyone, everyone, always hurt so much?

She laughed at herself. What kind of self-indulgent question is that? Silly girl. The smile lingered on her lips and she shrugged the pity off.

The night whipped by, and the lights of home crested on the hill. Home, at least for that moment. Even if it was a borrowed home with borrowed light, it was still light; it still glowed and was good. It held her children, and her lifelines, feeble though they may have felt, and it held, despite the oppressive heat of the late summer night, hope. There were no answers. But there was always hope.

23

Maybe It Was Time

IT WAS 1:43 IN THE morning. I was still in my workout clothes from what had become the day before and was finally flopping onto my soft, welcoming bed. The laundry had been piling up for days, and I simply couldn't put it off any longer.

Earlier that night, after the kids were fed and put in bed, I wrote a four-page paper on the effects of social expectation on the self-esteem of young women, and then I took a timed test online and submitted a PowerPoint presentation. Even earlier, I had run to the grocery store to replenish our depleted supply of food, and I visited with a friend who stopped by while I made enchiladas and English muffins. It was my day to drive the carpool. I had missed an assignment the night before because I didn't have the right software—and the professor was kind enough to give me an extension. There was a second note from the fifth-grade math teacher—my kid was still not making sufficient progress, and the teacher wanted to meet. The kids had brought home volunteer sheets and order forms for the book fair, and I had to disappoint them with my inability to volunteer or buy books. They wanted to go out for ice cream for family night, but with the paper and PowerPoint due, I had to disappoint them. Again. There were dishes from dinner piled in the sink, and I didn't want to think about the kitchen floor or the bathroom. A cursory wipe with some Clorox wipes was the best I could swing. There was an email from a friend who thought I was angry at her for not communicating much, and I stopped long enough to apologize and reassure her. My kids' Sunday school teacher called to ask where they were, and I explained that I had been in an all-weekend seminar and was unable to arrange to get them to church—despite the fact that I used my lunch break to speak in the women's meeting, as I had agreed to do long before I realized I had school that weekend. I had made it back to class on time, albeit in my Sunday clothes while everyone else was in sweats. My kindergartner was off, but the boys had school. Someone asked me to volunteer at the women's shelter downtown and reminded me that we have a big neighborhood activity coming up. The activity was scheduled from 10 am to 8 pm, but childcare was only available from 11-1. It was assumed that family or spouses would help. My car was making a funny noise and was past the time when the oil should be changed, but I couldn't figure out how or when to get to it, so I pushed it off until after my next eight-page paper was due. I lost a filling on Friday, but I couldn't figure out what to do about it; at least it didn't hurt.

That same Sunday, before running back to my seminar—while my kids were at home with a sitter—a woman sat down next to me as I was waiting to speak. She leaned close, complimenting me on my suit, and told me that her husband was traveling for four days. She said she was absolutely dreading the week and didn't know how she would make it. "I really hate being a single mother."

I just stared ahead; a burning lump lodged in my throat, and didn't move, lest I break into a million pieces.

Along with juggling my school load, I was asking professors for letters of recommendation and filling out grad school applications while having to think about decisions for a future I couldn't even see yet. *Maybe carrying nineteen units again wasn't the best plan?*

I wasn't sleeping well—mostly because there just wasn't time—and some days the stress was so bad I couldn't swallow my food. I had never struggled with disordered eating, and I told myself this was just stress and it would pass. (It was, and it did.) But the praise I got from people over my thinner appearance was confusing and felt shameful. I could see how a younger, less experienced woman could easily seek that kind of validation and control. It scared me.

David was sitting in his customary place at my kitchen table. "You need to take care of yourself." As usual, he wasn't fooled by appearances, and he could see me. He had been coming over more frequently and had made himself available to watch the kids for my two weeknight classes. It was working well—they liked having him around more, and he'd proven to be fairly dependable.

"I'm really sorry I can't do more to help," he said. It weighed heavily on him that he couldn't find work and wasn't able to contribute financially. His mother still tried to help out where she could, but she was on a limited income. I was getting royalties on the quilting book and keeping us above water. Barely.

I shrugged. I had made peace with the reality that he might never be able to help support us and was instead grateful that he was sober, present, and trying his best to be a parent again. "Will you be there on Sunday?"

Bean was getting baptized on Sunday. He had waited much longer than children typically do, but I didn't pressure him—it had to be something he wanted. Traditionally in our church, a child's father baptized them when they were eight years old, but that wasn't an option for David. A friend would be doing the baptism.

Due to very specific requests from Bean, we were not including any music or sermons or inviting any people. He wanted to go, get dunked, and be done. (We'd practiced in Mike and Nancy's pool.) So that's what we were doing—no frills.

David nodded, but I could see him swallow hard. There were so many little woven sorrows and pains built into our collective and individual lives. Church was still difficult.

"You'll meet us at the restaurant afterwards, right?" He nodded again. "I'm sorry this is so hard," I said quietly. I wanted to put my hand on his, but I was afraid to touch him—we could talk, and be open and honest, but touch was a barrier I just couldn't bring myself to cross. I still don't know why.

He looked at me, his face naked and open. "I am too. I cannot ever escape the reality that I did this. I did this to us, to you, to the kids, and all day, every day, without escape, it's my reality. I did this. But I am so grateful they have you. Please take care of you."

I nodded and went to the kitchen sink. I didn't trust my voice.

Always have a backup plan. My mom told me that once upon a time, and she was right. I wasn't great at front-end plans, but since the forest fire ran through my life a couple years earlier, I always had a back-up plan.

I was scheduled to graduate that spring. I had done well enough that I had several professors encouraging me to apply to their programs. One even suggested that I think about a PhD. I laughed. *One thing at a time.* I wondered if I could pull it off, but that it was even a possibility was amazing to consider.

My backup plan had been to apply to the Masters of Special Education at my college. My backup plan blew up when my school dissolved that program. I spent a chaotic few days racing around and trying to meet with advisors, but the program I had considered was gone. Poof. Utterly gone. While I was hoping and praying for options with other schools, in the back of my head I had been relying on the safety net of staying right where I was. It was safe.

Then I stepped back. Perhaps that was precisely what I needed. Was I playing it too safe, knowing there was a spot for me at my school? Was that too much of a cushion? Did I need to take a greater risk?

Silly me, for wondering.

24

Unbreakable

FEBRUARY 7, 2012

When I look back at the last five years, it makes me want to curl up and sob. I've always kept getting back up. Every. Single. Time. In retrospect, I'm kind of proud of that. But this last one? It feels like I've had the wind knocked out of me, and I'm seeing stars. I want to curl up and cry. I want to close my eyes and have someone else make it all better. I want someone to say softly to me, "I've got this one, Trace," and allow me to see what it feels like to be safe. Even if just for a moment.

Yesterday, I honestly doubted my ability to do this for the first time. I felt so flattened that I had to lay on the ground for a while and remember how to breathe. Today, still raw and sucking for air, I found that tiny spark. More fragile than it's ever been, barely sputtering…but it's there. I'm going to nurse it for a day or two, and hopefully, with a little care, the spark will turn back into the fire I need to finish this fight.

THE CHURCH SECRETARY TAPPED ME on the shoulder on my way down the hall to Sunday school. "The bishop would like to speak to you after church." My gut lurched—that would mean the kids would be with me, and any actual conversation would be impossible over their bobbing, hungry heads.

"Can I see him now?" I asked.

The bishop nodded when I knocked and invited me to sit in my usual chair in his office. He had checked in with me regularly since the divorce. He was always supportive and kind to me and the children. After some pleasantries, he said the words that I always knew would eventually come, even though I still wasn't quite prepared for the sucker punch they packed: "I'm so sorry, but the church cannot help you any longer."

"But…I'm almost done!" I pleaded. Four months from my scheduled graduation. My head swam, and I felt sick. Suddenly the black thread on the cuff of my blouse was fascinating, and I tried, briefly, to stop the waterfall of hot tears. He murmured words meant to comfort—*it wasn't my fault, it was a financial decision that came from above*—but no words could soften the reality. Tears dropped softly into my lap. It was clear that he took no pleasure in his task; he was simply doing what had to be done, and it was unfortunate.

I stumbled out to my car, leaving my children in their Sunday school classes, and let the waves of panic overtake me. I had to find a way to pay the rent on a house I couldn't afford. I was facing homelessness. No matter how I tried to spin it, I could not figure out how to finish the next four months of school, keep my GPA up, apply to grad schools, take the GRE, be a decent—or at least passable— mom, and keep our heads above water. I wanted to believe that living in my car was not an option, but I couldn't help but wonder whether I shouldn't have traded my Suburban a few months ago for the smaller, more fuel-efficient model in which I now sat clutching the steering wheel.

The rest of Sunday was a grey blur. I know that I picked my kids up, and I know that I got us home, but the details are lost. Not even when my marriage dissolved and I lost my home did I feel so utterly hopeless as I did that night. For the first time, I truly could not see what to do or where to turn. Over the last few years, there had been a lot of trials, but I had known what I needed to do, and there had always been determination, inspiration, a glimmer of light. Sunday night and into Monday, I knew a dark hopelessness that left me terrified. Waves of fear and fatigue engulfed me—I understood how a person going into hypothermia might imagine falling asleep as a blissful release.

Fear made my hands shake and my body curl up like wisps of smoke from a blown candle, but because I didn't know what else to do, I wrote.

Writing was always a solitary endeavor. I had kept my blog up for years, but unless a person commented I had no way of knowing who was reading. I would send my words out into the darkness, often never knowing if they mattered to anyone but me. But writing cleared my head and calmed my heart, so I continued. I had had a few essays published in collections, and I had written a few pieces for a magazine or two—but mostly I just wrote for myself, to stay sane, to make sense of an unplanned life. I didn't know who was reading. *I still don't.*

I sat down and poured my heart out. It was part of the ongoing narrative that I had been sharing for years. I opened a naked, raw window into my fears and my feeling of powerlessness. Sunday was awful—not because of my bishop, who was so kind and so sorry and had done so much to help us—I had only cause to be grateful and I knew it. I had been carried over some very sharp rocks, which had allowed me to focus and excel in ways that I never could have without that support.

It was awful because I didn't know what to do next. I had been singularly focused on finishing that last quarter; I didn't have a plan B. The part that was most frightening was the feeling that I just didn't have it in me to get up again. I had never felt that so deeply before. *Was this what it felt like to finally be defeated?* To really be at the end of all ropes and have the last thread fray and finally give way? I felt abandoned by God.

It was a very dark place.

Alone in my room, I looked for my rocks. I had to find a way to pay my rent and my bills on my own—rock. *But what if I couldn't?* I had to finish school, no matter what—rock. *What kind of job would I qualify for?* How would I pay for daycare? Daycare for three kids would eat up any money I made at a low-end job, and that brought me right back around to my starting point two years earlier—rock. David had no money—rock. He could help with the kids at my house, but he couldn't drive carpool with them. Dammit. My head spun as the logistics of the swirling moving pieces I needed to manage all crashed down around me. *I was so close*—rock.

I wrote all this down and sent it out into the dark.

I fell into a fitful, dreamless sleep. When I awoke the next morning there were a handful of comments on my site—kind words from familiar names—and some names that were new as well. People were asking how they could help. It was a lovely sentiment, and I appreciated the kindness and words of support. The friends—like Mo—and the community I found from writing were a safety net and an emotional life raft.

I didn't yet understand how deep and wide that net had been woven.

As the comments piled up, friends started asking for real ways they could help, and the conversation took on a life of its own. People who had never commented before started to email me. By the time I got my kids fed and delivered to school, my inbox was peppered with notes from kind and thoughtful strangers from all over the country—and even overseas. I never suspected that so many people read my words or cared about my story. I was wrong.

My first instinct was to curl up under a blanket and not look at the accumulating comments. My pride made me want to hide; instead, I made myself sit at my computer, a box of tissues in my lap, reading as the comments and emails continued to pour in. My own community was unveiling themselves to me in real time, and I owed it to them not to look away.

There was a short comment submitted from Reese Dixon, a woman who wrote at a sister blog, *Feminist Mormon Housewives*. They were much, much bigger than my little corner of the internet, but I had written guest posts for them and had become friends with the women who founded the site.

Reese quoted directly from my post: "Hey Trace, we've got this. Email coming."

I crumbled to my knees. Cradling my tear-swollen face in my arms, utterly humbled, I could not place a prayer coherent to any human ear, but I knew with a quickening of my soul that God had not forgotten me. God was reaching out to me with not one, but with a hundred different hands—beautiful, tender hands made of flesh and bone and sinew. That day my sisters' hands reached me, and were the hands of God.

Reese wrote me that the Feminist Mormon Housewives had been discussing starting a scholarship program for some time. They were deeply concerned with how motherhood affects education and poverty rates and felt compelled to do something about it, but they had been stymied at the prospect of finding a deserving candidate. She said they thought I was the perfect person to receive the inaugural FMH scholarship for mothers returning to school.

She gently told me that I didn't need to worry about anything—they were going to roll it out immediately for me. She would put up a notice on their website and take it from there.

For the next two days, between classes and caring for the needs of my children, I watched miracles unfold. My screen filled with beautiful, kind words that made my eyes swim and tears splatter onto my keyboard. And it wasn't only words. As I clicked back and forth between my own website and FMH, the generosity was inconceivable. With each gift to the scholarship fund or to me came a note, a meaningful exchange of humanity, a sharing of grief or of joy or of some small story from a person's life. My lamp was overflowing.

The support and love was overwhelming. I never could have imagined the ripples of one person choosing to spill her messy life out into the universe. By the next afternoon, there were so many emails that I wasn't sure how to answer them. People shared how my story had helped them or their mother, their sister, their cousin, their daughter. Some were grateful for my honesty about my doubts and struggles with my faith. Some shared how my stories of Bean and his diagnosis of autism had helped their own children, or how my openness about my divorce and David's addiction had given them strength in their own pain. Each letter was a personal pinpoint of light—each unique and beautiful in its own right, but together they turned into something miraculous.

Through the love of people literally all over the world, what had seemed like the darkest hour of my life, where I felt abandoned by God, became the single greatest moment of light and grace. God didn't abandon us. He cleared the space so blessings from others could overflow.

25

Only Everything

FEBRUARY 24, 2012

In the prolonged absence of light, with nothing to reflect back who you might be, you forget your own edges and question where the darkness ends and you begin. This is the place where your heart cleaves; the contents within spill into the deep darkness, you balk in terror at what seems like the end of the world. But the heart has to break for what's within to grow... to push out of the darkness, where all seeds sprout, and force its way up, through some miracle, toward the light.

In that moment, in some small measure, we might finally, in our own brokenness, understand the grace offered by Christ in His descending beneath all things. The contents of your shattered heart are the fertile loam that feeds the life as it pushes up, finally bursting into the light.

Perhaps there are other ways, gentler and kinder, to learn these lessons. Perhaps there is a different story for each of us written in the book of life. The single thing of which I am now certain is that the contents of our hewn, split, shattered, broken hearts—however they be torn asunder— is required for the seeds within us to find the light. Nothing less will do. Nothing more is asked. It's only everything.

"WHAT DO YOU THINK THE odds are of you moving?" I asked David. "I could help you find an apartment or a studio close by." He was on the floor, playing renegade dolls with Abby. He never obeyed her intricate rules, but at least there was a dad in her doll-house again. He'd been my first call the month before when I had heard back from a program I had applied to in Washington D.C. It was a new program, still waiting on full funding, but if it worked out, I could be part of an inaugural cohort with a certification in Autism Studies. It was riskier than going to Seattle or Salt Lake City where I had a large support system and friends, but it sounded perfect, and I was considering it.

His doll misbehaved and Abby giggled. "I hope to eventually, but I have to stay close to my mom for now."

There were a million details up in the air that all lacked definitive answers, but I was starting to get used to the moving ground. I still had to finish my last classes. No matter where I landed for school, we were going to be moving. I needed to find a place to live, in an area of the country I didn't know. I had to find decent schools for the kids, and I wanted to consider David and what he could man-age. I knew it wasn't going to be easy, but that really didn't scare me anymore. The last month had been a powerful lesson in trusting that things would work out and the path would be clear—just like in Indiana Jones, it didn't matter that I couldn't see the stones beneath my feet—the test was having the faith to take that first step.

I had spent the last month alternately writing my senior thesis and thank-you notes to countless people for sharing their stories, for donating to the FMH scholarship, and for reaching out to me and the kids. A thousand motherly hands had stretched down to carry us, and because of them, I could focus on school, I could take my last classes, I could keep a roof over our heads. I considered their gifts consecrated and sacred. Every day I offered my heart at the hearth of my sisters and at the feet of mercy and grace.

David smiled at me across the gentle divide between us. He knew what had happened with the scholarship and the blogs, and he was humbled. He looked so much older, his beard greying, lines etched around his eyes and crossing forehead. Things were not perfect, and we still treaded carefully around some of the emotional land mines, but there was a peace that generally attended us. As hard as it was to remember sometimes, we were all hurt. Because of his willingness to show up, I was able to forgive him and to forgive myself. It would have been so easy to lay everything at his feet, but it would have been so wrong.

"I'll help you," I said softly.

He moved the dolly toward Abby's toes, making her dissolve into a fit of giggles. "I know."

Just as we had created our marriage together, we were both the architects of our post-divorce life and how we would parent the children we both loved. As long as he stayed sober, I was willing to do whatever I could to help him be an involved father and a healthy part of our children's lives.

It wasn't until years later that I realized that, in so completely forgiving him, I had also freed myself.

There are two images of David seared into my mind. Both are looking back through a departing window.

The first is from the evening we left Little House. He had accompanied me that day to pick up the twelve-foot rental truck; I was nervous about driving such a large vehicle, and grateful for his willingness to help and again be present.

That evening, after the belongings of a household of four had miraculously been fitted neatly inside what seemed a ridiculously small truck by a crew of friends, it was finally just David and me standing in the warm twilight.

"You're going to visit us, right?" It was hard to talk over the lump in my throat. He pushed some gravel around with his shoe, his hands shoved deep in his jean pockets. He nodded and looked toward the kids running and laughing on the now-empty Little House lawn. The next day my neighbor was dismantling Bean's wooden fort and moving it to her backyard for her grandkids. It was the last vestige of us.

My car was loaded and secured on a trailer behind the box truck, and we were waiting on a friend to pick me and the kids up to spend our last night in the Northwest.

"I'm scared," I whispered.

He looked across the impossible space between us, his own eyes swimming. "I know. You've been scared all along, and yet you've still managed to do the right thing. You're the star, Tracy Leigh." There was an entire sky of love and tenderness in his ragged voice.

He tried to smile but turned and called for the kids. He sat down on the front steps of Little House, and took each child in his lap, holding them close and spoke quiet words of his love meant only for each of their ears. I stood apart, tears streaming down my face, giving them the room for their own memories.

Car wheels crushed over the gravel behind me, and it was time. David helped me buckle the teary kids in the backseat of my friend's car, leaning in to kiss their salty, rosy cheeks and feel their arms around his neck one more time. He stepped toward the back of the car, his hands shoved deep in his pockets again and his eyes red.

"I'm sorry," he whispered.

My chest felt like an anvil was lodged over my heart, where there were worlds built and destroyed between us. There was everything to say, and nothing left to say. "I know…me too."

"Go." He laid his open hand gently on the top of the car and tapped three times.

I clicked my seatbelt and turned around to check the kids. Over their three small faces, he stood alone in the driveway of Little House, slowly disappearing from sight as we headed east.

The second image is from his last visit.

He had flown out to see the kids in Virginia and had spent almost two weeks with us. We had talked about him moving, but his concerns for his mother still kept him in Washington State. His health had deteriorated, and he was feeling some of the lasting damage from his years of narcotic abuse. He spoke more slowly, and the poetry that once easily flowed took him much longer to mine. It worried him, he admitted, but he accepted it as a consequence of his life.

Over the years, we had fallen into an easy pattern, talking on the phone once or twice a week. Computers and social media made it easy to stay connected, despite the distance, and he talked with the kids and with me regularly. When he would call, he would let me know if it was a parenting call or a friend call, and we would laugh.

It was a good visit. He did some sightseeing with the kids and spent a lot of time just hanging out—helping them with their homework, listening to them practice their instruments, and telling silly stories about when we were young. The kids loved having him in our guest room.

When it was time to head back, we made plans for his next visit, and he said he might be ready to seriously consider moving. He missed the kids. I told him we could help him look for a two-bedroom place, so his mom could come too. The kids would love to have Nana close again.

When we dropped him off at the airport, there were no tears or sadness—we expected to see him again soon. Everyone hugged and laughed and parted ways.

As I drove away, the kids waving out the open windows, it was easy to follow the big man in a rainbow shirt moving slowly through the crowd toward his flight home.

26

Knocking on Heaven's Door

THE CALL CAME IN THE dim, gray light before dawn. She fumbled for her phone in the dark and saw the number; her stomach dropped as adrenaline and dread flooded her body, suddenly both wide awake and numb. The aging voice was fragile over the line, as she tried to make sense of the confusing jumble of words. David. Hospital. Collapse. Ambulance. Intubated. Heart failure. Non-responsive. Half-formed questions bubbled to her lips, interrupted by shock-formed half-answers from the frail woman on the other end. "Wait...? What...? How...? Is there a nurse...someone I can talk to...?" she pleaded into the phone.

She was in Utah for the summer, nestled near Cache Valley and the northern peaks of the breathtaking Wasatch Mountains. Her children were all still asleep in various beds around her new in-laws' house. They'd been playing outside the night before, getting to know new cousins and grandparents, and they were overjoyed with the deep azure sky, the pasture, the chickens, the enormous dog, and the sheep named Maverick.

She motioned for her husband to close the door—she didn't want the children to hear any part of this phone call. Six years before, they had seen their father overdose. They had seen him, during the divorce, seizing and convulsing on the floor of his mother's house where she had taken the kids for a supervised visitation. She had screamed for her mother-in-law to keep the kids in the front room, not to let them see as she rushed to call 911, but they saw anyway. They had seen the paramedics pounding on his chest, had seen the firemen rushing into their grandmother's genteel living room, had seen the mad, brutal rush to save his life. They were too young, but she could not protect them from it.

He survived that day. She had followed the ambulance at the paramedics' insistence, while protesting that she wasn't his wife anymore. She couldn't make any decisions for him. Her head swam as she tried to answer the doctor's questions in the ER. How many times? How much? Of what? He'd been in and out of rehab half a dozen times in the previous three years, before she finally filed for divorce. "If he does this again, he will die." Yes. She knew.

He knew it, too. And over the next few years, he got help. He followed a program. He stayed sober. It was hard. Every day. There is a reason twelve-step plans use the phrase "One day at a time." For an addict, it's often broken down into one hour, or one minute, at a time. A day seems too large a hurdle. But a minute? A minute can be done. Until someday, for some reason, it cannot.

Less than a year earlier, she had him fly out to stay with them on the East Coast. She had invited him many times, but he was finally feeling strong enough, and he came for almost two weeks. He stayed in their home, met her new husband and her step children, and immersed himself in his own children. It had been a singular joy watching the harmony between loved ones and seeing the kids bask in that light. It had been a beautiful visit, and they had spoken about repeating it again this coming fall.

They talked frequently. She valued him—not only as the father of her children, but as a constant for most of her life. They had met when she was still a girl. He was her former husband, but prior to, and after that, he was also her dearest friend.

Now the phone call she had feared for years had come. Waiting on a call-back from a nurse, her heart was leaden. He had been doing so well...But she knew the frailty of that protest. She knew how it could go, and how fast it could go.

Her husband joined her outside in the gathering dawn. His parents, out for their morning walk, were silhouetted against the rising sun as they approached. The cat had joined them and their giant dog on their walk—they made a peculiar and oddly beautiful quartet. Strange, the things you remember when the world is shifting.

It was Pioneer Day in Utah. July. It would be hot, and the roses were opening in ridiculous color and bloom despite the early hour. She remembers noticing that, too, along with a stray chicken wandering in and out of the flowers. The phone rang.

He was gone.

There are moments in life that transcend time, where everything stops, the birds hold their song, and the enormity of the silence is deafening in its vastness. There are moments where a person can, ever so briefly, see the curving arc of the horizon and can feel the curling crest of the wave of time under their feet. Thank God those moments are fleeting, because our earthly hearts really cannot breathe in that paralyzing intensity for long. In that moment, she understood why people fall to their knees before angels.

Before her lies the task of waking her children this beautiful summer morning and telling them their father is dead. She cannot protect them from the incapacitating unfairness of life or from the unforgiving hardness of the devastating reality of addiction. She wants to cry out for someone to shield them, someone more adequately prepared than her, someone who knows better than she how to shepherd children through a valley no child should walk. But there is no answer. So she will do it.

She can see the house over her husband's shoulder, backlit by the rising sun, where her children are asleep, safe and happy, surrounded by family, summer roses, giant dogs, chickens, cousins and a sheep named Maverick.

She takes a deep breath, and tries to rub away her endless tears, and moves toward the sunrise and what she must do.

2007

David was resting in the late-afternoon dappled sunlight filtering through the plantation blinds. He didn't open his eyes, but he was awake. "Well, how was it?"

I walked into my closet and set my bag down. I didn't know what to say. For Latter-day Saints, the temple was something utterly outside regular church—not everyone went, not everyone wanted to go, and the decision was not made lightly. It was a step of religious commitment beyond basic baptism made by every Christian.

I had put it off for years; so long that people stopped eagerly asking me when I was going and just left me alone.

When I was pregnant with Abby, David had been baptized, leaving behind his decades of Buddhism for this young form of American Christianity. Like so much with him spiritually, he didn't jettison who he had been; he just rolled it into himself, and he was the most Buddhist of Mormons.

With his baptism, our congregation renewed their excitement for us to attend the temple, but that only made David nervous. I finally asked all the well-intentioned people to just give us space.

When Abby was about a year old, after David had relapsed twice, I made the decision that I was ready to go. I didn't want our community to make a big deal out of it; I didn't want a dinner, and I didn't want any of the inevitable questions about David and why he wasn't joining me.

So one day, I just went.

It was nothing like I had expected, and I felt raw and slightly wounded. When you hear for years about a beautiful ritual shrouded in mystery, it might be inevitable that there will be disappointment or confusion. I didn't have parents or siblings with whom I could share the experience and talk about my feelings, and in that moment, standing in my closet, it felt like there was another wall between David and me.

"Well? Do you want to talk about it?" he asked gently.

"I can't." I looked down, feeling strange in my clothes.

He sat up and looked closely at me, his eyes sharp but kind. "Do you regret going?"

I considered his words. "I don't think so. I'm not sure what I feel right now. It's a lot." I paused, not sure what was okay to discuss with him. "It's really…weird."

He laughed gently. "Yeah, I bet. All religious ritual is weird if you stop and consider it. God is unknowable, and we do our paltry best to reach out to him, and out of context, it's all weird."

I nodded, unsure what to say, but trusting him.

He smiled and leaned back. "Did you at least have to knock?"

I looked up at him suddenly—*how would he know that?* There was a place in the ceremony where the participant does knock, but David wasn't the type of person to read about religious rites on the internet. He respected the traditions and things people held sacred, even if they weren't his holdings.

He smiled at the transparent surprise on my face. "So you do. Excellent…" he trailed off.

"How do you know that?" I asked.

He leaned forward, his eyes clear and bright. "Because of course you must knock. The act of knocking is the act of proclaiming yourself before God. In knocking, you are announcing *I Am* to the Most High, and you are asking to be acknowledged. You cannot enter the presence of God if you cannot proclaim *I Am*."

I didn't know he could still surprise me, but there it was.

He stood up and put his arms around me, and I could hear the deep rumble of soft laughter in his chest. He was never laughing at me—it was the joy he had for mystery, for life, for himself, for the divine ribbons that wrapped through our lives, binding us one to another.

He let go of me, and I could hear him softly humming Bob Dylan.

He kissed the top of my head and went downstairs, where the kids were making noise about dinner and clamoring for piggy-back rides. I could hear the happiness in his voice as he picked up a giggling child, and called over his shoulder, "Jesus did it first!" His laughter floated up behind him, and he began belting out the Dylan song.

Knock knock knocking on heaven's door. . . .

The Burning Point

Acknowledgments

Sitting in my friend's living room on an inky black winter night, she asks me what I am afraid of. "Sharks." I reply, smiling. She snickers.

I am knitting quietly, outside the circle of amber light cast by her low lamp, but my fingers and the roving know this rhythm and their tightly woven patterns seem to free my mind to wander and find the real answer.

I try and find the thread, that tiny place where there is a real answer to her question. She will laugh with me, but really she is gently coaxing me to look where I am afraid to look. She says nothing while I run the soft yarn between my fingers. She is holding space, protecting my margins, while I reacquaint myself with the dark.

What am I afraid of? I am afraid of the thousands of tiny moments of light and brilliance that make up the life of a person being lost, and forgotten, and swallowed by the breach. I am not afraid of dying; I am afraid of our stories—our precious sparks of madness and glory—being forgotten.

My hands are still knitting. My heart hurts, and I swallow hard. This is why I am a writer, a steward of some, a protector of others, a champion of myself and those I love. I am a writer. I must write to figure this out.

And so I wrote.

Not a single thing in my life looks the way I first thought it would. No painting, no essay, no book, no child, no marriage. They've all been better, greater, deeper, more painful, richer, or harder when juxtaposed against my feeble imagination and the impetus leading me to pick up the pen or brush. Always. This book is no different.

My deepest thanks and gratitude to my husband Jonathan, whose heart is vast and generous enough to have made room in our lives for David—both before and after his death. I am deeply grateful to both Jonathan and our children for their loving sacrifices that allowed me to write this story.

Additionally, this work could not have been undertaken without the support of Marissa Stewart-Glover, Kathryn Lynard, and especially, my editor, Michael Austin—each of whom acted as midwives and life-support at various points. Finally I would like to thank *Sunstone Magazine* and Stephen Carter for publishing my essay "Wonder," which was awarded the Eugene England Personal Essay Award for 2016 and forms the basis of Chapter 8 of this book.

This memoir is a work of creative non-fiction, mining my own life and experiences. The events and conversations portrayed in this book are true to the best of my ability, but human memory can be flawed. Some creative liberties have been taken to protect the privacy of living people.

~t.m.

Photograph by Melanie Awbrey Beus

Tracy McKay and her husband, Jonathan Lamb, are raising their combined family together near Washington D.C. They have a very large dog to match their very large family, and life goes on in its messy, beautiful way.

Made in the USA
Columbia, SC
05 December 2017